advertising

a cultural economy

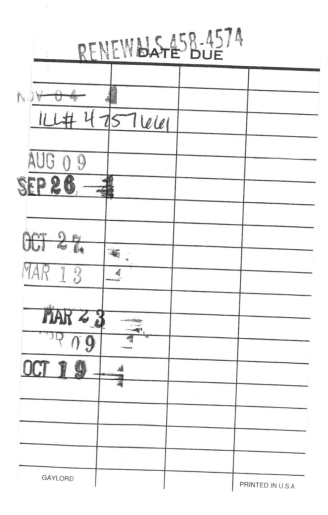

Culture, Representation and Identities is dedicated to a particular understanding of 'cultural studies' as an inherently interdisciplinary project critically concerned with the analysis of meaning. The series focuses attention on the importance of the contemporary 'cultural turn' in forging a radical re-think of the centrality of 'the cultural' and the articulation between the material and the symbolic in social analysis. One aspect of this shift is the expansion of 'culture' to a much wider, more inclusive range of institutions and practices, including those conventionally termed 'economic' and 'political'.

Paul du Gay is at the Faculty of Social Sciences at The Open University. **Stuart Hall** is Emeritus Professor at The Open University and Visiting Professor at Goldsmiths College, the University of London.

Books in the series:

Representing Black Britain
Black and Asian Images on Television
Sarita Malik

Cultural Economy
Cultural Analysis and Commercial Life
Edited by Paul du Gay and Michael Pryke

Advertising Cultures
Gender, Commerce, Creativity
Sean Nixon

Advertising
A Cultural Economy
Liz McFall

advertising

a cultural economy

Liz McFall

SAGE Publications
London • Thousand Oaks • New Delhi

First published 2004

Apart from any fair dealing for the purposes of research
or private study, or criticism or review, as permitted
under the Copyright, Designs and Patents Act, 1988, this
publication may be reproduced, stored or transmitted
in any form, or by any means, only with the prior
permission in writing of the publishers, or in the case of
reprographic reproduction, in accordance with the terms
of licences issued by the Copyright Licensing Agency.
Enquiries concerning reproduction outside those terms
should be sent to the publishers.

Every effort has been made to trace all copyright holders
of the material re-printed herein, but if any have been
inadvertently overlooked the publishers will be pleased to
make the necessary arrangements at the first opportunity.

 SAGE Publications Ltd
1 Oliver's Yard
55 City Road
London EC1Y 1SP

SAGE Publications Inc.
2455 Teller Road
Thousand Oaks, California 91320

SAGE Publications India Pvt Ltd
B-42, Panchsheel Enclave
Post Box 4109
New Delhi 100 017

British Library Cataloguing in Publication data

A catalogue record for this book is available
from the British Library

ISBN 0-7619-4254-8
ISBN 0-7619-4255-6 (pbk)

Library of Congress Control Number 2003110017

Typeset by C&M Digitals (P) Ltd., Chennai, India
Printed in Great Britain by Athenaeum Press, Gateshead

contents

list of illustrations

acknowledgements

It has taken quite some time for this book to emerge in its current form. To those who have helped shape it along the way I owe thanks, not only for their support and kindness, but also for their constancy. The book draws substantially on doctoral research supervised by Paul du Gay and Margaret Wetherall and I continue to be grateful for the training they provided and for the mixture of patience, commitment, inspiration and energy that they brought to the project. Paul du Gay in particular has been an ongoing and indispensable source of ideas, debates and 'damn fine' coffee.

I would like to thank the Open University, especially the Sociology Discipline and the Research School, for providing first the financial support and later the research leave to enable the project to be completed. I also owe thanks to those in the Open University in Scotland who encouraged me to begin the project in the first place, Graham Dawson, Bram Gieben, Katla Helgason and Gerry Mooney.

A non-historian conducting historical research into a subject as flimsy and ephemeral as advertising relies upon the skills and expertise of archivists and librarians. I am especially grateful to Michael Cudlipp and Margaret Rose of the History of Advertising Trust in Norwich and to Ellen Gartrell of the Hartman Center for Sales, Advertising and Marketing History, Duke University, North Carolina for generously granting me the space, time and help to allow me to navigate my way through their extensive collections. I am also grateful to staff at the British Library; the Bodleian Library, University of Oxford; the National Museum of American History at the Smithsonian Institute and the Guildhall Library, London.

Many friends and colleagues discussed ideas with me, read drafts and offered feedback. I want to thank in particular Daniel Miller, Sean Nixon, Graeme Salaman and Alan Warde for their responses to earlier versions of parts of this work. I also want to thank Rick Holliman, Sarah Seymour-Smith and Ramaswami Harindranath among others for breaking into the monotony just often enough to keep me sane while this was being written. Special thanks are due to David Featherstone who has listened, read and responded to numerous drafts with unstinting patience, generosity and insight. Extraspecial thanks to the little people, Eavan and Marni, for moderating my progress in the best possible way and to Linda Usherwood (aka Mary Poppins). The book is dedicated to Stephen.

introduction: the quaint device of advertising

[T]he time of men does not have the form of an evolution but precisely that of a history. (Foucault, 1981: 8)

An article in a 1652 issue of the *Mercurius Mastix* laments the appearance in the press of yet another variation on the already extensive gamut of trade announcements purporting to be 'epistles', 'petitions', 'iterations', or 'news from abroad'.[1] This new variation is referred to only as a 'quaint device in their trading', but it is clear that the object in question, though not yet known by that term, was an early form of advertisement. It took some time before the general term 'advertisement' was settled upon, with alternatives like 'puffs', 'bubbles', even 'impertinences', in circulation until well into the nineteenth century. Yet despite its antiquity, 'quaint device' is a perfectly apposite description and one that offers a subtle hint about the character of early advertising. In contemporary use the term 'device' connotes a deliberate, functional mechanism; in the seventeenth century, it carried stronger connotations of techniques of contrivance, manipulation and deception. Both these senses can be applied to contemporary advertising, but they are equally descriptive of early advertising and it is entirely likely that the writer in the *Mercurius Mastix* had the latter sense in mind. This is a clue that something might be amiss in the received characterisation of early advertising as an innocuous and naïve first foray into the realm of commercial promotion. Pre-twentieth-century advertising is almost universally portrayed as simple announcement, to be contrasted with the cunning sophistication and subtlety of contemporary versions (Williams, 1980; Dyer, 1982; Leiss et al., 1986). One of the first insights offered by historical research is that such judgements are generally made from the distance of time; they seldom, if ever, refer to advertising of the 'present day'.

A second and instructive sense of the term 'device' can be found in Callon's anthropologically informed work on markets (Callon, 1998a, 1998b; Callon et al., 2002). Callon revisits the debate between those who would have economies and markets as real, objectively existing entities, and those who would have them as pure 'fiction' or social construction. His distinctive formulation is that neither is the case. Instead economies and markets are the simultaneous outcome of the work of many different forms of calculative agencies, and the material devices employed therein. Economics, and related disciplines of management, marketing and sociology, work to 'perform' the economy and organise markets by evolving the techniques, tools and devices that define and measure what is meant by 'economy'. Advertising can be characterised as a material device employed in the definition or qualification of markets, and this is a role that merits much closer investigation than it has yet received (see Callon et al., 2002; Slater, 2002a). As a calculative institution, advertising originates in a very specific commercial impulse to promote sales. This foundational objective may have remained consistent over the years but the nature of the techniques, tools and devices deployed to meet it have varied enormously. The precise circumstances underlying these variations and, in particular, the ways advertising has been indelibly shaped by the interaction of institutional, organisational and technological arrangements, is a fascinating field of critical inquiry, but one that has thus far been left largely untouched by an academy that has preferred a different approach.

This approach has grown out of an enduring fascination not with advertis*ing* but with advertise*ments*. Advertisements seem to offer an insight into what one nineteenth-century author described as 'the wants, the losses, the amusements and the money-making eagerness of the people' (Anon., 1855: 183). Journalists, historians and social and cultural theorists concur – advertisements mirror dominant values, attitudes and habits and are thus prime source material for divining the 'spirit' or 'pattern' of the age (Salmon, 1923; Hower, 1939; Wood, 1958; Rowsome, 1959). This view of advertisements as socio-cultural source material structures critical academic work conducted principally, but not exclusively, within the disciplinary boundaries of sociology and cultural and media studies. The resulting characterisation of the socio-cultural and economic significance of advertising, and its empirical basis, is the central problem that this book addresses.

This will involve, in the first part of the book (Chapters 1–4), a close interrogation of the approach taken to advertising in critical academic work over the last few decades. Critical fascination with advertisements as source material is motivated primarily not by what they reveal about advertising, but by what they reveal about societies, cultures and economies. The academy, however, has tended towards the view that these insights are not simply offered up by advertisements, but are to be gained only from specific, technical methods of analysis. Advertisements may be society's mirror but, as Marchand (1985: xvii) insists, it is an odd sort of mirror – a 'Zerrspiegel' that both selects from and distorts the reality depicted. The true significance of advertising texts has to be 'decoded', and an extensive corpus of work has been devoted to the development of methodologies – like content analysis and semiotics – tuned to this task. Such methodologies are generally deployed to help provide grand explanations of how advertising goes beyond the stimulation of demand for specific products to 'produce' consumption as a specific mode of behaviour. At a fundamental level, critical academic work has bought into Galbraith's characterisation of advertisements as producing the sorts of consumer required by specific industrial systems (Galbraith, 1958).

This textually fixated approach to advertising has incurred certain costs. Foremost among these has been a sustained neglect, over the last 30 years or so, of production-side analyses of the institutions and practices of advertising. This is a particular instance of what has been considered a broader disdain of the market and the economic as proper objects of analysis within disciplines like sociology and cultural and media studies (Morris, 1988; Zelizer 1988). Such a disdain is in evidence in works that have achieved a near canonical status, but whose expositions of advertising's cultural and economic significance are extrapolated almost exclusively from analyses of individual advertising texts (Barthes 1977; Williamson, 1978; Wernick, 1991; Goldman, 1992; Goldman & Papson, 1996). The index entry for advertising in Goldman and Papson's *Sign Wars*, for instance, includes sub-entries like 'harvesting', 'semiotic obsolescence' and 'sign economy', but not 'agency' or 'practitioner'. Even works adopting a broader perspective tend to be conducted at a remove from the minutiae of everyday practice (Ewen, 1976; Schudson, 1984; Leiss et al., 1986; Mattelart, 1991; Fowles, 1996). By the middle of the 1990s, almost no detailed empirical study of the character or development of contemporary advertising practice existed. For an institution that plays a pivotal role in the grand narratives of economy, culture and society offered by Frankfurt-variant political economy (Horkheimer & Adorno, 1973; Haug, 1986), mainstream liberal economic theory (Galbraith, 1958), as well as a plethora of more recent accounts of the epoch (Jameson, 1984; Baudrillard, 1988a; Featherstone, 1991; Lash & Urry, 1994; Bauman, 2000, 2001), this is a particularly poor state of affairs, and one that is only slowly beginning to change.[2] Disregarding the practices and institutions of advertising is especially unhelpful when the object of critique, despite being derived from the evidence of advertisements, is advertising as a societal institution. This should raise eyebrows: Is it really adequate to found a critique that reaches far into the nature and organisation of contemporary societies upon textual deconstruction of the meanings of advertisements?

A preoccupation with texts, moreover, is not the only problem with advertising critique. In a move that springs directly from the treatment of advertising as a window onto the grand problematics of social, cultural and economic organisation, critical accounts have accorded advertising a very particular historical role. Advertising is conceived of as an institution that is steadily evolving in power and sophistication. As mentioned at the outset, early advertisements are generally characterised as simple, crude and naïve – the inevitable corollary of this is the view that contemporary advertisements are persuasive, subtle and intelligent. This is complemented by a perception that while contemporary advertisements are pervasive, ubiquitous, inescapable, earlier advertisements were rare and unusual. These characteristics are ascribed to much larger processes of transformation in which the integrity of culture, and in particular its autonomy from economy, is often thought to be at stake in a process sometimes referred to as culturalisation or hybridisation (Jameson, 1984; Featherstone, 1991; Wernick, 1991; Lash & Urry, 1994; Sternberg, 1999). If contemporary advertising is a persuasive, pervasive and hybrid form it is because the logic underlying societies defined epochally as commodity- or consumer-driven requires it to be so.

It is not really possible in this space to do justice to the many competing formulations of the contemporary epoch, and in the effort to tease out the functional role of advertising within them some important distinctions will no doubt be collapsed. Nonetheless it is fairly uncontroversial to note that both consumer- and commodity-driven designations of the epoch turn on a particular account of contemporary consumption (Jameson, 1984; Baudrillard, 1988a; Featherstone, 1991; Lash & Urry, 1994; Bauman, 2000, 2001). Exponential increases in the volume of consumption over the last half century are clearly of some consequence here, but the caesural distinction is not so much the quantity as the character of consumption. At stake, for many theorists, is a progressive decline in the importance of instrumental, utility-driven consumption, and a concomitant expansion in symbolic consumption (Campbell, 1987; Baudrillard, 1988a; Ferguson, 1992; Bauman, 2001). Contemporary consumption is all about the desire for difference and the expression of identity through the display of sign values. Advertising is thoroughly implicated in this shift and, by extension, in an array of related changes. The manner in which it seeks to promote consumption leaves advertising up to its neck in what Baudrillard (1988b) calls the symbolic exchange of sign values, and the consequences of this are hard to overstate. Advertising plays around with meanings drawn from a preexisting culture to make objects seem more significant, more desirable and more personal than they really are. In the process a sort of reconfiguration of otherwise more stable relations occurs between meaning and reality, subjects and objects, and culture and economy. Advertising is thus cast in a transformative historical role, where its evolutionary advances are tuned to the changing structures and organisation of the epoch.

This teleological characterisation is, intuitively, entirely reasonable. Technology has enhanced advertisements with colour, sound and movement in a way unthinkable even 50 years ago, while profiling and niche marketing techniques enable specific groups to be targeted on the basis of ever more finely tuned criteria. The problem, however, is that manifest changes in the form and appearance of advertisements, in themselves, are not sufficient evidence on which to pin such a vast historical transformation. An understanding of advertising's historical significance really has to encompass more than the deconstructive analysis of texts, no matter how skilful the exposition might be. For this reason the second part of the book (Chapters 5–6) seeks to reappraise advertising through the mechanism of a historically situated focus on the context of advertising production. Despite the importance accorded to advertising's transformative historical role in several branches of critical theory, the empirical history of advertising production has actually been much neglected. The preoccupation with interpreting changes in advertising format has tended to override the need to investigate the specification, formation and operation of advertising practices at a local, organisational level. This is much to be regretted, because the context in which material practices were conducted is crucial to understanding the format of advertisements and the broader role of advertising. It is a central contention here that the critical characterisation of contemporary advertising as an increasingly persuasive and pervasive transformational medium cannot be sustained in the absence of any detailed historical evidence. Such evidence is of limited use unless it is sensitive to the historical context of production – little can be surmised by comparing the advertisements of different historical periods without any regard to the circumstances in which they were produced. The book aims to reconstruct something of these production circumstances through a description of the institutions, practices and products of advertising prevalent in both the UK and the US in the period between 1780 and 1935.

This is not an attempt at a comprehensive history. Instead, the book offers a snapshot of how advertising operated as a way of generating different ways of thinking about its contemporary and historical formations. This approach is informed by Foucault's genealogical model of 'the accidents, the minute deviations – or conversely the complete reversals – the errors, the false appraisals, and the faulty calculations' that comprise history (Foucault, 1984b: 81). Genealogy endorses a history of advertising tuned, not to a predetermined evolution, but to how a diverse, haphazard and uneven array of institutions, practices and products adapted to fit specific contextual circumstances at different historical moments. The adoption of this approach is underscored by the conviction that, in providing a little more context, historical description offers a salient response to critical concerns about the increasing persuasiveness, pervasiveness and hybridisation of contemporary advertising. This is not a form of revisionism seeking to portray historical advertising as equally or more persuasive, pervasive or hybridised, but employs instead a different logic. This is a logic which insists that, outside the historical context of production, criteria like persuasiveness have little meaning. Their purchase is always and only in relation to an available external context upon which they are entirely contingent. Thus, the existence of persuasive twenty-first century television advertising cannot be thought to preclude the existence of persuasive nineteenth-century press advertisements, anymore than fast contemporary transport links preclude the fact that rail transport was experienced as fast in the nineteenth century. The concept of contingency runs through the second part of the book as a constant reminder that the features applied to distinguish contemporary advertising are not absolute, and are much tougher to measure across the distance of time than is often recognised in critical theory.

structure and organisation   This book is intended as a response to critical characterisations of advertising's role in sustaining societies driven by the logic of 'commodity consumption'. Such characterisations emanate from a range of critical traditions, employ different methodologies, and arrive at distinctive theoretical positions. Accordingly, the first part of the book (Chapters 1–4), comprises a close review of the literature, establishing the recurrence of certain themes and theoretical conventions that have dominated thinking, to the point where a historically situated, practice-based methodology offers a much needed alternative perspective. Such a methodology forms the core of Chapters 5 and 6, which focus on describing how the diversity of forms taken over time by the institutions, practices and products of advertising challenges their teleological characterisation in critical work.

Chapter 1 begins with a review of the defining importance of semiotic theory and method in the critical study of advertising. Semiotics describes how advertisements manipulate the relation between 'meaning' and 'reality' by appropriating pre-existing meanings to add value to unrelated products, and posits methods of decoding their true underlying significance. Having outlined this approach in some detail, Chapter 1 goes on to suggest that the semiotic pursuit of 'authentic' meaning is rendered problematic by recent work, foregrounding the contingency of meaning upon instances of use. This analysis is taken forward in Chapter 2 with a review of critical accounts that have adopted a broader institutional perspective on advertising. This 'institutionally focused' body of work is concerned less with the relationship between meaning and reality and more with that between subjects and objects. In particular, this literature addresses advertising's role in transforming the latter relationship in line with the changing requirements of consumer- or commodity-based societies through the production of ever more persuasive and pervasive advertisements. Empirical evidence in support of such claims, Chapter 2 goes on to argue, is surprisingly sparse, and rather at odds with emerging historical accounts of early consumption and promotion practices. Chapter 3 continues to work with this literature and incorporates emerging work on advertising practices in a shift of emphasis from subjects and objects to the 'domains' of culture and economy. Advertising's capacity to bridge and thereby transform the relation between economy and culture is a recurrent critical theme. This formulation deploys 'culture' and 'economy' as separate and opposed 'domains' that would function autonomously, were it not for the intervention of commodity systems of production that work to effect a 'de-differentiation' or 'hybridisation' of the domains. Chapter 3 posits as an alternative, a formulation of the 'cultural' and the 'economic' as provisional conceptual abstractions whose separation, however convenient intellectually, collapses in instances of material practice. Advertising might be more accurately conceived of as a constituent material practice in which the 'cultural' and the 'economic' are inextricably entangled. Chapter 4 reviews the foregoing chapters to build the case for a genealogical description of advertising practice as an appropriate response to the abstract epochalism of critical literature on the subject. It describes a marked tendency to theorise a historical role for advertising that is rarely historically empiricised, but argues that no matter how convenient the fit may appear, history does not offer solutions to theoretical problems. What history can do is provide a more sensitive and informed portrayal of the commercial, promotional environment of the past.

Chapter 6 addresses the characterisation of contemporary advertising as an exceptionally pervasive and hybrid 'culture industry' through an exploration of the institutions and practices of advertising in historical context. Direct comparisons of the role of advertising at different historical moments, relative to criteria such as pervasiveness and hybridity, are no simple matter, because historical comparisons do not compare like with like. Nevertheless, historical description offers an effective counterbalance to critical caricatures of early advertising by highlighting the context in which specific institutions, arrangements and practices prevailed at given historical moments. The chapter begins with a discussion of the institutional context of relations between practitioners, agencies, the media and advertisers, and highlights the sheer diversity and scope of arrangements and actors involved in the early development of the field. It then moves on to consider the impact of advertising on outdoor environments, and reveals an entirely unexpected saturation of outdoor environments which led one contemporary commentator to describe advertising as 'the monster megatherium of modern society' (Smith, 1853: 278). The next part of the chapter reviews the historical practice of advertising with the aim of revisiting the argument that a unique de-differentiation between the cultural and economic is currently underway. The first problem raised with this view stems from the presence of 'cultural' or, more accurately, 'aesthetic' competences among historical practitioners as far back as the early nineteenth century. The second problem is with the definition of culture as a separate and bounded 'sphere'. Chapter 5 shows, through a close description of the development of the functional specialisms – account management, media buying and research – that culture is necessarily constitutive of material practice.

Finally, Chapter 7 turns to the persuasiveness of advertisements themselves. Curiously, there are remarkably few contemporaneous discussions of advertising that do not describe the enormous superiority of contemporary advertisements over the 'naïve' 'crude' or 'quaint' attempts of earlier generations. Chapter 7 suggests that this anomaly arises because persuasiveness is not a function of the use of particular sorts of images, copy or psychological strategies, but is contingent upon the techniques, technologies and media available at a given historical moment. The chapter reviews the uses of 'persuasive' images, copy and emotional appeals within their contexts of production to uncover how different institutional, organisational and technical methods, as well as social, political and economic circumstances indelibly imprint themselves upon the forms advertising takes at different historical moments.

The concluding chapter draws together these different themes to reiterate the fundamental claim that advertising should not be theorised simply as the evolving tool of commodity-driven societies, but merits close study as a specific commercial device. Viewed in this light, the full capacity of advertising to 'reinvent' itself in an array of different forms, in response to low-level changes in the environments in which it is conducted, begins to emerge.

notes

1   Cited in Elliot, 1962: 102.
2   See Moeran (1996), Mort (1996) and Nixon (1996; 2003) for more detailed research into advertising practice.

colonising of the real

Advertisements do not simply manipulate us, inoculate us or reduce us to the status of objects; they create structures of meaning which sell commodities not for themselves as useful objects but in terms of ourselves as social beings in our different social relationships. Products are given 'exchange-value': ads translate statements about objects into statements about types of consumer and human relationships. (Dyer, 1982: 116)

introduction   Semiotic theory and method have been of defining importance to the development of academic approaches to advertising.[1] Pure applications of semiotic method may be rarer now than in the past, but concepts, ideas and methods deriving from the tradition continually resurface in theoretical work, and even inform commercial practice.[2] For this reason the aim of this chapter is to look closely at how advertising has been theorised within the semiotic tradition, in order to establish some of the insights, and some of the pitfalls, of the approach.

At the centre of the semiotic account of advertising is the relation between meaning and reality. Semiotics offers both an explanation of the relationship between meaning and reality and a method of getting at the meanings of texts. Its success in both these respects is radically dependent on how categories like meaning and the real are conceptualised. If the semiotic definition of these categories is accepted, its account of what and how texts mean is very convincing. Yet semiotics offers only one of a number of epistemological stances on meaning, not all of which are at all compatible with the semiotic account. One of the main aims of this chapter is to review some of these different stances, not in order to arrive at the *best* way of thinking about meaning, but rather to make the case for an approach to the study of advertising less centred upon the problematic of meaning. The simple reason for this is that while debates about the nature of meaning provide a fertile and fascinating philosophical challenge, in the end they reveal little about advertising. This relates to the overall argument of the book that critical debates about advertising are hampered by their focus on the *meaning* of texts and products, at the expense of the *practices* of the industry.

This chapter begins with a detailed review of semiotic theory and method. A variety of theorists have contributed to the development of the structuralist semiotic project originally envisaged by Saussure (1960); but insofar as the approach has been applied to the study of advertising, Barthes's expositions (1973, 1977) are the most interesting and influential. Accordingly, close attention is paid to how Barthes defined the semiotic project and the relationship between meaning, reality and society in *Myth Today*. For Barthes, semiotics is a science devoted to the problem of meaning, which, in combination with other sciences, provides a totalist explanation of how social systems function and are reproduced. This overview of semiotics as theory is followed by a discussion of semiotics as method, in a review of its application to the study of advertising by Barthes and by critical theorists like Williamson (1978), Dyer (1982) and Goldman (1992), among others. These semiotic analyses of advertising texts share a preoccupation with the way in which advertising dissolves, captures, abducts, colonises or otherwise corrupts 'authentic' meanings, so that 'reality' increasingly disappears from view.

The validity of semiotic method as a basis for such large, 'totalist' claims is considered in a section airing some of the criticisms which have been levelled at semiotics as a way of getting at meaning. These criticisms derive, in the first instance, from concerns about the objectivity of semiotics as an interpretive method, but also from the status of texts as discrete and competent sources of meaning. Theorists, particularly those working within or influenced by a loosely defined 'post-structuralist' tradition, have argued that meaning is 'intertextually' negotiated across a range of sites, not inherent within texts. These criticisms highlight some of the problems with textual analysis as a way of getting at meaning, but they also begin to suggest a deeper problem raised by the pursuit of meaning.

This arises because of the status of meaning as a contested category. Alternative conceptualisations of meaning uncover both the dependence of the semiotic account on what can be described as a materialist conception of meaning, and the availability of alternative approaches to the definition of meaning. The main goal here is not to 're-re-conceptualise' meaning, but to describe some of the pitfalls of placing meaning at the centre of critical accounts of advertising. The pursuit of meaning in literature critical of advertising is a potentially limitless task which, whatever it may yield in philosophical terms, explains very little about the commercial practice of advertising.

the semiotic project

Semiotics as science   This section sets out the main characteristics of the semiotic explanation. Semiotics offers not only a method but a comprehensive social critique – what Barthes, with Marx in his sights, calls a totalist explanation of social life. Barthes's vision of semiotics is quite in keeping with Marx's 'ruthless criticism of everything existing', which accounts for any phenomena in terms of the determinative action of the mode of production (Marx, 1844: 12). The goal is to outline the ways in which Barthes understood the links between semiotics as a formal method and the overall operation and reproduction of the social system. The key to this is in the status of semiotics as a 'vast science of signs' applied to 'the problem of meaning' (Barthes, 1973: 119). The operation of meaning is of concern to Barthes because it is intrinsic to the functioning of all aspects of social life. At the most fundamental level Barthes's method of exploring meaning depends upon an acceptance of semiotics as a formal science. What this means is that forms should be studied *apart* from their content. The study of forms may be an abstraction, but if so it is justified as a necessary aspect of scientific technique, and because it can provide the best insight into social life.

> Less terrorised by the spectre of 'formalism', historical criticism might have been less sterile; it would have understood that the specific study of forms does not in any way contradict the necessary principle of totality and History. On the contrary: the more a system is specifically defined in its forms, the more amenable it is to historical criticism. (Barthes 1973: 120)

The sort of formal, historical criticism that Barthes has in mind is based on the combination of semiology with other sciences. This is to be achieved through mythology, which deploys semiology, the formal science, in 'dialectical coordination' with ideology as 'historical science', to yield a totalist explanation of social life and its structures of order and reproduction (Barthes, 1973: 121). Barthes's definition does not stretch beyond describing ideology as an historical science, but his use is consistent with the Marxist conception of a tool elaborating the base/superstructure model, whereby the 'mode of production of material life conditions the general character of social, political and intellectual processes of life' (Marx, 1859: 67). Material production is caught up here in some form or pattern of determination with the superstructural forms of ideology and culture. At the risk of doing a disservice to the various Gramscian, Althusserian and post-Althusserian reformulations of the nature and relative degree of ideological autonomy, this is broadly what Barthes has in mind when he describes ideology as an historical science. Mythology is therefore rooted in two distinct but coordinated approaches: the specific historical science of ideology, and the formal science of semiology. An understanding of what this means in practice requires some detailed unpacking of the methodology of this formal science.

Semiotics, fundamentally, concerns the study of formal relations between different elements that are understood to produce meaning. The most basic element is the sign, which is the 'associative total' of two further elements: the signifier, or material object and the signified, its meaning. In practice a sign is always object plus meaning, as the separation of signifier and signified is purely an analytical device. Meaning in signs works at two levels in the first instance; the first level is denotative, the second, connotative. Denotation refers to literal, 'objective' meaning: a rose is a type of flower. Connotation goes beyond literal meaning and draws upon cultural codes, while still depending on the denotation: a rose is a flower that signifies love. In this system denotation is the site at which connotations can be expressed, such that 'the first system (denotation) becomes the plane of expression or signifier of the second system (connotation) ... the signifiers of connotation are made up of signs (signifiers and signifieds united) of the denoted system' (Barthes, 1967: 91).

A further relation studied in semiotics is that between signs. Saussure (1960) originally proposed the distinction between syntagmatic and paradigmatic relations. Syntagmatic relations refer to the possible ways in which signs can be combined together in a chain. In verbal language this is governed by grammatical syntax rules, but other types of language or code also employ syntagmatic or combinatory rules. Paradigmatic relations, on the other hand, refers to the association between different signs that share a function, such that they can appear in the same context but not at the same time. Barthes's famous example of these relations used the fashion code to clarify how syntagmatic relations were those between different elements of dress which could be worn together – for example, jeans–shirt–jacket – whilst paradigmatic relations existed between those elements which could not – for example, hat–veil–hood (Barthes, 1982: 211).

Mythology involves the study of how these relations operate at a more general, 'macro' level. For Barthes, myth is a kind of second-order system, 'staggered' in relation to language, the first system. Signs that function as total units of meaning at the first level are thus reduced to mere signifiers at the second. Meaning in myth comes from combinations of signs that collectively express broader, cultural ideas.

> We must here recall that the materials of mythical speech (the language itself, photography, painting, posters, rituals, objects, etc.), however different at the start, are reduced to a mere signifying function as soon as they are caught by myth. … Whether it deals with alphabetical or pictorial writing, myth wants to see in them only a sum of signs, a global sign, the final term of a first semiological chain. (Barthes, 1973: 123)

To clarify this point Barthes uses the example of a *Paris-Match* cover depicting a black soldier in French uniform saluting the French flag. Here, meaning is communicated not through the individual signs in the image but through the transformation of these individual signs into a single signifier of French imperiality. The signifier here then is 'a black soldier is giving the French salute' and the signified is 'a purposeful mixture of Frenchness and militariness' (1973: 125). It is at this level that ideology is in operation, transmitting specific, semiologically structured historical ideas about the nature of French society. Mythology thus concerns the distribution of specific ideologies through the dialectical coordination of historical and formal sciences. This dual nature underlies Barthes's account of the relationship between myth and meaning.

Myth has a peculiar function in relation to meaning. Analogous to the sign, the signifier of myth has two components: meaning and form. Meaning here is a full and authentic category made up of the history of the object, which is emptied or 'impoverished' by the form of myth. Historical meaning, whilst not finally nullified, is kept at a distance, close enough to sustain the form of myth but far enough to tame and reduce historical meaning. In the *Paris-Match* cover, for example, Barthes explains, 'one must put the biography of the Negro in parentheses if one wants to free the picture, and prepare it to receive its signified' (1973: 127). In this way historical meaning is transformed, through the formal action of semiology, to a state which will not threaten existing social and economic interests. Of particular interest for the purposes of this chapter is the status of meaning as a coherent, univocal 'truth' impoverished by myth.

If semiology explains the formal relations of meaning, ideology provides the connection between myth and what Barthes terms 'the interests of a definite society' (1973: 139). These interests are conceived in Marxist terms as those of the ruling class, the bourgeoisie. Through suppressing historical meaning, myth acts in the interests of a definite social order, the capitalist system of production, to 'transform history into nature'.[3] Even where the intention of myth is explicit, it is perceived as natural, 'not read as a motive but as a reason' (1973: 140). This naturalising of specific historical intentions is how myth operates as bourgeois ideology. For Barthes, as for

Marx, the world pre-exists language as a set of dialectical relations between 'man' [*sic*] and nature, but myth acts to transform the historical reality of these relations into a harmonious façade. Concealed beneath this façade is the struggle and contest of man's 'real' relation to nature, where nature is transformed through labour (1973: 155).

In Barthes's schema myth obscures the dialectical structure of the real and serves the interests of the bourgeoisie by concealing their existence. The bourgeoisie are made invisible because myth acts to transform bourgeois interests into the everyday, the apparently natural order of things, and in this it is distinct from left-wing myth.

> Left-wing myth never reaches the immense field of human relationships, the very vast surface of 'insignificant' ideology. Everyday life is inaccessible to it: in a bourgeois society, there are no 'Left-wing' myths concerning marriage, cooking, the home, the theatre, the law, morality etc. Then it is an incidental myth, its use is not part of a strategy, as is the case with bourgeois myth, but only of a tactic, or, at the worst, of a deviation; if it occurs, it is as a myth suited to a convenience, not to a necessity. (Barthes, 1973: 161)

There is then a clear structural separation of function and intent between bourgeois myth and myth on the left. Bourgeois myth has a natural, universal everyday status, a completeness that refers to all aspects of social order, rendering it unavoidable and inescapably deterministic. This is what Barthes is getting at when he labels myth 'depoliticised speech': the disappearance of particular political and economic intentions under a natural, quotidian appearance. Despite Barthes's assertion that every myth has its own history and geography, this account of the progress of myth stresses a linear top-down dissemination from 'high' to 'low' culture (1973: 163). There are no competing interests here; there are no fundamental differences between bourgeois and petit-bourgeois myth, as they all exist in the same 'naturalised' relation to history. While there is myth on the left it is not myth in the proper sense, as it can not disguise specific political intention as everyday knowledge, and is therefore separate in function and intent from myth proper.

Semiotics, at least for Barthes, was conceived as part of a much larger explanation of the operation and reproduction of given societies. As a method, semiotics is designed around the description and analysis of formal relations between elements that contribute to the production of meaning, but instilled within this is the view that the formal operation of meaning is strategically linked to particular historical intentions, in accordance with the interests of ruling groups. In its coordination with ideology, semiotics achieves this by suppressing authentic, historical meanings that derive from the dialectical reality of man's relation to nature.

Crucially, there are two different sorts of meaning operating in the semiotic account. There is formal meaning, which is communicated through the relational functionality of the sign, and there is historical meaning, which is suppressed through the action of the former. In this sense signification is understood as a sort of artifice on top of the real relations between meaning, history and nature. This is an interesting proposition, but it begs the question of precisely how and when the dialectical structure of reality started to fade from view. The question of periodisation is not one that Barthes really addresses; there is simply an assumed, distant past prior to the 'order' of capitalist societies. Barthes's semiotics thus evoke the enduring myth of a simpler, purer past where reality was less susceptible to signification. This sort of position has had an enormous influence on thinking about the role of advertising in contemporary societies. Advertising more than any other medium is precisely placed to transform 'real' meanings, to make what Barthes would call specific historical intention appear natural and inevitable. In the next section attention will shift to exactly how semiotics has been applied to advertising to make precisely this sort of argument.

the rhetoric of the advertising image: how it works

Because in advertising the signification of the image is undoubtedly intentional; the signifieds of the advertising image are formed *a priori* by certain attributes of the product and these signifieds have to be transmitted as clearly as possible. If the image contains signs, we can be sure that in advertising these signs are full, formed with a view to the optimum reading: the advertising image is *frank* or at least emphatic. (Barthes, 1977: 33)

Barthes's discussion of the application of semiotic method to advertising images, the *Rhetoric of the Image*, was first published in 1964, but it was to set the tone for much subsequent critical research into advertising for the next few decades. This section addresses how semiotics, both as a method and as an explanation, has influenced critical accounts of advertising since the 1970s. To this end the section will begin with a closer look at Barthes's take on the advertising image, before moving on to consider how other authors have extrapolated on the method. The seminal treatment here is Williamson's *Decoding Advertisements* (1978), and this will feature prominently alongside the accounts of other writers including Leymore (1975), Goldman (1992) and Goldman and Papson (1994; 1996). These accounts interpret semiotics in distinctive ways and apply varied technical approaches, but they share some fundamental ideas about the relationship between advertising, meaning and reality in contemporary societies. Indeed, for a certain period it became almost impossible to think critically about advertising outside this framework. Moreover, whilst dissatisfaction with 'pure' or rigid applications of semiotic method have been increasingly expressed by critical writers on advertising,[4] the method continues to inform questions about the meaning of advertisements raised in a wide range of recent work (Giaccardi, 1995; Cross, 1996; Fowles, 1996; Kang, 1999; Myers, 1999; Cronin, 2000).

In his well-known analysis of an advertisement for *Panzani* foods depicting a string bag spilling out its contents of *Panzani* pastas, parmesan cheese, tomato sauce and fresh vegetables, Barthes deconstructs three messages contained within the visual text. The first message Barthes identifies is the linguistic message. This has denotational and connotational elements, and two main functions – anchorage and relay. Relay has a narrative function to carry the story forward, and although crucial in film it is rare in the fixed image. Anchorage is the most significant function of linguistic text because it represses the proliferation of multiple and undesirable meanings and 'it is at this level that the morality and ideology of a society are above all invested' (Barthes, 1977: 40). The second message inherent within the denoted image is described as 'a non-coded iconic message' (1977: 36). At this level the image appears as a message without a code, its nature is 'absolutely analogical', in that the objects presented have an apparently natural status in the photograph (1977: 42–3). The function of this second message, in accordance with the key semiotic principle, is revealed through its *relation* to the third, coded iconic message. The non-coded 'denoted' image's special function is to naturalise the coded, 'symbolic' message. This function is crucial as the third message operates at the level of connotation, where 'semantic artifice' is deeply embedded.

In the coded iconic message there is a series of discontinuous signs. Barthes isolates at least four signs or cultural connotations provoked by the *Panzani* advert: a return from the market, *Italianicity*, a total culinary service and the 'still life'. Barthes suggests that there is a further information pointer that reveals that the image is an advertisement. This arises from the place of the image in the magazine and from the emphasis on labels. In a move consistent with semiotics' reification of the text, Barthes reaches the obscure conclusion that this information eludes signification, as the advertising nature of the image is purely functional. The external system of which advertising is a part is thereby ruled outside the construction of meaning.

This is not to imply that semiotics offers an account of meaning as self-evident or inherent within texts in an unproblematic way. Rather, semiotics stresses the plural and active nature of meaning-making as a process. Barthes, for instance, acknowledges that the number of readings of the advertisement will vary between different individuals. The image is a 'lexical unit' combining a range of different lexicons, which are portions of language relating to specific bodies of practices or techniques, such as tourism and housekeeping (1977: 46). Some individuals will lack certain lexicons, but it is still possible for one individual to have all lexicons referred to in a single lexical unit or advertisement. This is important because, for the method to be tenable, it has to be possible for a single individual to 'own' all the relevant lexical units; otherwise the analyst would be unable to provide a complete description. The multiplicity of possible readings is anchored by the 'common domain of *ideology*, which cannot but be single for a given society and history, no matter what signifiers of connotation it may use' (1977: 49).

This, critically, allows semiotics to invoke a more universal explanation of social order through reference to the ideological nature of meaning-making, and it is precisely what Barthes means when he refers to the dialectical coordination of semiotics and ideology. Not only does ideology explain how semiotics as a formal process of signification relates to given interests; semiotics explains how ideology works. For instance, Barthes maintains that not all elements within the image are transformed into connotators – there always remains a certain denotation within the image, and it is this that perfects the system. The denotative, literal elements of the image function to naturalise, or in Barthes's terms 'to innocent the semantic artifice of connotation' (1977: 45). Thus, coordination is the key to how semiotics and ideology work. Ideology provides the bridge between the structural layering of the text, multiple individual readings, and the interests of a given society, while at the same time the relations of signification enable ideology to be disseminated.

Among the earliest detailed applications of structuralist method to advertising was Leymore's (1975) discussion of advertising's operation as a mythic system. Leymore situates her analysis as an attempt to use the structuralist principles outlined by theorists like Saussure, Levi-Strauss, Jacobson, Chomsky and Barthes to determine how the *system* of advertising was constituted. It is perhaps this focus on the system that most strongly differentiates Leymore's approach from other semiotic analyses of advertising. Although structuralism enshrines, in principle, the significance of the relations between elements in a system, most applications of it, as we shall see, are based around the analysis of individual advertisements as self-contained entities within that system. Leymore's approach is based on the 'realisation' that all advertisements for all competitive brands constitute a 'true advertising system' (Leymore, 1975: viii). For this reason her analysis is applied to product categories like baby foods, washing powder and butter/margarine. This gives Leymore the enormously complex task of producing a comparative description of relations between different elements in a range of different competing advertisements. She achieves this by identifying a range of dimensions – background, product, setting, personage – and considering the value of relation, defined as abstract versus concrete, between them. These different structural elements are then subjected to elaborate algebraic and statistical analyses. She applies this analysis to questions like the difference between static (print) and dynamic (television) advertisements, and the success of different Exhaustive Common Denominators (ECDs) or structural themes in advertisements. This enables her to draw the following two conclusions.

> (a) At the .98 confidence interval a significant correlation was found to exist between the ECD dimensions and consumer response as measured by volume sales. ...
> (b) It is possible to tentatively conclude that the dimensions have different impacts on consumer's response, some affecting it positively and others negatively. The most effective campaign, according to the present analysis, is the one using Happiness/Misery, and the least effective is Eternal Time/Profane Time. (Leymore, 1975: 117)

At the risk of doing a disservice to the intricacies of Leymore's mathematics, the conclusion that themes relating product use to happiness are most successful seems a profoundly banal place to end after such a difficult deconstruction of the system. The reason for this is certainly related to the challenge of trying to track meaning across the advertising system, even where that system is tightly defined and complex mathematical tools are deployed. This challenge arises from the nature of meaning as a dynamic, actively negotiated and plural entity. The implications of this for the study of advertising will be discussed in greater detail below, but for the moment it is worth returning to how Leymore relates her findings to the question of advertising's social role.

While Leymore's methodological focus on the advertising system sets her apart from the other theorists under consideration in this chapter, her conception of the social role of advertising shares more common ground. One of her main conclusions is that advertising obeys 'the same laws of construction and the same rules of order and classification as myth' (1975: 154). What is different for Leymore is that advertising is a simpler, 'degenerated' form, which has taken on the role of traditional mythic forms to reinforce accepted forms of behaviour and to reduce anxiety. Advertising is a sort of 'hidden myth' whose surface manifestations conceal a more complex underlying structure that for Leymore, among others, is where meaning resides. The key distinction between Leymore and other semiotic theorists is that her method of tracking this structure focuses on the system rather than the individual text. This however seems to have placed Leymore in the unfortunate position of relying on a vastly complex methodology to arrive at some disappointingly simplistic conclusions.

It is perhaps unsurprising then that subsequent exponents of the semiotic method chose to focus on elaborating the structural relations *within* individual advertising texts. The most detailed and influential treatment in this vein is Williamson's *Decoding Advertisements* (1978). According to Williamson, in order to sell, adverts have to *mean* something, and this is achieved through connecting people and objects, making the two interchangeable. Adverts thereby 'sell us ourselves' in a society where the *real* origins of identity are obscured by the distortions imposed by consumption. These distortions conceal the true basis of identity in production-based class differences behind false consumption-based distinctions fabricated by the 'ideological overlay' of advertising (Williamson, 1978: 13). Williamson deploys the terminology of semiotics to describe how a currency of signs enables the transference of meaning on to products. This transference is crucial in advanced capitalist economies because of the need to differentiate basically similar products. To this end, bizarre and illogical juxtapositions of products and objects/meanings take on a natural status, and this is construed, as in Barthes's formulation, as an ideological process. Adverts utilise a pre-existing referent system of meaning, because the product, prior to signification in the advert, has no meaning. Having captured meaning, the product becomes the signified – so, Chanel No 5 equals Catherine Deneuve. This is a step towards the product itself as a signifier of meaning, having taken over the 'reality' from which its meaning was originally abducted. In this way products can generate the feelings they represent, as in 'Clairol equals happiness'; or they can offer themselves as the currency for something else, as in 'Anne French equals clear skin equals boyfriends'. This process is carried out by the 'subject' as an active creator of meaning. The advertisement 'must enter the space of the receiver, it is he or she who completes the circuit through which, once started … a current of "meaning" flows continuously and apparently autonomously' (1978: 41).

This is what Williamson terms the 'vicious circle' of meaning exchange between advertisements and subjects. There are four simultaneous stages in this process. In the first stage we create the meaning of the product through our recognition of signifiers from the referent 'myth' system, which we then attribute to the product. The crucial factor here is the implication of the subject in the exchange process, and this provides the key to the ideological nature of the process. As for Barthes, the subject's active involvement in the formal production of meaning ensures a simultaneously ideological moment in which constructed meanings appear natural. We make the exchange and complete the links set up in the advert, and in doing so we enter a transformational space and become the signified. In this second stage, subjects take on meanings from the product.

Products whose only meaning derives from a re-hash of mythological elements already present in society, develop such an aura of significance that they tell something about their buyers and actually become adjectival in relation to them. There are the 'Pepsi People', the 'Sunsilk girls', and so on. ... We are thus created not only as subjects but as particular kinds of subjects, by products in advertisements. (1978: 45)

For this sort of appellation to be successful, Williamson maintains, you must *already* recognise yourself as the kind of subject represented. Adverts address the subject as special, individual, and in this third stage individuals recognise themselves and are simultaneously constituted as particular sorts of subject, at once individuals and part of a group. This works particularly well in English through the perfect ambiguity of the pronoun 'you' that permits diverse individuals to be addressed as one imaginary unified subject. Finally, through the advert, we create ourselves. Having constituted subjects as members of a group, then as individuals, adverts, in their depiction of multiple aspects of the self, break the individual down into a 'fragmented ego to be reunited by the product' (1978: 55). Williamson characterises this appeal to a coherent, conscious self as an appeal, not to an inherent subject essence, but to an ideologically constructed consciousness. Fundamentally, adverts act ideologically to reproduce subjects in a mould suited to the demands of capitalist economies. Williamson's explanation of how this happens is far more elaborate and sustained than Leymore's, but they end in a markedly similar place: while the overt function of adverts is to sell goods, their hidden function is to conserve society in a given form by resolving contradictions and reproducing consuming subjects.

These themes continued to appear in work by authors like Winship (1981), Dyer (1982) and Vestergaard and Schroder (1985) produced throughout the 1980s. Winship emphasises the active involvement of subjects in the meaning-making process and stresses the need to analyse the 'ideological problematic' enshrined within the means of representation adopted by advertisements. This commitment to the terms of the semiotic account is also pronounced in Dyer's analysis of ads as actively negotiated 'structures of signs' (Dyer, 1982: 115). Dyer explains, in accordance with Williamson's and Winship's accounts, that adverts create 'structures of meaning' in which goods are sold, not on the basis of intrinsic value, but on the basis of artificial, constructed human and social values. Again, this process is termed ideological in the way that the formal structure of signification in adverts helps render the specific, historical condition of contemporary capitalist economies as natural and inevitable. These principles can also be found in Vestergaard and Schroder's analysis of the language of advertising. Their account rehearses Williamson's position that, as an ideological process, advertising imposes 'behavioural normalcy' and makes specific phenomena appear natural and inevitable (Vestergaard & Schroder, 1985: 145).

There are undoubtedly other applications of the semiotic approach in work on advertising, but the next significant re-working of a semiotic mode of analysis is that provided by Goldman (1992) and Goldman and Papson (1994; 1996). Goldman's account begins by identifying advertising as a key institution in 'producing and reproducing the material and ideological supremacy of commodity relations', a system he terms 'commodity hegemony' (Goldman, 1992: 2). This indicates a move away from the Althusserian model of interpellation favoured by Williamson, where subjects are 'hailed' by the ideological messages of advertisements, towards a more Gramscian framework. Hegemony derives from Gramsci's analysis of the exercise of ideological leadership through the articulation of a range of different cultural elements to appeal to the broadest possible range of opinion (Williams, 1977). For Goldman, adverts contribute to a system of commodity hegemony because they reproduce a sense of commodity relations as a natural and inevitable part of the lives of different individuals. Their ideological significance however can be observed through skilled deconstruction offering an insight into 'how commodity interests conceptualise social relations' (Goldman, 1992: 2).

Goldman's particular contribution to the technique of deconstruction is the proposal of the mortise and the frame as structural elements. The mortise and frame function, like linguistic text in Barthes's analysis, to steer interpretation in a preferred direction. The term 'mortise' refers to a joining device, a cavity that another part fits into or passes through.

In consumer-goods advertising, the mortise conventionally takes the appearance of a hollowed-out box insert containing a picture of a named, packaged product. ... In this joining and fastening function – the constituting of relationality between parts of the ad – the mortise presupposes an underlying set of interpretive rules or codes defining a logic of visual organisation. The mortise is an encoding practice that conveys decoding instructions to viewers: as part of the advertisement's formal structure, it is a framing device that guides interpretation of the ad's content. (1992: 63)

The mortise acts as a formal device, structuring the creation of meaning within the advert. In 'routing' the transfer of meaning, it establishes the connection between the image as signified and the product as signifier. Through the mortise, irrespective of the content of individual ads, 'an ideology and practice of commodity fetishism at a deep level of communicative competence' is reproduced (1992: 65). The mortise thus constructs commodity signs that use fetishised codes to legitimate consumption.

The emphasis here is slightly different from that of many other semiotic theorists, in that greater significance is attached to the embeddedness of meaning within the system of advertisements and its extension beyond single texts to products as commodity-signs. Where Williamson's product is blank prior to signification in the advert, Goldman's product is a commodity-sign, carrying meaning from previous advertising and from the system of advertising. Here Goldman acknowledges his debt to an 'inter-textual'[5] account of meaning but, as shall be seen below, there are limits to how far this revision is allowed to modify his application of semiotics.

Before moving on to review more closely some of the problems raised by semiotic methods of 'getting at meaning' it is worth briefly flagging a further theme which flows through these accounts. If, in all these accounts, advertisements are understood to manufacture artificial structures of meaning, illogically connecting products with pre-existing cultural and human values, they do this as an ideological feature of the 'modern capitalist economy'. Advertising is thus a necessary companion to the evolving needs of capitalist societies. The belief that things were not always thus is the essential corollary of this. Semiotic accounts refer to advertising's role *today* as quite distinct from anything that has gone before. Contemporary advertisements are pervasive, ubiquitous, unavoidable and increasingly sophisticated, or as Dyer puts it 'more and more involved in the manipulation of social values and attitudes, and less concerned with the communication of essential information about goods and services' (Dyer, 1982: 2). In Vestergaard and Schroder's terms this amounts to a reversal of the 'pre-capitalist state of affairs' where cultural relationships between people and goods came from the relations of production (Vestergaard & Schroder, 1985: 155). Through advertising, the original, organic interaction between man and nature is superseded by the alienated manufacture of identity through the consumption of commodities.

It should by now be clear that semiotics formulates the relationship between advertising, meaning and reality along very specific lines. This formulation provides a complete, 'totalist' explanation of how advertising works and how it fits the structure of capitalist societies. Its dependence on very particular ways of thinking about meaning and reality is also evident. Semiotics is characterised by a dualistic conception of meaning which contrasts authentic meaning, based in the real, historical relation between people and nature, with the constructed, artificial meaning that is the ideological product of mechanisms like advertising. The remainder of this chapter considers some of the problems inherent in this approach to the question of meaning.

meaning and the text One of the most frequent criticisms of semiotics refers to the status of the analyst/interpreter, the figure that Barthes terms 'the mythologist'. For critics such as Leiss et al. (1986: 214) and Moeran (1996: 30), semiotics depends entirely on the impressionistic insights of individual analysts, with varying abilities to reach the 'deeper levels of meaning construction'. Other authors have complained that the semiotician is set apart from the recipient of meaning, mysteriously equipped to stand outside the ideological universe that structures all other interpretations (Cook, 1992; Nava et al., 1997). These criticisms are sometimes linked to arguments that semiotic method lacks objectivity and produces vague findings from specific texts that cannot be generalised. Such criticisms hark back to the methodological spat between quantitative and qualitative approaches as if, in discipline areas largely premised on the constructedness of facts, an irreproachably objective method was really an option.[6]

For present purposes, however, the most interesting problem raised by semiotics is not objectivity but the location of meaning. A deep paradox in relation to this question runs through semiotic approaches to advertising, because while the *theory* understands meaning as resident within the structural relations persisting across a system of representation, on the whole the *method* tracks meaning within individual texts. The reason for this is clear: the structural analysis of texts as self-contained, competent objects for analysis presents a complex but manageable task, while the analysis of relations that persist across a whole system of representation is quite a different matter. To make this point clearer it is worth returning briefly to Leymore's systemic analysis. Leymore defines an advertising system as constituting all the advertisements of competitive brands. To this, she applies algebraic and statistical analysis of the relations between elements to enable her to draw conclusions like 'good : evil ≈ washing powders : not washing powders' (Leymore, 1975: 75).

This relation demonstrates that the brand closest to the theme 'washing powders equal good', is the one that achieves success in the market; a powder which deviates from the theme 'condemns itself to be identified with the signifier of the "not washing powders", which is Evil' (1975: 75). Many of the conclusions that Leymore draws from her analysis are similarly crude and reductive, and this is certainly a function of the difficulty of identifying meaning in systems. Leymore's algebraic method may enable her to track oppositions and relations across an advertising system, but in order to make the task analytically manageable these relations have to be expressed in very simple terms. It would simply not be possible to conduct a comparative analysis of an 'advertising system' along the lines of Barthes's deconstruction of the *Panzani* advert.

Still, this is not the only problem with Leymore's approach. Equally troublesome is how the boundaries defining an advertising system should be drawn temporally and in market terms. Semiotic analysis is synchronic, freezing the object of analysis at a moment in time, but individual advertisements reference a whole universe of prior advertising; they are not bounded within a given 'season'. The competitive advertising market for many products is also much more fluid than Leymore acknowledges. Soap powder is an exceptionally well-defined and relatively stable market. Other markets are drawn not from common product characteristics but from common instances of use. Thus games consoles, mobile phones and branded sportswear may compete in the same market as teenage Christmas gifts and therefore constitute an advertising 'system'. Markets are 'structures of mediation' constituted through the application of specific commercial practices and technologies that refer back, through market research for example, to the social practices of consumers (Slater, 2002a).

Locating meaning in advertising systems does not therefore offer any easy solutions to the semiotic problematic of attributing meaning *externally* to relations between elements within a system, but conducting analysis *internally* within individual representations. This problematic is exacerbated by the shift towards intertextual definitions of meaning as 'plural, shattered, incapable of being tabulated' (Kristeva, 1984) and located across different systems of signification. Goldman's (1992) and Goldman and Papson's (1996) accounts attempt to accommodate intertextuality whilst retaining a method of analysis focused primarily on individual texts. They accentuate the increasing prevalence since the 1980s of rapid, absurd and pastiche recombinations of sign values in the 'mature sign economy' of advertising. Opaque messages and techniques like parody and self-mockery proliferate in a spiralling, self-referential generation of intertextual 'not-ads' (Goldman, 1992; Goldman & Papson, 1996). These shifts are part of an acceleration of meaning prompted by a change in the form and structure of commodity hegemony.

In American TV advertising during the 1980s hegemony no longer comprised a single dominant ideological account nor did it depend on a closed model of subjectivity. The hegemony of capital now rests on a flexible, and extremely privatised, system of individuated meaning production. Dominant political–economic institutions no longer require a *coherent* legitimating ideology. As concentrated corporate capital has found greater profits in a splintering of market niches, structuring meaning to suit this fragmentation of markets has contributed to fragmented public discourse. (Goldman, 1992: 174)

'Individuated meaning production' is accommodated within the logic of contemporary commodity hegemony as the very openness of 'not-ads' blocks counter hegemonic readings (1992: 198). The openness of interpretation wards off resistance while at the same time ensuring that the crucial connection is made between the commodity name and the interpretation of the advertising sign. This 'closed circuit' between the commodity name and the reading is crucial to Goldman's account because it maintains the link between ads, meaning and a given economic order, characterised as commodity hegemony. Despite the emphasis on negotiation and intertextuality the account that he, and later Papson, provide remains very close to the semiotic explanation expounded by Barthes and Williamson. For the latter, readings are always drawn from a shared ideological universe, while for the former, freedom of interpretation ultimately serves, rather than challenges, a hegemonic system.

This is an uneasy position. Advertisers 'steer meanings' but cannot guarantee interpretations that will either ratify 'preferred' meanings or produce 'aberrant' meanings (1992: 40). Yet the emphasis on the closed circuit between commodity and reading leaves little space for a truly oppositional reading – one that breaks the circuit – outside the ideological/hegemonic universe. This tension also characterises Williamson's and Barthes's accounts. Both stress the active involvement of the subject in the creation of meaning but as Williamson explains, this freedom is not quite what it seems. Freedom is illusory, a 'position given to you by the advertiser' (Williamson, 1978: 71). Subjects may be required to actively complete the circuit of meaning in adverts, but this process is largely predetermined, 'restricted to the carefully defined channels *provided* by the ad for its own decipherment' (1978: 72). Conversely, both Williamson, and Goldman and Papson maintain that people are wise to advertising and adept at resisting its messages. This is characteristic of the awkward fluctuation in semiotics between preferred and open, predetermined and active readings, that are at once resisted and irresistible.

Goldman's more fluid, 'intertextual' approach to meaning relies primarily on an acknowledgement of advertising techniques like parody, pastiche and cross-referencing to deflect criticism; a function that had, in any case, already been recognised by writers like Williamson (1978: 175–8) and Dyer (1982: 185–7). The notion of intertextuality, however, is intended to summon up more than simply cross- and self-referentiality. It also involves recognition of the transposition of signifying practices across a range of different systems. This means that the regime of signification in advertising shapes, and is shaped by, other regimes like film and television, popular music and literature. While many semiotic theorists acknowledge in principle the play of influence across these regimes, advertising texts are treated in practice as complete and self-contained systems of meaning. Even where, as in Goldman and Papson's (1996) analysis, more weight is given to cross-referentiality across signifying regimes, the relationship is unilinear with advertising always cast in the role of insatiable cultural appropriator, coloniser or 'cannibal'.

A further problem with the textual location of meaning, disregarded even by intertextual accounts, is the relationship between meaning systems and other dimensions of social life and practice. It is all very well to acknowledge how meaning is negotiated across texts, but what of the role of practices? Referentiality across film, music and advertising clearly establishes chains of meaning, but material practices – patronising certain sorts of bars, shopping for certain sorts of clothes, employment in certain sorts of work – also produce meaning. The relation between meaning and practice is followed up below, but for the moment it is worth considering how two specific aspects of practice have fared in the semiotic account.

One of the most acute manifestations of the view that meaning is located in discrete systems of signification arises in the status attributed to the product. Advertising exists in semiotics to instil meaning in products. In Williamson's account the *only* meaning of products is that instilled by the advert: the product is effectively a *tabula rasa* (Williamson, 1978: 45). The dissimilarity between many products and appropriated meanings is taken as evidence that ads are free, indeed are compelled, to harvest any attractive referent meanings. This is a paradoxical treatment in a theoretical system that privileges the symbolic character of all objects – wine, milk, steak and chips (cf. Barthes, 1973). Advertising meanings somehow take precedence over any other meanings that may be associated with the brand, product or company outside advertising.

An allied problem arises over the status of the authors or producers of advertisements. The intentions, aims and strategies of advertising producers are left out of all the accounts reviewed in this chapter, an omission which springs directly from the semiotic challenge to the idea of originary authorship. 'Obviously', Williamson argues, 'people invent and produce adverts, but apart from the fact that they are unknown and faceless, the ad in any case does not claim to speak from them, it is not their speech' (1978: 14). The absence of the author is consistent with the theoretical tenets of a method that refers back to a structuralist Marxist conception of social relations. If the consciousness of producers is derived from a common ideological universe, the texts they produce necessarily transmit over-determined ideological meanings, rendering their explicit intentions of little significance. The tenability of this position has been challenged on the basis that, whilst producers clearly do not in any straightforward way dictate the meaning of advertisements, their specific modes of production are crucial to a robust assessment of advertising (Nixon, 1996, 2003; Moeran, 1996; Miller, 1997; Slater, 2002a). Micro-level production practices pale in semiotics next to the ideological role of advertising, but the absence of an account of how advertisers actually conduct practice forces semiotic analysis into disembodied abstractions.

Excessive abstraction, in fact, haunts the semiotic pursuit of meaning. The assumption that meaning is available for textual analysis to 'get at' raises difficult questions about the character and location of meaning, which the emphasis on intertextuality does little to solve. Indeed, accentuating the relations and references across different systems of signification only raises more questions about how 'systems' and the boundaries between them should be defined. But this is not yet an end to the problematic raised by the semiotic approach to meaning. An even more intransigent problem arises in the guise of the connection between meaning and concrete material practice. The nature of this connection and the questions it raises for the critical study of advertising will be the focus of the final section.

meaning, discourse, genealogy　　The approach to meaning in semiotics, then, raises some awkward questions about the status of meaning as a category. Meaning in semiotics is conceived along dualistic lines that at once set up an opposition between meaning and reality, and between authentic and artificial meaning. Further, when meaning is conceived as having a plural, fluid and negotiated nature, the textual approach to tracking meaning encounters real difficulty. This section argues that these two issues are absolutely related. The main problem with textual analysis is not really methodological but arises from the epistemological stance on meaning. Semiotic method makes sense only insofar as its underlying dualistic approach to meaning is accepted. To make this clearer it is worth first revisiting some of the key principles of the semiotic conceptualisation of meaning, and their links to a historical-materialist way of thinking about the world. Some problems with this conceptualisation are then reviewed, before consideration is given to the way meaning is formulated within a broadly Foucauldian perspective of discursive constitution. This helps clear the path for the overarching argument that, ultimately, debates about the nature of meaning reveal surprisingly little about the developing nature, role and practice of advertising in contemporary societies.

In Barthes's analysis, the role of myth, defined as the coordinated action of ideology and semiotics, is to transform history into nature, neutralising or 'depoliticising' the explicit historical intentions of the bourgeoisie (Barthes, 1973: 149–50). In a bourgeois society all 'proper' myth is bourgeois myth. 'Public philosophy' – the rites, practices and norms of everyday life in the media, the legal system, cultural institutions and daily rituals – are all driven by the interests of the bourgeoisie. The relation between everyday myth and the bourgeoisie is opaque as a function of the ideological conversion of history into nature. Underpinning Barthes's analysis is the notion of a reality prior to myth. If myth transforms historical *reality*, the world must somehow offer up the real for transformation. Barthes concurs with Marx's view that the world exists prior to language as a dialectical relation characterised by struggle and contestation between human actions and nature (cf. Gaukroger, 1986: 303–12). In Barthes's account the dialectical nature of this relation is transformed through the action of myth.

> The world ... comes out of myth as a harmonious display of essences. A conjuring trick has taken place; it has turned reality inside out, it has emptied it of history and has filled it with nature, it has removed from things their human meaning so as to make them signify a human insignificance. (Barthes, 1973: 155)

Myth is defined as depoliticised speech, a meta-language which 'speaks of things' (1973: 156). Meta-language is symbolic, representational, in some way at a remove from a more direct relation to things, and is to be distinguished from the language-object, the form of language that 'speaks things'. This line of thinking relates to Marx's proposal that labour should be understood as the constitutive activity of man (cf. Gaukroger, 1986). Barthes's opposition of meta-language to the language-object derives from the idea that all natural objects bear traces of the human labour which produced or used them. These traces are traces of political reality that can be spoken only by the 'language-object'. Only in the language-object is language operationally related to its objects, such that the woodcutter felling a tree speaks the tree rather than 'of' the tree. This, for Barthes, is the only political speech, in that it refers to objects only insofar as they are transformed by human action.

> There is therefore one language which is not mythical, it is the language of man as a producer: wherever man speaks in order to transform reality and no longer to preserve it as an image, wherever he links his language to the making of things, meta-language is referred to a language object, and myth is impossible. (Barthes, 1973: 159)

This is an obtuse line of argument. It assumes the existence of a clear and settled demarcation between forms of productive activity or labour that transform reality and those that preserve it as an image. Yet it should be immediately clear that many forms of labour and the accompanying language do both. Landscape architects, commercial illustrators, academic botanists and conservation activists may be simultaneously involved in the transformation and representation of trees. Gaukroger's discussion of Marx's concept of labour offers an explanation of how this problem arises.

Marx conceives wage-labour as the typical form taken in exchange economies of the more broadly conceived category of labour as the constitutive activity of man. But, Gaukroger argues, this involves the conflation of two quite different notions of labour that do not cover 'all and only the same phenomena'.

Constitutive activity, if this is defined simply as labour which issues in a product, will include, amongst other things, many forms of leisure activity. Wage-labour, on the other hand may not result in a product at all: there are many kinds of service and other forms of activity that wage-labourers perform which are 'unproductive'... (Gaukroger, 1986: 310)

Gaukroger's analysis raises a fundamental problem with the proposition that political, language–object speech is functionally distinct from all other forms of meta-language or mythical, depoliticised speech. Is the woodcutter's language as a producer defined by the issue of a product or by the payment of a wage? If it is the former, what is to be said of the speech of those who transform reality through the production of services? And if it is the latter, what is to be said of those who fell trees in their own gardens? This is crucial because it bears directly on how the real outside of myth is to be defined.

A further dimension of this problem is the dialectical separation between material reality and symbolic meaning. Barthes's formulation of the relation between reality and meaning again refers back to the historical-materialist conception associated with Marxist tradition. At the simplest level this conception involves the idea that there is a determinative relationship of some form between the physical properties of objects and their use-value. This is what Barthes terms the 'historical meaning' of objects, and it is this which disappears from view with the dominance of exchange-value in capitalist societies. There is not the space here to engage in a detailed review of everything Marx had to say on the subject. The existence of contradictions in the sheer volume of Marx's writing leaves plenty of scope for debate between authors like Sahlins (1976), who regard Marx's materialist view of meaning as denying the cultural dimension of utility, and those like Jhally (1987), who think Sahlins misinterprets Marx. In Jhally's view Marx *did* recognise the cultural constitution of use-value: he simply did not see it as limitless. According to Jhally, Marx's view was not that there was a single, inherent truth or use-value within physical properties, but that these properties constrain use, as is clear in the passage he quotes from *Capital*.

> The usefulness of a thing makes it a use-value. But this usefulness does not dangle in mid-air. It is *conditioned* by the physical properties of the commodity, and has no existence apart from the latter. ... Use-values are only realised in use or in consumption. They constitute the material content of wealth, whatever its social form may be. (Marx, 1976, quoted in Jhally, 1987: 43)

Regardless of which interpretation is preferred, the crucial point is that the historical-materialist conception of meaning regards meaning as having some sort of basis in material reality. This informs the semiotic critique of advertising's effect on historical or authentic meaning. Advertisements are culpable of 'ransacking nature' and colonising 'real' meanings to construct exchange-value for goods (Barthes, 1977; Williamson, 1978; Goldman, 1992; Goldman & Papson, 1996).

> ... it is probably little noticed how much of the human symbolism of advertisements carries over into 'real life'. ... If meaning is abstracted from something ... this is nearly always a danger signal because it is only in material circumstances that it is possible to know anything and looking away from people or social phenomena to their supposed abstract 'significance' can be at worst an excuse for human and social atrocities, at best a turning of reality into apparent unreality, almost unlivable while social dreams and myths seem so real. (Williamson, 1978: 169)

For Williamson, as for many other critical theorists, the symbolic processes of advertising are accelerating, appropriating an ever-increasing array of 'real' values. A decisive break is underway from earlier societies, where people were more closely connected to the material basis of reality. These arguments are coherent and compelling in the context of the dualist opposition of authentic and historical, to artificial and constructed meaning. Problems begin when this approach to meaning is challenged, as it increasingly is, particularly in anthropologically informed work. Appadurai (1986) and Sahlins (1976), for instance, reject the notion of a materialist base to meaning, arguing that, while systems of classification describing the functions of objects are an inherent feature of most cultures, such systems are inscribed in patterns of use, and intrinsically subject to change. The meanings of objects, they insist, derive from their uses, their forms and their patterns of circulation, and this is not related in any inevitable way to their material characteristics. Appadurai and Turner accept Simmel's argument that value and meaning are not inherent in objects but are judgements conferred by others. The meaning of phenomena, in this sense, 'is not inherent in a real process'

(Turner, 1992: 73), but is fluid, negotiated and inextricably interwoven with patterns of use.

This is related to the view elaborated in Wittgenstein's philosophy that defines meaning as comprised of both semantic and pragmatic elements. Use cannot be easily separated from meaning precisely because use is itself a major factor in the determination of meaning, as Pitkin points out.

> Wittgenstein argues that meaning and use are intimately, inextricably related, because use helps to determine meaning. Meaning is learned from, and shaped in, instances of use; so both its learning and its configuration depend upon pragmatics. ... Semantic meaning is compounded out of cases of a word's use; including all the many and varied language games that are played with it; so meaning is very much the product of pragmatics. (Quoted in Laclau & Mouffe, 1990: 101–2)

There is no inevitable relation between the material existence of an object and its meaning; meanings are established in a system of socially constructed relations with other objects. This systematic set of relations encompassing both language and practice is what Laclau and Mouffe term discourse (1990: 100). In Foucauldian terms discourse can be defined as 'ways of referring to or constructing knowledge about a particular topic or practice: a cluster (or formation) of ideas, images and practices, which provide ways of talking about forms of knowledge and conduct associated with a particular topic, social activity or institutional site in society' (Hall, 1997: 6). More specifically, Laclau and Mouffe explicate discourse as a total realm encompassing both linguistic and non-linguistic elements of practice.

> Let us suppose that I am building a wall with another bricklayer. At a certain moment I ask my workmate to pass me a brick and then I add it to the wall. The first act – asking for the brick – is linguistic; the second – adding the brick to the wall–is extralinguistic ... Obviously if this totality includes both linguistic and non-linguistic elements, it cannot itself be either linguistic or extralinguistic, it has to be prior to this distinction. This totality which includes within itself the linguistic and the non-linguistic is what we call discourse. (Laclau & Mouffe, 1990: 100)

This is in sharp contrast to the materialist conception of meaning, and to Barthes's opposition of myth as meta-language to the transformational speech of the language-object. It is a formulation that better accommodates the phenomenon of labour, which is neither solely transformational nor solely representational, but intrinsically both. The notion of discourse then centrally involves recognition of the simultaneously semantic and pragmatic dimensions of meaning. This opens up a sense of the contingency of meaning upon specific systems of relations and practices that are, of necessity, subject to change. This contingent conception of meaning is hard to reconcile with the semiotic anxiety over its abduction: if meaning is a contingent construct, the logic of attributing to advertising the degree of efficacy required to produce such a devastating effect on meaning is questionable. For meaning to be the casualty of advertising, advertising has to be understood as having privileged status over all other potential sources in the determination of meaning. But if the meaning of objects shifts over time, space and context, and between users, evaluating the impact of advertising becomes a speculative and potentially limitless interpretative task.

It is this feature of meaning that motivated Foucault's decision to set aside the inexhaustible and ultimately futile techniques of semiotics as 'a task that nothing could limit' (in Dean, 1994: 16). Discourses, Foucault maintained, 'are transparent, they need no interpretation, no one to assign them a meaning. If one reads texts in a particular way one perceives that they speak clearly to us and require no further supplementary sense or interpretation' (Foucault, 1980: 115). This encapsulates many of the criticisms that have been levelled at semiotics regarding the status of the interpreter and the location of meaning. Meaning, for Foucault, is the plural outcome of ongoing, active processes, and therefore has no single, essential core accessible only to the skilled analyst or semiotician. This is why, finally, criticisms of semiotic method are not really methodological at all. Rather they are criticisms of the conception of meaning and its place in a totalist explanation of 'everything existing'. But if semiotic method cannot get at meaning, if the nature of meaning is really a matter for philosophical debate, the question arises of what direction future work on advertising should go in. In *Nietzche, Genealogy, History* Foucault enlarges on his refusal to be drawn into the pursuit of essential, 'original' meaning and offers an alternative possibility. Following Nietzche's rejection of the notion of a reality prior to language in which the exact essence of things existed in their purest 'immobile' forms, he advocates genealogy as an alternative to the deconstruction of the origin of things (Foucault, 1984b: 78). Genealogy can uncover

'something altogether different' behind things: not a timeless and essential secret, but the secret that they have no essence or that their essence was fabricated in a piece-meal fashion from alien forms. … What is found at the historical beginning of things is not the inviolable identity of their origin; it is the discension of other things. It is disparity. (1984b: 78–9)

This genealogical investigation of the piecemeal fabrication of forms offers an alternative approach to studying advertising from the endless semiotic pursuit of meaning. Informed by a genealogical perspective, the study of advertising could embrace instead the patchwork of historical conditions and accidents that have shaped the field.

conclusion   This chapter has focused primarily on the relationship between advertising, meaning and reality to establish how the totalist form of explanation semiotics provides is linked to a dualist, materialist conception of meaning. This conception underlies the logic of applying techniques of structuralist deconstruction to advertisements to ascertain how 'real' material circumstances are subsumed by the semantic artifice of signification. The latter is understood as a progressive, linear process in which 'reality' steadily gives way in the construction of advertising myths. Semiotic critics talk about advertising 'today' in a way that makes it absolutely clear that things were not always this way. Advertising is characterised as an increasingly pervasive, persuasive, symbolic medium because of its connection to the historical evolution of capitalist economies. The story of advertising is thus the story of the progress of capitalist economies, and the cultural analysis of advertising has to be conducted 'in the context of the historical development of capitalist political economy and class relations (Goldman, 1992: 22).

This formulation of advertising, however, is destabilised by rethinking the definition of meaning as a contingent construct, formed in instances of use. If meaning is always contingent it cannot simultaneously be the historical casualty of the signifying regimes upon which capitalist economies depend. The materialist account of meaning makes great play of the distinction between the present and the past – the origin, when things were not as they are now. The problem with this is that it invokes an often idealised precommercial past that is simply assumed rather than known. There is no patient, abundantly detailed record of how advertising was conducted at other moments in time. It is for this reason that genealogy is advocated as an approach that could 'record the singularity of events outside of any monotonous finality ... sensitive to their recurrence, not in order to trace the gradual curve of their evolution, but to isolate the different scenes where they engaged in different roles' (Foucault: 1984b: 76). An historical account of advertising less invested in superimposing a final destination on singular events, and alert to their contingent formation in specific assemblages of institutions, processes and practices, is an appropriate mechanism to counter the tunnelled vision of critical teleology.

notes

1 The term 'semiotics' is primarily used throughout this chapter, although Barthes himself preferred 'semiology'. Semiology was the term originally coined by Saussure, but 'semiotics', a word deriving from the work of American theorists like Charles Peirce, has become the most commonly used term. Deely (1990) provides a more detailed discussion of the historical development of the approach.

2 *Semiotic Solutions* formed in 1987 to sell market research insights derived from semiotics to the advertising industry. See *Semiotic Solutions* website: www.semioticsolutions.com.

3 See Barthes, 1973: 139. This aspect of Barthes's account has strong resonances with Marx's thesis of commodity fetishism, in which the mystical, enigmatic character of commodities derives from the mistaken attribution of value as inherent in commodities, rather than as the result of human labour (Marx, 1978: 319–29). See Chapter 2 for a more detailed discussion of the influence of the commodity fetishism thesis on critical literature.

4 See for example writers like Wernick (1991), Leiss et al. (1986), discussed in Chapter 2, and the more extensive critique levelled by writers like Moeran (1996), Miller (1997), Mort (1996) and Nixon (1996), featured in Chapter 3.

5 The term intertextuality was developed by Kristeva to refer to the transposition of several different sign systems into one another such that meaning is always polyvocal and never finally decided. 'If one grants that every signifying practice is a field of transpositions of various signifying systems (an intertextuality), one then understands that its place of enunciation and its denoted "object" are never single, complete and identical to themselves but always plural, shattered, incapable of being tabulated' (Kristeva, 1984: 59–60).

6 See also Goffman (1979) on the representativeness of large-scale advertising surveys, and Fish (1994) on how the notion of social construction informs disciplinary approaches.

the persuasive subject
of advertising

introduction   In spite of the impact that semiotic analysis had across the academy, some of the best known and most influential critical accounts of advertising produced since the 1980s took a quite different approach. Probably the most significant difference was a shift away from an exclusive reliance on the text as the object of analysis towards a more generalised focus, which also encompassed the institutional position and historical development of the industry. The primary aim of this chapter is to consider the types of explanations of advertising that accounts in this vein have offered, and in particular to explore how the relationship between advertising, people and objects is characterised. This relationship is widely understood to have shifted to complement changes in the structure and organisation of advanced industrialised societies, and particular explanations have emerged of how advertising both reflects and facilitates such changes. Foremost amongst these explanations has been a concern with how advertising has refined its persuasive capacity.

It would be hard to overstate the significance of the issue of persuasiveness. Persuasiveness is used throughout academia as an index of advertising's power to stimulate demand, to manipulate behaviour and to manufacture meaning. It is widely invoked as *the* criterion differentiating contemporary advertising from its predecessors. Persuasive advertisements manipulate the relationships between people and objects to maximise appeal, and are thereby deemed culpable in a way that information-based advertisements are not for facilitating the transition to a different sort of society. The critical fascination with describing the 'consumer', 'post-Fordist', 'post-modern', or 'information' epoch thus frequently calls upon persuasive advertising as an enabling tool.

Critical accounts over the last two decades renewed interest in the relationship between subjects, objects, advertising and the broader organisation of society, but this is not a new concern. Interest in the effects of specific modes of production on people and objects stretches back to Marx, and has subsequently been developed most notably in reference to advertising by Frankfurt School theorists like Adorno, Horkheimer, and latterly Haug. These theoretical precedents are reviewed briefly to pave the way for a more detailed consideration of how commodity forms of production have been understood to intervene in the relationship between people and objects, in recent accounts such as those of Leiss et al. (1986) and Wernick (1991).

The focus then shifts to the question of how advertising is supposed to get in between people and objects. Critical explanations have settled upon two associated factors – that advertising in the twentieth century became simultaneously more persuasive and more pervasive. These factors go hand-in-hand; for many commentators, advertising's increased everyday presence is a necessary prerequisite to its growing potency. The section considers the prevalence of this view in the literature, examines the nature of some of the evidence available to support it, and suggests two main problems with such evidence. First, some of the most comprehensive surveys of the changing historical content of advertisements are surprisingly inconclusive. Second, supportive evidence comes almost exclusively in the form of textual analyses that provide only a very partial insight into the contemporaneous significance of historical advertisements. These problems prompt questions about the adequacy of this type of evidence in supporting arguments citing profound changes in the subject/object relationship.

This line of thought is developed further in a discussion of how historical work on material practices of consumption and promotion renders the types of relations that existed between subjects and objects. Here the degree of fit between historical evidence and critical claims about the transformed subject/object relation in consumer societies is explored. The underlying aim throughout is to signal the need for a theoretical approach to advertising grounded in a contextualised historical study of material practices. This need arises because of the types of claims critical theories have made about advertising's unique transformative potential. Such claims have generally relied upon very specific and quite circumscribed forms of evidence. This evidence is frequently thin on historical detail about relations between people and things in the societies against which the contemporary moment is contrasted. In this critical vein the past is always known, but the minutiae of historical practices calculated to promote consumption unsettles such assumptions.

advertising masks

Commodity fetishism: advertising and the subject/object relation   Perhaps the defining feature of critical work on advertising is that it addresses itself to questions about the broader effects and role of advertising in society. In the previous chapter the focus was on the perceived effects of advertising on the categories of meaning and reality. In this chapter the focus is primarily on the related issue of the impact of advertising on the relationship between people and objects. One of the strongest themes in the literature is that advertising has done something fundamental and probably irrevocable to that relationship. It has masked the true nature of objects and subjects, and in doing so produced a different sort of society. But if this is the case it has not acted autonomously. Rather, advertising is understood, in a wide range of critical work, as a tool of a particular economic system, defined as capitalist commodity production. There is not the space here to engage in a detailed exploration of competing theories of economic organisation.[1] It is, however, important to consider briefly the Marxist account of the relationship between people and objects under capitalism, because this, more than any other explanation, has had a formative influence on the place attributed to advertising in subsequent work.

In Marxist theory the specific form of the person–object relation in capitalism arises because the system of production is motivated by the need to *exchange* rather than *use* the goods produced – a situation widely characterised as the subordination of use-value to exchange-value (Haug, 1986; Jhally, 1987; Adorno, 1991). According to Jhally (1987: 27–35) Marx's theory of commodities distinguished between two levels, 'essence' and 'appearance'. 'Essence' refers to the underlying social relations of production, concealed by the appearance of things in capitalist systems of production. 'Appearance' is not illusion, but an aspect of reality, 'the form in which essence shows itself' (1987: 28). For Marx, the dual-use and exchange-value nature of the commodity is the key to the social relations of production. Both types of value have an essence and an appearance, but in use-value the two are instrumentally related – an object's appearance suggests its use. In exchange-value, in contrast, products are endowed with qualities that they do not in themselves possess, and there is therefore no real relationship between essence and appearance. This is the basis of commodity fetishism. In Marx's view people make a fetish out of commodities when they see values as inherent in objects, rather than as the result of human actions. Commodity fetishism 'naturalises' a social process by rendering essence – the human labour of production – invisible beneath the appearance of intrinsic value. The appearance of commodities in the market thus masks the relations of production.

The view that historical social relations are naturalised in commodity systems of production underpins the semiotic account of advertising, but it has also had a profound influence on a number of other critical explanations of advertising. Marx himself may not have integrated advertising into the theory of commodity fetishism, but other theorists in the Marxist tradition soon identified how neatly advertising slots into this explanation. Advertising is one of the primary tools whereby products can attain exchange-value, where an appearance unrelated to use-value can be instilled. In Adorno's (1991) and Horkheimer and Adorno's (1973) expositions of the operation of the culture industry, advertising plays a crucial role. Advertising substitutes the story of the product's origination in production with its own symbolic story. In the culture industry this advertising story ultimately becomes the reality.

> The poetic mystery of the product, in which it is more than itself, consists in the fact that it participates in the infinite nature of production and the reverential awe inspired by objectivity fits in smoothly with the schema of advertising. ... If the real becomes an image insofar as in its particularity it becomes as equivalent to the whole as one Ford car is to all the others of the same range, then the image on the other hand turns into immediate reality. (Adorno, 1991: 55)

This is a serious state of affairs. In this schema the effect of advertising as the ultimate tool in the fetishisation of commodities alters the reality not only of objects but also of subjects. The 'reification' or objectification of people, for Horkheimer and Adorno, is so complete that the notion of individual personality is reduced to the characteristics – white teeth and fragrant odours – defined in advertisements (Horkheimer & Adorno, 1973: 167; Adorno, 1991: 82). Adorno talks about people donning 'culture-masks' to enable them to participate actively in the mystification of reality that structures the culture-industry. Authentic behaviour is overtaken by false, copied performance – 'it is this rather than self-expression or individuality which forcibly produces the behaviour of the victims which recalls St Vitus's dance or the motor reflex spasms of the maimed animal' (Adorno, 1991: 82).

Adorno and Horkheimer's bleak and sinister polemic is replicated in many subsequent explanations of advertising. Ewen's (1976: 33–5) account, for example, sees advertising as creating consumers with 'fancied needs' that transcend basic needs, to produce consumption in line with the historic needs of capitalist commodity production. The immediate effect of advertising might be only a momentary act of consumption, but the long-term aim is the development of a 'critical self-consciousness' where 'real' personal and social frustrations would seek solutions in the marketplace. Advertising produces the 'commodity self' – an objectified body split into separate portions, each with a product to match. Personal and social success in this system depends upon 'a commodity defined *self-fetishization*' where using the right product can solve any problem (Ewen, 1976: 47). A similar logic underscores Haug's (1986) account of commodity aesthetics. In his terms, the subordination of use-value produces a context in which sensuality, expressed in the appearance of products, has a primarily economic function. Advertising here, in controlling the appearance of products, can also control people through sensual appeal (Haug, 1986: 16–17). Commodity aesthetics is a form of beauty specifically designed to enhance exchange-value, whereby the commodity itself stimulates a desire to possess. Useful objects are transformed into commodities that can speak to people's instinctual drives and trigger a 'sensual understanding'.

[Capitalism] subjects the whole world of useful things ... to an incessant aesthetic revolution in the course of their inclusion in monopoly capitalist commodity production. Aesthetic innovation, as the functionary for regenerating demand, is thus transformed into a moment of direct anthropological power and influence, in that it continually changes humankind as a species in their sensual organisation, in their real orientation and material lifestyle, as much as in the perception, satisfaction and structure of their needs. (Haug, 1986: 44)

In all these accounts advertising is directly implicated in the transformation of the subject/object relation which is understood to occur under capitalist modes of commodity production. The relentless dominance of appearance over use is inherent in the logic of the commodity itself, and the particular contribution of advertising is to reproduce that dominance.[2] Despite important differences in the ways the debate about the social role of advertising has been taken up, this basic position has indelibly imprinted more recent work.

Who is behind the mask? – what advertising does to the subject   Leiss, Kline and Jhally describe contemporary advertising as a 'privileged form of discourse' that has taken on the role traditionally performed by institutions like the church, the state and the broader community. Advertising defines the relationship between people and objects, and is therefore an 'integral part of modern culture' which appropriates and transforms 'a vast range of symbols and ideas' (Leiss et al., 1986: 5). This conception is broadly reminiscent of the semiotic position outlined in the previous chapter, but what sets Leiss et al. apart is their methodological approach. For them the deconstruction of individual advertisements is not sufficient; rather, they combine economic, socio-cultural, institutional and textual dimensions of analysis to enable them to describe advertising's provision of a 'cultural frame for goods'. This term signals how advertising, through its proximity to major economic concerns and its pervasiveness in everyday life, defines the interplay between people and objects in a 'consumer society', where goods act primarily to communicate meaning rather than to satisfy wants. Advertising's place in the transition to consumer society is evidenced by historical changes in the format and content of advertisements.

In this formulation Leiss et al. stay quite close to the key terms of the commodity fetishism thesis. Market economies, they argue, at the most basic level, misrepresent the true nature of material objects. As the market–industrial economy expands an increasing array of natural and human elements are drawn into the realm of commodities, as 'objectified forms' which conceal 'any adequate representation of the *social* character of production and consumption activity' (1986: 323). Advertising feeds this systematic distortion by masking the material nature of objects through the construction of branded images. Market societies can be characterised as 'masked balls' hosted by advertising and marketing, where the desire for meaning is displaced onto commodities, disguising the underlying social relations and processes (1986: 348).

Wernick begins in a similar vein, by expressing the need for the critique of advertising to encompass more than the decoding of individual advertisements. An understanding of advertising's role, he argues, must also take into account the broader promotional system spanning production, marketing and design. To this end he provides a cogent description of the promotional significance of Josiah Wedgwood's copy of the Portland Vase. Wedgwood borrowed the Portland Vase to make a replica in the full knowledge that the project would be unlikely ever to yield a profit. Yet the project, as Wernick explains, was not an idle indulgence but part of a strategy to use the copy as a marketing device for the profitable product ranges at the core of Wedgwood's business operation. The connotations of classical aesthetic achievement attached to the vase enabled it to function as an advertisement for the Wedgwood empire. Thus the entire matrix of activities surrounding the production and distribution processes were implicated within the promotional, symbolic function. For Wernick, Wedgwood's use of the Portland Vase epitomises the arrival of 'artificial semiosis' – a process involving the industrial manufacture of meaning and myth (Wernick, 1991: 15). In artificial semiosis, ' "imaging sites" construct the promotional sign through advertising, packaging and presentation, and materially stamp the commodity through the design process, creating a dual character object, the *commodity-sign*' (1991: 16).

The crucial departure is not the symbolic character of objects per se, but the manner in which this character is instilled. Artificial semiosis instrumentalises the acquisition of meaning, and it is this 'type and modality of promotion' that is distinct from earlier pre-industrial forms (1991: 17). In the industrial phase promotion becomes a strategic and integrated aspect of production. Advertising is fused with symbolic manufacture and the resultant 'commodity-sign' is an entirely new sort of product. For Wernick commodity-signs are different from pre-industrial goods primarily because of the way in which image is manipulated to enhance their 'actual use-value'. This, in his terms, is an 'ideological' process in that advertisements act to unite commodities with attributed subject positions.

> The commodity they project as the object of desire is simultaneously presented as a cultural symbol charged with social significance; and the ego they seek to engage as the subject of desire is induced to adopt the socio-cultural identity attributed to those who already use the product. (1991: 31)

There is not that much difference between this and Williamson's (1978) or Goldman's (1992) accounts of how advertising works through an Althusserian model of ideological interpellation. This is surprising because at various points Wernick seeks to distance his analysis from more classically Marxist accounts of advertising's ideological action. Yet the main distinctions between Wernick and accounts in the latter vein are actually quite subtle. As mentioned above, Wernick locates advertising within a much broader promotional system spanning production and design. This foregrounds his acknowledgement that advertising, however important, is only part of a much more extensive production process in which signification occurs at various stages. Unfortunately, Wernick stops short of allowing this assertion to alter his own methodological approach, but it nevertheless marks a less restrictive way of thinking about how and where signification occurs. This also emerges in his acknowledgement of the difficulty of disentangling promotional symbolism from other cultural meanings.

> It is almost as difficult in the real world to make a rigorous distinction between the commodity and its manufactured symbolic aura as in the advertising text. What complicates the distinction is that products, even physical and practical ones, are inseparable from language (including visual language) and from patterns of use that are overlaid with ceremonial and cultural significance. (Wernick, 1991: 32)

This difficulty is related to what Wernick calls the 'promotional intertext' that connects advertisements not only to their commodity-signs but to other ads, and to a shared cultural vocabulary which is both articulated and re-worked within advertising (1991: 92–3). Pushing these myriad semantic entanglements to one side, Wernick goes on to claim that the differences between generic cultural conventions attached to products and the specific brand identities that advertisers attempt to construct are 'obvious'. This insistence upon the singularity of advertising's role in attaching meanings to commodities leads Wernick back to the key terms of the structuralist/Marxist account.

> By addressing individuals always as potential customers, and so attributing them *a priori* a social identity linked firmly to that role, advertising builds the standpoint of consumption into the design of its every text. … The consumerist address imprisons the subjectivity it projects into a totally commodified ontology. Being is reduced to having, desire to lack. … Production as human praxis – the satisfaction of human need through non-alienated self-activity – is obliterated as a thinkable thought. (1991: 35)

This closely parallels the structure of accounts in the tradition of commodity fetishism. In particular there are resonances with Haug's concerns about the effects of commodity aesthetics on the sensory organisation of the human species. Yet for Wernick, Haug's conceptualisation does not go far enough – instead it reduces the transformative effect of commoditisation to an externality, a 'dressing up' (1991: 190). Promotion, in Wernick's view, does not just embellish commodities but fundamentally alters their very being, with implications for subjects as well as objects. Subjects in a 'de-referentialised' culture face the challenge of 'how to build an identity and an orientation from the materials of a culture whose meanings are unstable and behind which, for all the personalized manner in which its multitudinous messages are delivered, no genuinely expressive intention can be read' (1991: 192). Matters are worsened still with the involvement of consumers in promotional culture as its authors as well as its readers. In Wernick's expanded definition of promotion, ultimately everyone is drawn in to the promotional process. Even those who avoid it in the workplace inevitably undertake some form of self-promotion in finding a school, accommodation or a partner. This is especially problematic because the author and the product are one.

> Just like any other artificially imaged commodity, then, the resultant construct – a persona produced for public consumption – is marked by the transformative effects of the promotional supplement. The outcome … is a self which continually produces itself for competitive circulation: an enacted projection … The contemporary subject … is faced with a profound problem of authenticity. If social survival, let alone competitive success, depends on continual audience-oriented, self-staging, what are we behind the mask? (1991: 193)

All the authors featured here share an underlying preoccupation with advertising as a device with the facility to transform the nature of objects and subjects. This is why the term 'mask' is invoked so frequently to signal some basic essence that advertising, as the tool of a 'consumer-' or 'commodity-'driven society, conceals. There are significant differences between the authors in terms of precisely how they understand this action. For Adorno and Horkheimer, as for Ewen and Haug, advertising operates as an explicitly political tool of a society driven by the logic of capitalism, while for Leiss et al. and Wernick, the logic of advertising is driven by commercial rather than political aims. In addition there is a sense in Adorno and Horkheimer, and Ewen and Haug, of advertising as a new departure in the manipulation of meaning for political/commercial ends that is less pronounced in Leiss et al. and Wernick's accounts. Both the latter accounts acknowledge the persistence of the symbolic dimension of exchange in prior forms of society. Furthermore, Wernick in particular insists that it is not just advertising that is implicated in the process of symbolic manufacture. Nonetheless both Wernick and Leiss et al. retain a sense that there is something tangibly different and peculiar about how symbolism is produced in 'commodity capitalist' societies. These differences are sufficient to return both accounts to the question of advertising's effects on objects and subjects, and this merits closer examination.

If advertising can transform not only the appearance but the ontological 'reality' of objects and subjects, this poses questions about what sorts of entity objects and subjects are. The previous chapter suggested that meaning derives ineluctably from both symbolic practices and patterns of use. According to this line of reasoning, advertising cannot really do anything new and irrevocable to the underlying nature of objects and subjects: it only feeds into an ongoing negotiation of meaning. This signals a conception of objects and subjects as *contingent* categories, which raises some difficult questions for the critical accounts featured here. These difficulties arise because critical accounts adopt a simultaneous investment in a conception of meaning as a stable category located *outside* promotional culture, and as a fluid and vulnerable category manipulated *within* promotional discourse.

Wernick, for example, is well aware of the challenge that the notion of contingency poses to his characterisation of the subject in promotional culture. He concedes that, in tracing the effects of promotion on contemporary subjectivity, his account is broadly aligned with an intellectual tradition describing the alienation, reification and collapse of the subject under the condition of capitalist modes of production. This involves what Wernick terms a 'classical liberal' (1991: 191) view of the subject as an essentially stable identity position characterised by attributes typically including freedom, autonomy and consciousness. Yet Wernick also wants to make space for the oppositional view of the subject as a contingent historical and anthropological category. He argues that this latter view is based on the notion that subjects are constituted by language, and is therefore very relevant to his analysis of promotion as itself a linguistic, communicative form. But this is not an unproblematic move. Leaving aside the emphasis in recent work on the subject as formed not exclusively through language but in the 'prestigious imitation' of material forms of *practice*, this is still a poor compromise.[3] Promotion may be a language, and for some theorists this may explain its involvement in shaping subjectivity, but this does not in itself square his concerns about its transformative and largely detrimental impact on subjectivity. For the key point here is that contingency means that transformation is inevitable. It makes no sense to express concern about changes in the essential characteristics of human subjects if there are no such essentials. As Rose has argued, the tendency in critical theory to regard changing forms of subjectivity as causally related to wider social transformations makes sense only if subjects are viewed as stable, ontological categories.

> These kinds of analysis regard changes in the ways in which human beings understand and act upon themselves as the outcome of 'more fundamental' historical events located elsewhere – in production regimes, in technological change, in alterations in demography or family forms, in 'culture'. ... Changing relations of subjectification, I want to argue, cannot be established by derivation or interpretation of other cultural or social forms. To explicitly or implicitly assume they can is to presume the *continuity* of human beings as the subjects of history ... (Rose, 1996: 130)

Although Leiss et al. talk about people rather than subjects, their emphasis on advertising's masking of 'important' human concerns demonstrates an equivalent commitment to a 'classical', essentialised view of what it means to be a human subject. Their use of the term 'mask' is meant to draw attention to the systematic distortion of the 'true' nature of objects in market societies. This distortion conceals any 'direct connection between goods and the enduring sources of contentment in life' (Leiss et al., 1986: 326). Advertisements are 'fetishes' which distract people from more satisfying, reciprocal forms of participation in social life. In consumer societies affiliations with social groups are based primarily on arbitrary lifestyle groupings, such as 'hippies' and 'punks', with products to match. These fleeting forms of collective participation emerge from the dissolution of more traditional, stable forms of collectivity organised around community, custom and religion.

Although in quite moderate terms, advertising is again characterised as feeding the objectification and alienation of the subject. The subject is still fundamentally regarded as an entity which, outside of the vestiges of market societies, would be fairly stable, conscious, free and autonomous. But there is a basic theoretical inconsistency in this sort of argument. If the subject has an ontologically stable essence comprising these sorts of fundamental attributes, how can capitalist/market societies in general, or advertising in particular, 'get into' it? In some respects this sort of position implies a contingent view of the subject as having specific social, political, economic and cultural conditions of existence.[4] But this is not, overall, how critiques of advertising view the subject. The explanation they offer is rather different. Advertising, in this critical tradition, 'gets into' the subject because it is quite unlike any previous sort of cultural or economic institution. In its unique mixture of commercial and symbolic messages; in its technologically mediated pervasiveness; in the psycho-cultural persuasiveness of its appeal; and most particularly in the interplay of all three, advertising is different. The next section explores the sorts of evidence that have been deployed to support this idea.

the pervasiveness of persuasive advertising

The real business of the historian of advertising is more difficult: to trace the development from processes of specific attention and information to an institutionalized system of commercial information and persuasion; to relate this to changes in society and in the economy: and to trace changes in method in the context of changing organizations and intentions. (Williams, 1980: 170)

Raymond Williams's admonition to advertising historians was originally written around 1960. Subsequently, at least one part of it has been enthusiastically pursued by writers on advertising. While these writers may have, to some extent, neglected the context of changing organisations, methods and intentions, no one could fault the degree of attention they have paid to the development of advertising as a persuasive system. Persuasiveness is widely characterised as an index of all the ways in which contemporary advertising is supposed to be different from its historical antecedents. Persuasive advertising is image-laden, rhetorical, and emotional. It does not trouble much with product characteristics, but stresses instead the transformational benefits of product use, enhancing appeal by framing products alongside unrelated personal and lifestyle attributes. In all these respects persuasive advertising stands in contrast to its more 'innocent' predecessor – informational advertising, which simply announces the details and availability of products. These ideas have enormous currency, and form a crucial part of the critical characterisation of advertising as a transformative medium. This section considers some of the evidence on which the increasing persuasiveness thesis is based. One of the most important sources of evidence is the extensive historical study of the content of advertisements conducted by Leiss et al. (1986) and this is therefore considered in some detail alongside Pollay's content analyses (Pollay, 1984, 1985).

Williams was not the first writer to emphasise a shift to more persuasive forms of advertising. This theme can be found in the earlier writings of advertising historians like Hower (1939), Rowsome (1959) and Turner (1952). By the time Leiss et al. first published the results of their influential historical survey of advertising content in 1986, Schudson had already commented on the 'common view both in the advertising industry and outside that, once upon a time, ads were primarily informational, appealing to the rational consumer, but that ads in the twentieth century have become increasingly persuasive, oriented to a non-rational, impulse driven consumer' (Schudson 1984: 58). Yet Leiss et al.'s survey was significant because it not only provided systematic evidence in support of this view, but also elaborated a framework explaining how changes in advertising content were related to changes in the relationship between people and objects.

Leiss et al. describe advertising as 'the privileged discourse for the circulation of messages and social cues about the interplay between people and objects', a status deriving both from its proximity to economic concerns and its pervasiveness (1986: 50). This privileged position has been attained through a gradual evolution in advertising's persuasive capacity. Throughout the twentieth century, Leiss et al. maintain, agencies have concentrated less on the communication of information about products, and more on the transformation of consumer attitudes towards products (1986: 153–8). They describe the institutional development of the industry as comprising four main stages. In stage one (1890–1925) 'product oriented' advertising, involving mainly print-based media and rationalistic arguments about product benefits, dominates. This gives way between 1925 and 1945 to a phase described as 'product symbols', which involves a greater use of new media like radio and 'limited' market research information to make rudimentary associations between products and desirable qualities. This in turn is superseded by the 'personalisation' stage in the post-war years, where use of television and new research techniques enables advertising targeted at the psychological make-up of consumers. Finally the market segmentation stage, between 1965 and 1985, takes a multi-media approach to targeting different consumer groups.

These phases, in Leiss et al.'s formulation, are integrally related to the developing institutional structure of advertising. The use of different sorts of media, research techniques and other working practices all feed into the types of approach which dominate at different stages. In addition, they recognise that the phases are not as neatly demarcated as their periodisation suggests; the characteristics of appeal types do not completely disappear, rather they become subordinate components in a varied marketing environment. This is all very reasonable. Leiss et al.'s emphasis on the changing institutional framework is a welcome attempt to relate changing working practices to the final appearance of advertising. But their discussion is conducted at quite a generalised level, flagging primarily major institutional developments such as the introduction of new media and research techniques. In one chapter they cannot really do justice to the breadth and variety of institutional arrangements over the course of a century. The main evidence they do provide in support of their evolutionary framework comes later in the book, in the form of an extensive historical survey of advertisements. Ultimately, for them, only 'analysis of the complete "set" of advertising messages' (1986: 197) can apprehend 'the meaning of modern society's grand spectacle of people and products' (1986: 193).

Before embarking on their own investigation, Leiss et al. review the two major approaches used in the academic study of advertising: semiotics and content analysis. Their conclusions cover familiar territory, and the strengths and weaknesses they identify follow closely the terms of standard methodological debates on the trade-off between qualitative and quantitative approaches.[5] They opt for a 'middle range methodology' in an attempt to combine the insights of each method while avoiding their pitfalls. This combined method is then applied to an historical study of magazine adverts to produce a delineation, consistent with their four phases of institutional development, of four advertisement formats: product-information, product-image, personalised and lifestyle. These formats do not *precisely* supersede each other, but they do achieve 'dominance' at given periods, resulting overall in a move away from utilitarian representations of the relationship between people and objects.

This century opened with rationalism and the objective characteristics of goods at the centre of advertising, implying a predominantly pragmatic relationship between persons and objects; but this mode of representation has systematically been eroded and replaced by one in which products have been 'reanimized' and given meaning, transporting them from the rational-physical universe of things to the world of human social interaction. (1986: 279)

This point of view has become almost axiomatic in critiques of advertising. What Leiss et al. and Jhally describe as a switch in format, from information and utility at the turn of the century, to lifestyle and social context by the 1980s, is understood elsewhere as a shift from announcement to advertisement (Dyer, 1982; Pope, 1983, 1991; Falk, 1994), or from simple to compound advertisements (Fowles, 1996), or away from crude attention-seeking (Myers, 1999). Its influence on critical theory more generally should also be recognised, as this 'decline in printed text and concomitant rise in visual imagery' has been cited in broader accounts of epochal transitions in societal formation (Lash & Urry, 1987: 290; Featherstone, 1991: 86–8).

The increasing persuasiveness thesis is also inextricably linked to the notion that advertising has proliferated in the public arena. Advertising is persuasive in this sense partly because of its ubiquity, its saturation of the media, its pervasion of everyday existence. Advertising here is 'the most pervasive of all forms' (Myers, 1999: 212) weakening the influence of more traditional institutions on the generation of meaning (Leiss et al., 1986; Jhally, 1987; Goldman & Papson, 1994; 1996), and feeding the reproduction of societies structured according to a promotional logic (Wernick, 1991). Yet few of these accounts provide detailed evidence to support this proliferation. In most cases it is simply assumed that the level of saturation that advertising messages have achieved in both public and private spaces is unprecedented.

Two exceptions to this are Leiss et al. (1986) and Pope (1983), who both provide some figures which seem to support the idea of the increasing pervasiveness of advertising. But these figures are far from conclusive. Leiss et al. provide three graphs, recording advertising expenditure after 1920 in the United States, Canada and the United Kingdom respectively, which all suggest sustained increases. Pope's (1983) review is more detailed, and records increases in the volume of advertising placed, tracing these increases as a proportion of gross domestic product (GDP). His figures for advertising expenditure as a proportion of GDP reveal much smaller increases over time. In addition, as Pope points out, changes in the way statistics are collected, and the absence of reliable statistics prior to 1930, make historical comparisons very approximate. Moreover, even proportional comparisons cannot tabulate expenditure on the dominant nineteenth-century media of poster, street and transport advertising. Quantitative historical comparisons also tend not to factor in broader contextual changes in demographics, and in social and cultural life, which are germane to assessing pervasiveness.[6]

Evidence in direct support of increased pervasiveness, then, may be a little thin, but the same could not be said of the evidence that has been presented to demonstrate increased persuasiveness. Leiss et al.'s survey is among the most systematic that have been conducted, and spans 15,000 advertisements over 70 years in two Canadian mass-circulation magazines: *Maclean's* and *Chatelaine*. The study employed a scrupulous empirical method, and there is no real basis for challenging its findings about the dominance of distinct formats throughout the period in these magazines. Questions do arise, however, over the generalisability of their findings. Leiss et al.'s assertions are based on an overall analysis of changes in advertising format which makes only passing reference to the influence of the product in patterning advertising strategy. Yet as Pope (1983) has argued, the nature of the product itself has a major influence on the type of strategy adopted. This point is supported by the predominance of particular forms of appeal in particular product categories: perfume, for example, does not tend to be advertised on the basis of technical specification, while agricultural equipment adverts tend not to rely on romantic appeals. Styles or methods of appeal are not dictated in any simple way by the nature of the product, but there is nevertheless a need to allow for the influence of product type in the selection of particular types of approach. As Lury and Warde have argued:

An analysis of the differentiation in ad formats between products would, we believe, provide a more complex view of the development of models of the consumer and advertising images. A preliminary investigation of ads for food products in weekly and monthly magazines (Warde, 1994) indicates that the ad format identified by Leiss et al. (1986) as typical of contemporary advertising – with the emphasis on lifestyle – did not account for the content of food advertising in the British press. (Lury & Warde, 1997: 91)

Further, the restriction of Leiss et al.'s survey to two magazines is problematic. Even a cursory glance at the advertising featured in different media reveals vast differences in content, style and format, even in the same historical period. Moreover, as advertising historians like Pollay (1984), Pope (1983) and Nevett (1982) have highlighted, historical shifts in the availability and capacities of different sorts of media undoubtedly have some sort of influence on the uses of particular types of appeal in any given medium. Indeed the contemporary advertising specialism of media planning is devoted to the task of attempting to make informed judgements about the suitability of different sorts of media. Nor is media planning simply a response to the proliferation of media and markets at the end of the twentieth century; as Chapter 5 demonstrates, media planning was one of the functions that even the earliest advertising agencies conducted.

These issues, however, are not the only ones which cast a shadow on the thesis of increasing persuasiveness. Also worth considering are the less conclusive results of one of the other major surveys of the information/ persuasion balance in historical advertisements. In the early 1980s Richard Pollay led a research project into the content of 2000 print advertisements which appeared in ten of the largest-circulation Canadian magazines between 1900 and 1980 (Pollay, 1984; 1985). The aims of the project included testing whether advertising had become less informative during the twentieth century, and whether its focus had shifted to 'emotional' rather than 'logical' forms of argument. The question of informativeness was of particular significance because of the way in which the debate about the role and effects of advertising had been conducted.

> Ads that are intensely persuasive because they use atmosphere and association and because they stimulate our 'feeling' capacities are the cause of much moral misgiving on the part of many social observers. These observers are typically much less concerned with the appropriateness of 'thinking' ads dense in information. (Pollay, 1984: 56)

One of the first difficulties that this survey encountered was how informativeness should be defined. Pollay points out that whilst many ads feature illogical arguments and deceptions, judgements about the informativeness of such claims are always subjective and require further sources of independent information. For this reason the study measured the maximum potential informativeness, rather than actual informativeness, as 'this is all that can be measured reliably' (1984: 62). What Pollay found was that information richness did seem to have been declining steadily throughout the period, with ads from the first four decades emerging as the most informative. Yet the survey also produced some unexpected results. Despite the overall downward trend in informativeness, Pollay's results also revealed an unexpected resurgence in information richness, and a decline in more persuasive assertions in the 1960s and 1970s (1984: 66). This is what Pollay refers to in a later article as the 'subsiding sizzle' (Pollay, 1985). This term is used to invoke the decline in advertising structured around product benefits, 'the sizzle', against product characteristics, 'the steak'.

> Thus in this post-war era, print ads are less likely to portray human users and use situations, less likely to push benefits of consumption, and less likely to use emotive rhetorical styles. Growing in frequency are portrayals of only the product and text descriptive of product features. At present, roughly one-half of print ads sell the steak, a reversion from the 1950s when more ads were focused on the sizzle, the consumer use situation, the consumer benefits to be realized and the emotive portrayal of these. (1985: 33)

Pollay's conclusion was that specific historical periods do not in themselves determine the persuasiveness of advertising. In his view a much more significant factor came in the form of the beliefs and strategies dominant within the advertising community at given points in time (Pollay, 1984: 73; 1985: 34).

The salient point here is not whether Pollay's or Leiss et al.'s findings are the most compelling. Their respective studies employed quite different sorts of methodology, sample type and size, each with their own relative strengths and weaknesses. Leiss et al., for example, considered the greater number of advertisements, whereas Pollay's study featured a broader range of print media. In addition, Leiss et al.'s use of a combined analytic method can be contrasted with Pollay's more quantitatively based content analysis. But while these methodological debates may be of some consequence, there is a much more fundamental issue at stake concerning the adequacy of textual analyses for supporting assertions about fundamental shifts in advertising style from rationalistic, information-based formats to emotional, transformative and persuasive formats. Pollay's conclusion about the role of the advertising community in defining advertisement style and content suggests an alternative avenue for investigation. His is one of the few major pieces of research conducted in this period in which what Williams above termed 'the context of changing organisations and intentions' (Williams, 1980: 170) was really thought to figure in the changing appearance of advertising. One of the primary arguments of this book is that a meaningful understanding of the nature and intentions of individual advertisements cannot really be achieved in the absence of an attendant knowledge of the historical context in which they were produced. Specific institutional, organisational and technical arrangements comprise the production context and pattern the final form in which advertisements appear. For these reasons, persuasiveness is not best approached as an objective feature of advertisements, but as a contingent dimension of appeal.

The notion of contingency is not something that accounts of the evolving nature of advertisements really address. Although Leiss et al. do relate their schema to the institutional development of advertising, this is done on the basis of secondary information about large-scale trends and innovations in the institutional scene. These trends are not related to the specific methods and practices which comprise the production of individual campaigns. In this respect the product orientation phase may be related in general terms to the dominance of print-based media and the absence of formal consumer research mechanisms, but this is not related in any more explicit a way to how given advertisements were actually produced. This is something of a problem. Leiss et al. present their analysis of the economic, socio-cultural and institutional dimensions of advertising as a way of overcoming the 'interpretative' limitations of textual methods of analysis. But these other dimensions of their analysis are mainly scene-setting; the overwhelming weight of their argument is derived from their primary survey data.

An analogous situation persists in Wernick's work. Wernick does not explicitly take up the issue of historical changes in advertising format, but his emphasis on the gradual evolution of promotional culture implies a similar logic. For Wernick the systematic manufacture of meaning through artificial semiosis begins with industrialisation, and evolves gradually into the contemporary situation. But although his account initially emphasises the 'promotional matrix' encompassing production and distribution, his description of the 'contemporary promotional condition' is supported primarily by semiotically inspired analyses of individual advertisements. This, Wernick concedes, is a provisional abstraction, as 'there is no empirical way to disentangle, from among all the other environmental influences which impinge on consciousness, the specific impact, as such, that advertising has' (Wernick, 1991: 45). This ultimate reliance on studying the text in isolation from the broader promotional system is one reason behind the slightly paradoxical tension in Wernick's work that simultaneously flags both the longevity and the novelty of the promotional use of symbolism. As has been pointed out elsewhere, Wernick's story of Wedgwood's promotional exploitation of the Portland Vase reveals a manufacturer who 'knew a thing or two about the symbolic dimensions of commodities' (Nixon, 1997: 187). This begs the question of whether Wedgwood's promotional knowledge emerges because Wernick's description is not restricted to individual advertising texts. It is Wernick's discussion of Wedgwood's broader commercial strategies, intentions and activities which gives a sense of the persuasive orientation of his promotional activities.

Before moving on to consider in more detail the types of promotional activity engaged in by some of Wedgwood's closer contemporaries it is worth considering one further contribution to the debate about the increasing persuasiveness of advertising. Barnard's discussion questions the validity of the 'informing/persuading dichotomy' in advertising theory from a different perspective (Barnard, 1995). In his analysis of the rhetorical focus of advertising he points out that even advertising which appears overtly informative intends to influence behaviour; that information is 'any difference that makes a difference and that only in so far as information influences or modifies behaviour is it information' (1995: 36). If this view of information is accepted then the ethical distinction between informative and persuasive advertising is wrongheaded, as 'all ads are morally questionable and no change in quality such as is perceived by Dyer, Williams and Leiss, Kline and Jhally, took place around the end of the nineteenth century' (1995: 38).

If advertising has transfigured relations between subjects and objects in societies designated as consumer- or commodity-based, then one of the most influential explanations of how this has been achieved cites its growing sophistication. Advertising is widely characterised as a medium that has become increasingly persuasive through evolutions in content and an increased presence in 'everyday life'. This section has highlighted some difficulties with the evidence on which this view is based. Specific problems arise in documenting increases in both pervasiveness and persuasiveness. The primary difficulty with the latter is the reliance on textual analyses. This approach is flawed because persuasiveness is not an objective characteristic of advertisements, but a contingent dimension of the appeal advertisements make. Without knowledge about the specific historical context in which advertisements were produced, very little can be surmised about their intentions. The aim in the remainder of the chapter is to make this clearer through a review of historical evidence that highlights the existence of explicitly persuasive intentions in promotional practices.

historical subjects and objects

It is as though our interest in material culture would be pragmatic and related to some concept of basic needs and true interests were it not for the blandishments of capitalism. Sociologists, in particular, almost inevitably write about consumption as though contemporary society were a decline from some earlier state in which our main relationship to objects was constructed through some form of utility or need. But ... an abstract principle of utility or basic need is something of a cultural rarity. It is extremely hard to find evidence for merely functional or utilitarian relations to material culture in any non-industrial society. (Miller, 1995: 26)

While some theorists acknowledge the longevity of the symbolic dimension of exchange, there remains a very pronounced tendency in critiques of advertising to regard the contemporary condition as a decline from a former, less commercially mediated state. In this prior state the relationship between people and their things may have had a symbolic dimension but it was primarily defined on a more pragmatic, utilitarian basis. In this context people consumed things in order to satisfy needs or wants, not to communicate meaning (Leiss et al., 1986; Jhally, 1987). In such circumstances a persuasive promotional system was scarcely necessary, and it is therefore not entirely surprising that this system is widely supposed to be of fairly recent origin. Yet advertising critique, on the whole, is remarkably thin on historical detail about precisely what 'things' people in prior societies had, how they related to them, and what sorts of factors might have influenced their acquisition. This section aims to show, through a brief review of some historical studies of consumption and promotional practices, that such practices may well have been rather less pragmatically oriented than critiques have assumed.

Glennie's review of the historical literature on consumption highlights the distinction drawn in many accounts of consumer society between modern 'consumers of commodities' and pre-modern 'users of things' (Glennie, 1995: 165). Few theorists, as Glennie concedes, insist upon the model of a purely utility-driven society, but nonetheless the theoretical pre-occupation with large-scale transitions tends to produce a caricatured version of the past in which the significance of patterns and practices of consumption is diminished. Glennie traces this view of consumption to the assumption that widespread poverty prior to the nineteenth century prevented many people from having direct experience of goods. Inadequate means may have prevented poorer classes from having access to goods, but these circumstances, he argues, did not preclude the development of knowledge about consumer goods. Rather, 'the comparative economic insignificance of labouring class consumption conceals the existence and development of strong working-class discourses about consumption and social interaction. Moreover, there were strong qualitative differences among the consumption discourses of different classes' (1995: 177).

Glennie demonstrates the existence of such sophisticated and discrete understandings of the symbolic dimensions of goods among classes with severely limited economic means in a discussion of clothing. The clothing of the poor, as evidenced by eighteenth-century newspaper descriptions of runaway servants, was highly nuanced. Historical information about poor people's clothes reveals a detailed and expressive knowledge of fashion, comprising what Glennie terms, a 'syncretist and hybrid discourse of smartness'. These ideas about fashion were not a result of social emulation but arose from a plurality of social, cultural and personal influences. Consumption, he insists, 'did not depend on unthinking emulation. Goods usually had multiple meanings, frequently combining utilitarian, ornamental and private associations, and these meanings connected to notions of identity and social ideology' (1995: 179).

That eighteenth- and nineteenth-century subjects had other than instrumental, pragmatic orientations to goods is important, because it bears directly on the nature of historical promotional work. If goods had multiple-layered social, cultural and personal meanings in addition to their 'use' functions, it seems less intuitively plausible that producers would base all their promotional energies on simply informing consumers. That this was not the case emerges very strongly in Robinson's (1963) and McKendrick's (1982) accounts of the promotional work of late eighteenth-century entrepreneurs like Matthew Boulton, Josiah Wedgwood and George Packwood.

McKendrick is well known for his revisionist placing of the birth of consumer society not in the wake of industrialisation, as many writers have supposed, but much earlier, in the eighteenth century. His analysis has been criticised by authors like Glennie (1995) for his emphasis on a 'trickle-down' view of consumption from upper to lower classes and it is certainly true that his discussion of the commercialisation of fashion and potteries stresses the rapid, downward spread of fashion (McKendrick 1982: 112). But this emphasis should be considered in the context of the types of evidence on which his account was based – primarily documentary records relating to the commercial strategies of entrepreneurs like Wedgwood. These records reveal the extent to which some entrepreneurs explicitly employed a 'trickle-down' philosophy in their promotional work. As Wedgwood put it: 'begin at the head first and then proceed to the inferior members' (1982: 141). Of greater interest is how varied and well developed were the range of marketing techniques employed by the partnership of Wedgwood and Bentley.

> They used inertia selling campaigns, product differentiation, market segmentation, detailed market research, embryonic self-service schemes, money back if not satisfied policies, free carriage, give-away sales promotion, auctions, lotteries, catalogues (illustrated and in translation), advanced credit, three tier discount schemes, including major discounts for first orders and almost every form of advertisement, trade cards, shop-signs, letterheads, billheads, newspaper and magazine advertisements, fashion plates and fashion magazines, solicited puffs, organized propaganda campaigns, even false attacks organized to provide the opportunity to publicize the counter attack. (McKendrick, 1982: 141)

These techniques were articulated to a widespread, feverish and passionate desire to possess Wedgwood's pottery. This desire may seem hard to comprehend from a contemporary perspective, but it is perhaps no more bizarre than the contemporary fascination with DIY and garden centre shopping. Neither passion makes much sense from a purely utilitarian perspective; they are made sensible only through an acknowledgement of the significance of the symbolic dimensions of objects. It was this symbolic dimension that Wedgwood's promotional work keyed into when, for example, he produced black china teapots to better display the feminine fashion for white hands, or when he cloaked the nude Greek figures on pottery aimed at the 'middling classes' (1982: 113). As Wernick (1991) argues, promotion was not simply an 'add-on' to enhance demand for goods already produced, but an integral part of Wedgwood's production process.

Wedgwood and Bentley's partnership may have produced some exemplary promotional tactics, but it would be a mistake to consider them a unique first foray into the realm. As McKendrick acknowledges, many of the strategies listed above were common to their competitors. This also emerges in Robinson's discussion of Matthew Boulton's marketing techniques. Boulton is best remembered for his role, as the business partner of James Watt, in the arrival of the steam revolution, but he also played, in partnership with John Fothergill, an important role in the Birmingham toy trade. The unfortunately named 'toy' trade embraced the production of an array of objects – buttons, belts, buckles, chains, snuff boxes, instrument cases, trinket boxes and a wide range of plated goods in a range of materials, including silver, gold, platinum, tortoiseshell, steel and gilt. This was a trade dependent upon an ability to respond to and manipulate fashions, and Boulton employed tactics later taken up by Wedgwood 'of using buttons as an advertisement of his craftsmanship' (Robinson, 1963: 48). By around 1770 Boulton had begun to manufacture ormoulu and had decided to launch his new range on the 'fashionable world' through an auction sale at Christie's. Such a sale, Robinson explains, would be an event on the social calendar, and Boulton prepared for it very carefully, ordering special display cabinets and catalogues. Boulton also had very clear ideas about how it should be advertised.

> I would have the Advertisement continued for a week together and in about 6 days after we will publish something else and so soon as the day is fix'd for Sale we will publish that: for tis necessary the Town should talk a little on the subject before the important week, and be brought into proper tune. (Boulton, quoted in Robinson, 1963: 51)

These advertisements made deliberate use of references to Royal patronage to enhance their impact, a strategy also much favoured by Wedgwood. Boulton also employed the advertising technique of making anonymous announcements or 'puffs' designed to attract attention to his trade. This strategy was closely monitored by his competitors, and as McKendrick points out an anonymous puff for Boulton would soon be followed by another for Wedgwood. The most crucial point here is that the types of advertisement that Boulton, Wedgwood and their contemporaries used were not deployed as stand-alone promotional techniques. Insofar as they made references to patronage in advertisements, they did so as part of a much more extensive campaign to build a diffusing 'snob appeal', which was repeated across the design of the commodities, their commercial stationery, publicity, and the location and timing of auctions and sales. Similarly individual advertisements for Wedgwood's or Boulton's wares yield only a very partial insight into promotional intent, when they were so often part of a series or a response to competitor's advertisements. This is one reason why content or textual analysis of individual historical advertisements is an inadequate method of assessing persuasive intent.

This is also evident in McKendrick's description of the promotional tactics of George Packwood, an eighteenth-century razor strop manufacturer. If McKendrick's discussion of the commercialisation of fashion and potteries put too much emphasis on a trickle-down view of consumption, the same cannot be said of his account of the commercialisation of shaving. George

Packwood may have employed a great many tactics to bolster the demand for his razor strop, but an appeal to social emulation was not among them. Rather, Packwood employed a quite different but nevertheless inventive and versatile set of strategies to promote his product. Packwood produced over 60 different advertisements in two years, and placed them in 26 different newspapers, as part of what McKendrick calls 'a remorseless attempt to imprint the brand name on the public memory to ensure that they sought and bought, indeed insisted on buying the right product' (McKendrick, 1982: 152).

These advertisements employed a vast range of different styles of appeal, from testimonials to parody, jokes, topical link-ups and true confessions. None of the numerous samples McKendrick quotes look like simple announcements of availability, although this is certainly something they do. Rather, they suggest an irrepressible effort to entertain, amuse, puzzle, irritate, or otherwise arouse the audience. Where the likes of Boulton and Wedgwood may have sought to manipulate the aspirational desires of consumers, Packwood and the numerous other small businessmen McKendrick describes as operating similar strategies were content to bludgeon consumers into submission. These very different promotional strategies were well suited to the nature of the respective products. Whereas pottery was a durable and relatively expensive acquisition, razor strops and shaving soap were inexpensive and disposable. Thus these different promotional strategies were adapted to suit the nature of different products and markets.

That strategies for stimulating consumption through manipulating the meanings and desirability of goods were fairly well developed in the eighteenth century also emerges in Walsh's historical studies of retailing and promotion (Walsh, 1999; 2000). Walsh's work responds to the characterisation of the department store in the nineteenth century 'as the analogue of "industrial revolution", Marxist alienation and the beginnings of mass consumption' (Walsh, 1999: 46). There is, she argues, little empirical support for this overdramatised characterisation of the differences between the department store and prior approaches to retailing. Eighteenth-century retailing is set up as a primitive age of dark and unappealing shops doing little to promote sales. Her description of the design of mainly high-class shops in eighteenth-century London suggests a very different picture.[7]

[I]nventories of high class London shops of the eighteenth century reveal the use of an impressive display of expensive interior fittings. These range from mirrors, glass display cases lining the length of the shop, mouldings with features such as festoons and cherubs, moulded and gilded cornices, and the arrangement of classical pillars or sculpted archways at dramatic points in the shop, often framing the customer's progression upstairs or into back shops. (1999: 47)

The construction of shop interiors, according to Walsh, was meant to invoke the opulence and style of wealthy private homes. Where you shopped in the eighteenth century was a mark of social distinction, in the same way as being seen at public events like the theatre. High-class retailers employed promotional strategies designed to play upon social aspirations, in a similar way to manufacturers like Boulton and Wedgwood. These strategies ranged from shop decor to the display of goods and the deferential attitudes of shopkeepers, which all helped articulate 'sophisticated social and cultural messages which were intended to be associated with the goods on sale' (1999: 52).

This is a significant point. If retailers in the eighteenth century were guided by the need to enhance the social and cultural associations of their products, if the same motivation can be traced in the promotional work of manufacturers, and if evidence can be found supporting the existence of 'syncretist and hybrid discourses' about the meanings of goods in all classes, the view that people had a primarily pragmatic orientation towards goods begins to look even less convincing. Goods in all these examples could be classed in Marxist terms as having 'fetishistic' dimensions, in that they were promoted on the basis of intrinsic values quite separate from the human action which produced them. These promotional efforts were designed to *persuade* through enhancing the symbolic meanings and associations of goods, not simply to let it be known that goods were available. This suggests quite a gap between the role attributed in critical literature to early forms of advertising and promotion and the actual intentions, strategies and activities which comprised promotional work. As suggestive as the promotional work in these particular instances is, much more research is needed before a more general picture of promotional knowledge and approaches in the eighteenth and nineteenth centuries can be gained.

concluding comments

The half century between 1880 and 1930, then saw the full development of an organized system of commercial information and persuasion as part of the modern distributive system in conditions of large scale capitalism. ... Slowly after the war, advertising turned from simple proclamation and reiteration, with simple associations, of the earlier respectable trade, and prepared to develop, for all kinds of product, the old methods of the quack and the new methods of psychological warfare. (Williams, 1980: 179–80)

The primary aim of this chapter has been to review the role attributed to advertising, most specifically in those branches of the critical literature which have sought to broaden the scope of analysis from the text to take account of the institutional position of advertising. This trajectory of critical analysis has been structured by the view that advertising, over time, has increasingly intervened in the relationship between people and objects, until the contemporary state in which it is advertising, more than any other medium, that defines that relationship. The literature draws heavily on the critical tradition of Marxism to explain how advertising acts to mask the true nature of products as an inevitable feature of the capitalist commodity system of exchange. Advertising is thus understood as systemically related to the emergence of commodity or consumer societies. It is the needs of such societies that, at the most elemental level, underscore the profound transformation of people, and objects and the relation between them.

The most influential explanation of how this transformation has been achieved has invoked the changing content of advertisements. Advertising is characterised as an evolving medium which increasingly colonises everyday life through an inescapable presence and irresistibly persuasive messages. The most systematic surveys of advertising volume and persuasive content, however, leave unanswered important questions about how historical advertisements functioned. Even extensive surveys of the quantity and quality of advertising make little, if any, allowance of the historical context in which the advertising was produced. Yet this context is entirely germane to assessing the persuasive intent of advertisements. Persuasiveness is not something that can be read across time and place. Even advertisements which, from a contemporary vantage point, seem purely informative were calculated to influence. To this extent the ethical and practical distinctions drawn between persuasive and informative advertising have been seriously overplayed.

The object of this argument is not to make the very real changes in the way advertising and promotion has been managed over the centuries disappear. Rather it is to suggest that the critical emphasis on interpreting these changes as part of an irresistible and inevitable move to a different sort of society risks overlooking the range, variety and inventiveness of approaches to promotion at different historical moments. There is much to be gained from striving for a more *precise* understanding of the different sorts of commercial mediation of the relationship between people and objects in place prior to the growth of the 'modern' advertising industry.

notes

1 Slater (1997), especially Chapters 2, 3 & 4, includes a fuller discussion of the relation between people and objects in different theories of the economy.
2 See Sahlins (1976) and Jhally (1987) for more detailed interpretations of Marx's conception of the use-value/exchange value relation.

3 See Foucault (1980), Hunter and Saunders (1995), Rose (1996), du Gay et al., eds, (2000).
4 Hirst and Wooley (1982) give a powerful exposition of this view.
5 See Chapter 1 for a more detailed discussion of semiotic method, and Dyer (1982) for a review of semiotics and content analysis.
6 These difficulties are discussed more fully in Chapter 6.
7 No doubt Walsh's study could be criticised because of this emphasis on high-class shops, but as she points out (56–7), despite their 'democratic' associations, nineteenth-century department stores themselves targeted mainly lower- and upper-middle-class shoppers.

the hybridisation of
culture and economy

[T]he expanded role of promotion, indeed of the circulation process as a whole, has led to a mutation in the relation between economic 'base' and cultural 'superstructure' such that the latter has become absorbed into the former – as the zone of circulation and exchange – while the former – as the zone of production – has itself become a major cultural apparatus. (Wernick, 1991: 19)

introduction   This chapter shifts the focus from how advertising has 'interfered' in the relationship between people and objects to how it has disrupted the 'spheres' of culture and economy. Concerns about advertising's impact on culture and economy have exercised writers in a variety of traditions. In the post-war period advertising has been characterised as the force responsible for: the production of 'false' demand (Galbraith, 1958); sustaining capitalist modes of economic organisation (Ewen, 1976; Haug, 1986; Jhally, 1987) and devaluing 'authentic' culture (Barthes, 1977; Williamson, 1978). These accounts are all preoccupied, at root, by the capacity of advertising to act upon the relation between economy and culture. Advertising is represented as an institutional link, a 'bridge' between 'economic' production and 'cultural' consumption, and it is this position which fuels concerns about its ability to do things to economy, to culture and to relations between them.

'Culture' and 'economy' are among the most problematic categories in the social and human sciences.[1] They are enormously difficult to define, yet they appear self-evident. They can refer to the most abstract dimensions of human experience and, simultaneously, to the most specific of daily transactions. The various critical writers featured in this chapter, moreover, understand and use the terms in subtly different ways. 'Culture' and 'economy' represent an enduring theoretical problem, which this discussion can neither fully solve nor entirely avoid. What it will do is track how a particular approach to 'culture' and 'economy' as *properly* separate and opposed 'spheres' has dominated critical thinking almost to the point of paralysis. Culture and economy are widely treated in critical literature as stable and coherent entities that would function autonomously and according to their own internal logic, outside the vestiges of commodity systems of production. The critical project therefore becomes a matter of tracking the damage – at a macro or global level – advertising does to culture and economy. This has tended to override the need to investigate the specification, formation and operation of advertising practices at a local, organisational level. This is unfortunate because it is at the level of local, material practice that the difficulties of applying a sharp delineation between culture and economy are most readily apparent. These difficulties arise precisely because culture and economy are not stable and coherent entities but provisional and historically contingent modes of conceptualising and organising social life. What they mean, at any given time and in any given context, is really a matter for philosophical investigation, not for an account of advertising practice. The approach taken here, therefore, is to leave the matter of comprehensive definition to more qualified sources, and to focus instead on the theoretical and practical grounds for an approach which treats the 'cultural' and the 'economic' as constituent dimensions of material practice, not discrete spheres.

To help build a case for such an approach it is necessary to examine in detail how critical work has approached the question of advertising and its impact on culture and economy. Accordingly, how culture and economy fare in two roughly distinguishable 'branches' of the literature – that based around the institution and that based around the practice of advertising – forms the main thrust of the discussion. First, I examine the role of a broad heritage of critical formulations and reformulations of the culture/economy relation, from the Frankfurt School onwards, in shaping approaches to advertising as an institution. This paves the way for a review of the influence of such reformulations on literature based on practice. Here attention shifts to authors whose work is characterised by a desire to ground any assertions about the nature of advertising in a more detailed understanding of its practices rather than its products. This literature makes a substantial contribution to the theoretical profile of advertising, and its insights merit careful consideration. Practice-based accounts help counter the hyperbole of critical claims about the potency of advertising's impact on culture and economy, offering instead more cautious and tempered assessments. Yet these accounts retain some ambiguity about what exactly is going on, and whether advertising does, finally, have some kind of role to play in the progressive blurring or hybridisation of culture and economy.

The chapter ends by turning to some of the broader epistemological and practical, empirical issues raised by these accounts of culture and economy. Here the focus is on tracing the development of the conceptualisation of culture and economy as separate and bounded spheres. Against this conceptualisation, work emerging from the anthropology of science and techniques (AST) and the Foucauldian governmentality tradition offers an alternative approach that rejects the general analytic definition and distinction of culture and economy. This approach foregrounds instead the idea of the cultural and the economic as performed in diverse instances of material practice that deserve detailed empirical investigation. Undertaking such a project promises an escape from the dualist preoccupation with maintaining the fragile boundary between culture and economy, and a richer understanding of how they necessarily interact in the everyday conduct of advertising work.

a transformative institution?

The commercial character of culture causes the difference between culture and practical life to disappear. (Adorno, 1991: 53)

The institution of advertising is supposed, by a range of critical theorists, to act in some (generally negative) way, upon culture and economy. The term 'institution' is being deployed to signal those authors whose comments are directed to the broad effects of advertising, based largely on analyses of the nature and impact of its products and institutional positioning between production and consumption. Works in this category include those by Leiss et al. (1986), Wernick (1991) and Jhally (1987), which explicitly tackle advertising's impact on culture and economy; but these are far from the only places in which assertions about this relationship can be found. A broad corpus of critical thought has also commented on the role of advertising, and this merits a short review before a more detailed consideration is made of how these critical themes have been developed in substantive work.

The idea that industrialisation and the associated emergence of a consumer society acted to transform the relation between culture and economy has a long history. That the expansion of capitalist production necessitated the construction of new markets, leading in turn to the commodification of culture through advertising and other media, is a theme that can be found in the Frankfurt School theories of Horkheimer and Adorno (1973), Marcuse (1964) and Lefebvre (1971). For Horkheimer and Adorno the commodity logic and instrumentalised rationality of industrialised systems of mass production also increasingly characterised the production of culture in the 'culture industries'. This account sees the autonomous spheres of the arts and 'high' culture diverted through the culture industries, culminating in a dumbed-down, homogenised *ersatz* cultural product for passive mass consumption.

Through this process, the distinction between culture and practical life erodes, as a mundane commercialised 'culture' takes over, which refuses the humanist pursuit of total fulfilment that defines authentic culture (Adorno, 1991).

This debasement of culture is driven by the commodity logic of capitalist systems of production. The commodity fetishism thesis refers to the subordination of the original use-value of goods to their exchange-value.[2] The triumph of exchange value leaves goods free to take on new meanings, and this is where advertising comes in. As Jhally puts it, 'the system of capitalist production empties commodities of their real meaning, and the role of advertising is to insert meaning into this hollow shell. In this way use-value is subsumed by exchange-value (Jhally, 1987: 173). This analysis of the relation between advertising and exchange-value is further developed in Baudrillard's work (1988a; 1988b). Drawing on insights from semiotics, Baudrillard argues that use-value is not obliterated by exchange-value, but becomes a subordinated part of it under the auspices of the 'commodity-sign'. The sign – autonomous and floating free from its signified material object – is thereby the crucial component of exchange-value. This means that advertising has almost limitless scope to mark objects with new associations. These objects, commodity-signs, are consumed for their cultural meanings in contemporary society, not for their material characteristics. This symbolic character, rather than the quantity or scope of consumption, for many theorists, is what defines contemporary society.

> The distinctive mark of the consumer society and its consumerist culture is not, however, consumption as such; not even the elevated and fast rising volume of consumption. What sets the members of consumer society apart from their ancestors is the emancipation of consumption from its past instrumentality that used to draw its limits – the demise of 'norms' and the new plasticity of 'needs', setting consumption free from functional bonds and absolving it from the need to justify itself by reference to anything but its own pleasurability. (Bauman, 2001: 12–13)

Although Bauman uses the term 'needs' he goes on to qualify this by arguing that consumption in consumer societies is not about needs at all. 'Needs' in consumer society are not based upon material objects, but on the desire for difference or social meaning catered for by the symbolic exchange of sign values. This view of present-day consumption as built around feverish processes of desire, fantasy, daydreams and wishes animated by advertising runs through much academic writing on the subject (Baudrillard, 1988a; Campbell, 1987; Ferguson, 1992; Schor & Holt, 2000). Advertising here presides over older, ritualised social systems in the production of meaning, defining the consumer society as cultural rather than social.

Many of these themes are reworked and elaborated in Wernick's more detailed account of the operation of 'promotional culture' (Wernick, 1991: 16–18). For Wernick, alongside industrialisation came the industrial manufacture of meaning, or 'artificial semiosis', whereby the commodity-sign is constructed through advertising, marketing and product design. What is new in artificial semiosis is not the symbolic character of objects *per se*, but the manner in which meaning is instilled. Industrialisation transforms promotion into a strategic, integrated business practice that alters the nature of products and ultimately remodels the links between economy and culture. Through 're-coding' products with psycho-cultural appeal to enhance their 'actual use-value', advertising is pivotal to this transformation (1991: 30). In a move strongly reminiscent of the structuralist conception of meaning discussed in Chapter 1, Wernick maintains that this systematic association of commercial products with cultural symbols devalues authentic meaning. Advertising thus dissolves the boundaries between the material and the symbolic, between the economic regime of accumulation and the symbolic regime of signification.

[C]ulture has lost its autonomy thereby, while the (market) economy has hypostatized into an all engulfing dynamic ... it has further come about that the (superstructural) domain of expressive communication has been more and more absorbed, not just as an industry but as a direct aspect of the sale of everything, into the integral working of a commodified economic 'base'. (1991: 185)

A similar perspective on advertising's effects as an institution appears in Mattelart's analysis of the global development of the advertising industry (Mattelart, 1991). Mattelart distances himself from the critical preoccupation with advertising texts, but his focus on the institutional development of the industry arrives at similar conclusions. Advertising, he argues, is a new form of power and social mediation, which has caused an upheaval in the nature and autonomy of culture.

The moment has arrived to ask not what culture can do in the face of the abuses of advertising and marketing, so much as what advertising and marketing have done to culture. Because like it or not, commoditised space has become so pervasive that it becomes impossible to think of culture as a reserved uncontaminated terrain. (Mattelart, 1991: 216)

Raising some analogous issues, Leiss et al. (1986) categorise advertising as a 'privileged form of discourse' that has increasingly assumed the role of traditional discourses of church, state and community in defining the relationship between people and objects. They describe advertising as a bridge transferring information between the sectors of production, media and consumption. This places advertising in an unrivalled position to influence consumption through its role in the generation of cultural meaning, and production through its imbrication in marketing. It is this institutional position that enables advertising to function as an 'effective tool of socialisation and persuasion' (Leiss et al., 1986: 193). Ultimately, advertising provides a 'cultural frame for goods' which has helped shift the essential function of goods away from the satisfaction of wants to the communication of meaning (1986: 327–48). As in Wernick's account, the epoch-making shift lies not in the symbolic dimension of objects but in the means by which this symbolism is communicated: '[in] earlier societies individuals became acquainted with the meanings carried by objects through culture and customs. In a consumer society, needs and commodities must be introduced by some other means, marketing and advertising become the chief match makers' (1986: 327). Again, consumer society is marked by the decline of stable, traditional institutions organised around religion, kinship and state, and the concomitant rise of promotional industries. Leiss et al. echo the critical trend which sees in consumer societies a profound transformation of culture and economy, occasioned by the combined effects of industrialisation, mass production and the acceleration of technological innovation.

This idea carries enormous critical weight. The heritage of Marxist political economy has made the culture/economy dualism a central critical preoccupation which theorists since the Frankfurt School have continued to reformulate. Writers like Harvey (1989) and Jameson (1984), for example, have developed the Frankfurt School and post-Althusserian tradition of analysis to provide an account of the ways in which culture in the late twentieth century has increasingly been colonised by the economic imperatives of capitalist modes of production. In another branch of theoretical work, the relation is reformulated so that influence runs in the opposite direction, from the cultural to the economic, as cultural knowledge gains precedence in the system of production. This is the version of culture and economy presented in Lash and Urry's analyses (1987; 1994). Here the boundaries between economic and symbolic processes in the contemporary or 'disorganised' phase of capitalism have eroded (Lash & Urry, 1994: 64). A number of forces, from growth in the prominence of 'culture industries' and cultural goods to the increasing role of 'signifying practices' in different forms of work, are implicated in this transition, but the role of advertising is of particular significance. For Lash and Urry, advertising acts as a crucial enabling technology in the transition from one mode of societal organisation to the next.

> If in organised capitalism underconsumption, or an 'underload' of demands created the conditions for advertising and the consumption and hegemony of the image, then in disorganised capitalism this now fetishized image is at least partly responsible for positional consumption and demand *over*loads. (Lash & Urry, 1987: 293)

Advertising here is central to the dominance of consumption that they, among others, regard as definitive of the 'post'-industrial information- and knowledge-based society (Featherstone, 1991; Beck et al., 1994; Sternberg, 1999; Davis & Scase, 2000). By merging economic objectives with cultural knowledge, advertising is precisely the sort of institution which produces new combinations between economic 'system' and cultural 'environment', a trend exemplified by the symbolic work undertaken by advertising practitioners (Lash & Urry, 1994: 64). Here, Lash and Urry draw heavily on Bourdieu's formulation of the structural positioning of the new fraction of the petit-bourgeoisie he described as 'cultural intermediaries'. Bourdieu attributes the new structural position of cultural intermediary to recent economic changes, 'in particular, the increasing role of the symbolic work of producing needs, even in the production of goods – design, packaging, sales promotion, marketing, advertising etc.' (1984: 345).

Despite the volume of work devoted to the topic of cultural intermediaries in the years since *Distinction* was first published, Bourdieu had remarkably little to say on the topic. Nevertheless it is clear that he saw the juxtaposition of symbolic practices with economic knowledge as a new departure related to a much broader set of changes in the economic organisation of 'post'-industrialised societies. In this he was clearly not alone. However, contemporary society is designated – 'consumer', 'post-industrial', 'information', 'disorganised capitalist' – a broad range of theorists see in it a different relationship between culture and economy, between consumption and production. In accounts of advertising written from an institutional perspective, this difference is often considered to be about the proliferation of images and symbolic representation – what is broadly construed as culture – in spaces previously considered more exclusively economic. Whilst theorists differ over whether this is a sign of the subjugation of culture to the economy, or a sign of a blurring or mutation of the spheres, there is at least some agreement that the delineation between culture and economy is no longer as clear as it once was. According to institutionally focused accounts, advertising plays a major role in these changes, but not all branches of the literature characterise this role in quite the same way.

the practice of advertising and the new 'cultural economy'

> ... the sociology of cultural products must take as its objects the whole set of relationships ... between the artist and other artists, and beyond them the whole set of agents engaged in the production of the work ... (Bourdieu, 1993:139)

One of the unintended side-effects of all this emphasis on the altered relationship between culture and economy, the expansion of the culture industries and the associated increase in symbolic, intermediary types of work, was to highlight how little was actually known about these fields of activity. Whilst by 1990 critics working within cultural studies had subjected the advertising text to extensive analysis for what it could reveal about the culture of capitalism, by the same point comparatively little investigation along the lines envisaged by Bourdieu had been conducted into the field of advertising production. This situation began to change as the 'turn' to all things cultural slowly resulted in practice-based research into the 'cultural intermediary' occupations of workers in the fields of the music industry, publishing, fashion, graphic design and advertising.[3] This section reviews some of the insights afforded by work focused on advertising practice, and lights on three facets as particularly important in the dynamic between advertising, culture and economy. First, the ethnographic empirical approach adopted by some authors provides evidence of advertising working less as a device in the transformation of culture and economy, and more as an illustration of the inescapable fusion of economic calculation with what would be informally regarded as 'cultural' knowledge in routine practice. Second, discussions of creative work in particular privilege its increasing dependence on novel, 'hybrid' combinations of economic and cultural knowledge. Practitioners appear as archetypal cultural intermediaries at work in the new 'cultural economy'. Third, the underpinning definitions of culture and economy in this literature merit some excavation to establish whether traces of a general, normative distinction between these 'spheres' remain, and to begin to build a case for rethinking how, and whether, the terms might be applied in material practice.

The cultural economy of practice Accounts of advertising practice have taken issue with the critical tendency to accord advertising a 'magic' or mystical power over the collective unconscious of a defenceless public.[4] Schudson's (1984) *Advertising: The Uneasy Persuasion* was one of the first to challenge overblown claims about the power of advertising. Advertisements, he argued 'ordinarily work their wonders, to the extent that they work at all, on an inattentive public' (1984: 3). Schudson gave voice to a sentiment that industry practitioners had long cited in their defence, that within the industry itself considerable uncertainty exists about whether, and exactly how, advertising actually works. In particular the effectiveness of individual campaigns is notoriously difficult to assess. Advertising is only ever one of a much broader range of marketing and promotional tools, and it is never possible to disentangle entirely the effect of any individual campaign from the range of other influences upon demand. As Lury and Warde (1997: 89) suggest, in a complex trading environment advertising is as much a 'function of producer anxiety' as anything else.

While Schudson's and Lury and Warde's remarks are plausible, they reveal little about the detail of how decisions to advertise are made. A fuller insight into this is provided in the ethnographic accounts of Miller (1997) and Moeran (1996).[5] Miller's account locates the decision to advertise explicitly in the context of anxiety about competitors' activities. Through the case study of a campaign for a milk drink, *Cal*, Miller identifies the importance of competitors' activities, the relationship between the agency and the client, and the internal politics of the agency, in the decision to advertise. These factors are implicated throughout the advertising process, from the initial decision to the level of expenditure (the 'appropriation'), and the content, style and media selected for the campaign. Moeran provides a similar picture of the motivations of Japanese advertisers.

Advertisers do not advertise because they wish to sell their products so much as because their rivals are advertising. They are afraid that somehow they might lose status – and, perhaps, as a result, market share (which ultimately boils down to status) – by not advertising in the same magazines in which their competitors are advertising. (Moeran, 1996: 221)

This resonates with the approach advocated in Fine and Leopold's (1993) analysis of the dynamics of consumption. For them it is the 'system of provision' linking production and consumption that is a crucial determinant of the specific marketing mix adopted for given commodities. This points to the significance for individual advertising strategies not of the kind of global, contemporary norm assumed in critical literature but of local, market and organisationally specific factors. Advertising's continued importance as a commercial strategy cannot, in this view, be reduced to pure economic calculation. Rather, it can be traced to an intricate interplay of economic and cultural norms across the institutional field of given markets, industries and organisations.

The nature of the institutional field, in this literature, casts a shadow across the entire advertising process. Agencies occupy an intermediary position between newspaper, magazine, radio, television and other media that carry advertising and clients who wish to advertise. This intermediary status is complicated by the long dominance of the commission system of reimbursement. The commission system generally operates by media granting recognised agencies an agreed level of commission for space or time booked. Agencies pay the media up front, then bill the client for the full cost, retaining their commission. The system has been the subject of enduring controversy within the industry, due in part to the ambiguity of the structural and financial basis of agencies whereby they provide a service to their clients but are paid by the media. This ambiguous intermediary position means that agencies effectively have to court both media and potential clients.

Moeran's account of the relations between the agency he studied and the media suggest something of the significance of this relationship. Demand for media space in Japan generally outstrips supply, and this means that there is considerable competition for the most desirable 'spots'. The superior bargaining ability of some agencies, Moeran points out, is not the outcome of the smooth operation of the laws of supply and demand, but of patterns of influence and obligation between business associates.

> It is these extra-curricular aspects of a media-buyer's and space-seller's working lives which enable them to practise their persuasive skills when necessary, while at the same time entangling them in a complicated and unyielding web of obligations which continue until one or the other of them drops dead. (Moeran, 1996: 220)

A failure on the part of the agency to secure the highest status 'spots' is understood as symptomatic of a much deeper problem of status and influence. This does not bear any straightforward relation to the likely commercial effectiveness of given media positions. In his consideration of magazine advertising, for example, Moeran noted that advertisers uniformly preferred the outside back cover (OBC), regardless of the kind of product they were advertising.[6] Any attempt to persuade clients to choose a different position, regardless of supporting research data, would be interpreted as a failure on the part of the agency to secure a higher status location.

The significance of managing what Moeran terms 'human chemistry' across the institutional field is also apparent in descriptions of agency–client relations. This is illustrated in the pitching system where agencies attempt to win new business by 'pitching' their ideas to clients. This system is unpopular with agencies as it can involve an enormous investment of staff time and other resources in preparing a speculative campaign with relatively little chance of winning the account. Moreover, according to Moeran's description of an agency pitch for a car manufacturer's account, it is quite possible to provide the best presentation and still lose the account. This, he maintains, arises because of the difficulty of orchestrating the right personality mix between key people in the agency and in the client's firm. It was the failure of this mix, rather than the weakness of the proposed advertising strategy, that led to the ultimate loss of this account. The elaborate networks of pre-existing obligations and loyalties are seldom fully apparent to both parties in the negotiation, and this, for Moeran, made the process particularly fraught. Pitching is not just about the reallocation of advertising business but about 'defining and maintaining the advertising *community* as a whole' (1996: 93). Account switching thus acts as a sort of 'tournament of value' which feeds the 'pedigree' of accounts and creates a history and identity to be recorded in the trade press.

> The Agency may have failed to win this account, too, but it did as a result procure the account of another major European car manufacturer, and thereby maintain its legiti-macy as a top-ranking Japanese advertising agency able to serve foreign clients. Thus ... presentations are designed to *re*produce 'markets, player positions, and collective wisdom'. (1996: 94)

This point is of some significance. It is a reminder of Granovetter's argu-ment that economic goals are always embedded in socially oriented goals and activities, here the reproduction of the community (and culture) of advertising as a whole (Granovetter, 1985; 1992). This also emerges in ethnographic descriptions of the internal organisation and management of the advertising process. Most agencies are organised around four main functional specialisms: account management, media, creative, and research or planning. Account managers provide the interface between agency and client; media plan, place and buy space and time; creatives produce the visual and copy content of advertising; and researchers are responsible for providing relevant information to situate the advertising. As might be antici-pated, these four specialisms traditionally tend to view the key priorities and objectives of advertising in quite different ways, providing a well-documented source of tension (Schudson 1984; Myers, 1986; Fowles, 1996; Nixon, 1996; 2003).

That these disagreements are about something other than competing assessments of how to 'do' advertising is clear in Miller's description of the re-launch campaign for *Cal*. At the initial campaign briefing the client's product manager (PM) called for dramatic and aggressive advertising, yet when creative staff provided a storyboard for a campaign along those lines, the account manager insisted the creatives had naïvely confused what was said and what was meant to be heard.

> It was quite clear that the original meeting was understood by the 'experienced' advertising executive as having very little to do with the actual intentions behind the campaign. The exciting bravado of the PM at *Cal* was seen to be a necessary public performance in the presence of his MD … Despite the fact that they had all sat around in the first briefing and discussed the detailed proposals for hours with complete seriousness, it was evident back at the agency that no-one was expected to take any of that discussion as having any further significance. (Miller, 1997: 186–7)

The advertising process here is shaped by a series of negotiations and interpretations between the client and the agency, and between different groups within the agency. Moeran makes similar observations of the production of a campaign for a contact lens *Ikon Breath*. The agency and the client had very different ideas about advertising strategy – proud of the technical achievement of the product, the client favoured a stress on product features, while the agency advocated emphasis on the consumer. This clash of ideas bordered on open conflict.

> The account executive in charge suddenly found himself caught between two warring parties. Clearly in sympathy with his creative team and unable to agree with his client's advocated approach, but at the same time desperate to make sure that no open rupture occurred (after all as account executive he was there to serve the client's interests) he adopted the only possible strategy open to him: compromise. (Moeran, 1996: 147)

In both Miller's and Moeran's ethnographies advertising emerges as a fraught collective process to which different participants bring a plurality of perspectives. This diversity of interest groups, according to Moeran, necessitates the use of 'a system of conventions' to enable coordination between groups (1996: 160). This notion flags the generalised and stereotyped ways in which particular groups understand and relate to each other. As Miller also observes, meetings on the *Cal* campaign followed an almost ritualistic logic whereby 'arguments were evoked that seemed to belong to a standard rhetoric that was more to do with the establishment of the structural relations between sections within the company than about the actual advert' (1997: 187). This standard rhetoric relates to what Miller describes as the 'best known structural fault within advertising agencies' (1997: 188) – the disparity between creative and account management perspectives. It is simply assumed that creatives will have artistic ideals, and that these at times will clash with the economic goals of advertising. This 'ritualised' conflict, Miller argues, is summoned up to structure disagreements between organisational groups, regardless of whether it has any bearing in the particular circumstances. Exchanges between groups and individuals were thus as much about the 'reaffirmation of organisational roles' as the creation of adverts.

The instrumental production of advertising, in these accounts, is bound up with the production and 'reaffirmation' of organisational roles and occupational 'habiti'. To be imbricated in any given aspect of production is simultaneously to be caught up in the *re*production of particular organisational identities, a process which itself inevitably involves reference to very particular interpretative tropes. Functional specialists in agencies and external advertising partners might thereby be thought of as 'interpretative communities', distinguished by particular meanings, goals and strategies (Fish, 1980: 14). Members of the same interpretative communities

'necessarily agree because they will see (and by seeing, make) everything in relation to that community's assumed purposes and goals; and conversely, members of different communities will disagree because from each of their respective positions the other 'simply' cannot see what is obviously and inescapably there. (Fish, 1980: 15)

The practice-based literature describes a process in which functional specialists construe the advertising task in distinct ways, resulting in ritualised patterns of agreement and disagreement which simultaneously help reproduce the identities of discrete occupational communities. This is instructive because it starts to suggest something of the embedded nature of economic calculation in other apparently 'non-economic' goals and practices. What is missing, however, is a more detailed sense of what goes into the formation of these different specialist groups. What are the specific techniques, devices and practices that constitute different functional specialisms and shape their distinct modes of calculation? These questions have to be addressed if the goal is to arrive at a better understanding of how the economic and the cultural interact in routine practice. One group that has received some close attention, specifically because of its blending of the economic and the cultural, is advertising creatives.

The increasing hybridity of creative practice   Despite the increasing critical interest in the practice of advertising there has been little detailed research into what advertising workers actually do on an everyday basis. The literature does, however, provide some valuable insights into the nature, characteristics and values of creatives as an occupational group. Advertising creatives emerge from this literature as a predominantly young, metropolitan, well-educated and well-resourced group (Mort, 1996; Nixon, 1996, 1997, 2003; Thornton, 1999; Soar 2000; 2002). They are also characterised by quite distinctive, often strikingly juvenile and laddish, codes of behaviour (Thornton, 1999; Nixon, 2003). Thornton's description of the following incident is a typical, if fairly mild, example.

> Creatives are not supposed to wear business attire ... This might undermine their claims to creativity. For example ... when the chairman recommended that staff refrained from wearing jeans or shorts ... a good proportion of the creative department came in wearing shorts, some of them obscenely short. What would have been seen as childish behaviour in others was not only seen as acceptable but as reassuring evidence of the 'creativity' of creatives. (Thornton, 1999: 63)

Mort (1996: 101) describes the creative identity and the importance of conforming to an agreed standard of non-conformity in similar terms. In order to meet their organisational brief, creatives *had* to adopt lifestyles and modes of behaviour quite separate from 'stiff business culture'. These patterns of behaviour are seen as necessary to enable creatives to perform as 'sovereign consumers', 'cognoscenti' who can provide taste leadership through their specialist knowledge of new trends in film, television, music, media, products and services (Mort, 1996: 96; Nixon, 2003). Through using their own cultural experiences and knowledge in the construction of advertisements, creatives are considered exemplary cultural intermediaries.

Crucially, as in Bourdieu's formulation, these cultural intermediaries are a new fraction responding to 'broad-based economic and cultural change' (Mort, 1996: 93). The 1980s, as Mort (1996: 91–102) and Nixon (1996, 2003) observe, were widely characterised within the advertising industry as a 'third wave' in which creativity achieved a new prominence. This new emphasis on the creative was based around claims that image-driven, artistic and emotional advertising was the most assured route to added commercial value. While some practitioners' claims about these shifts were undoubtedly overstated, Mort maintains these shifts in industry practice were a response to concrete changes affecting the industry.

> As the third wave agencies saw it, the core problem confronting the whole profession was the massive increase in the levels of material provision since the Second World War. ... Traditional messages of social improvement or price competitiveness, needed to be replaced by an approach which was more in tune with the demands of a generation of advanced customers. Today's advertisers needed to suggest philosophies of living and styles of behaviour, rather than simply pushing the product. (Mort, 1996: 97)

For Nixon (1996: 76) too, the 'creative revolution' reconfigured the priorities of advertising, altering ideas about effectiveness and how the consumer should be addressed. Changes in creative priorities were matched by parallel changes in account planning and media buying practices that fed a move towards creative advertisements structured around an 'Emotional Selling Point' (ESP).[7] These were image-laden adverts that combined specific filming, editing and lighting conventions to produce a more emotionally articulate representational technique. These new priorities, Nixon concedes, were foreshadowed to some extent, but the 1980s creative wave emerges nonetheless as a 'revolutionary' break with past practice.

This new creative identity was sustained, according to the literature, partly through the enshrinement of practice in an exclusive self-referential culture (Schudson, 1984; Mort, 1996; Nixon, 1996, 1997, 2003). Creative practice is introspective, characterised far more by studied reference to peers and competitors than by a 'scientific' analysis of the target audience. Moeran (1996: 161) also identifies the significance to creative practice of continual reference to the 'image pool' of work by other agencies, as well as other cultural forms. The work of creatives is thus not really about originality, but about 'bricolage' aimed at attaining a sort of marginal innovation, which will keep the campaign 'half a pace ahead of society' (1996: 138). This sentiment is echoed strongly in Nixon's (2003: 74–84) account of advertising's magpie-like cultural appropriation. Despite the rhetoric surrounding creativity in advertising he suggests that claims to creativity are often based on an 'extrapolation of quite small differences' (Nixon, 2003: 77). Advertising practitioners work within established 'genres' or 'styles', with boundaries that shift only very slowly. These descriptions of creative styles offer a distinctive perspective on the changes in the appearance of advertising which have occurred over the years. The emphasis on self-referential practices, where new styles result from incremental and 'precedented' changes suggests a potentially fruitful way of thinking about advertising as a practice which moves tidally, rather than in a pattern of relentless linear advancement. As outlined below, however, this is not something that the practice-based literature pursues.

As previously explained, the 'orthodox' critical view understands changes in advertising's appearance as symptomatic of advances in persuasiveness causally related to epochal patterns of social and economic change. The claims of writers like Mort and Nixon are more circumscribed, but their emphasis on the 'emotional' third wave in advertising agencies as a response to post-war conditions of plenty implies a similar logic. This logic is one in which advertising practice moves towards an increasing utilisation of aesthetic, style-based *cultural* knowledge in order to pursue its *economic* aims more effectively. This is broadly in line with Lash and Urry's (1994: 139) characterisation of advertising's historical development from a free professional business service, through a Fordist industry, to a fully fledged 'culture industry' in post-Fordism. Accounts of creative practice thus feature a sort of teleological undercurrent, whereby advertising's culture industry, staffed by cultural intermediaries, provides evidence of a new hybridisation of culture and economy. There is, though, a problem that runs through these (and many other) theoretical reformulations of the dualism concerning what, exactly, is being hybridised. This merits closer examination before a more concerted effort to rethink these terms can be attempted.

Culture and economy in the practice-based literature   The writers on advertising practice assembled here have their sights on goals as diverse as capitalism in Trinidad and contemporary masculine cultures of consumption. Providing an explicit theorisation of the nature of relations between advertising, culture and economy is therefore not a priority for them, and there is little manifest discussion of the culture/economy question. Nevertheless, the structural position of advertising between the economic and cultural spheres of consumption means that ideas about what these 'spheres' are, and how advertising intervenes between them, filter through all of this writing. To help make the case for an alternative analytical approach to culture and economy it is necessary first to unpack in a little more detail how writers on practice use the terms.

The relationship between culture, economy and advertising does not figure prominently in Moeran's account until his final chapter, where he describes how people, objects and activities are imbued with added advertising values in a manner which sustains consumption and 'the political economy as a whole' (Moeran, 1996: 281). Advertising here unites production and consumption by improving the capacity of the production sector to add the values that will best facilitate exchange. These values derive from the intended uses, technical characteristics, worth and social cachet of different objects, and they coalesce into commodity exchange-value and symbolic exchange-value. Commodity exchange-value is based around people's calculations of the monetary worth of objects, while symbolic exchange relates more to the non-monetary meanings invoked in the exchange process (1996: 290–6). For Moeran this notion of value, rather than culture or cultural meaning, is the stock-in-trade of advertising in contemporary societies:

> ... consumerism makes the category of 'culture' irrelevant in societies like those of the United States and Japan, since – thanks to global marketing practices and the workings of advertising and the media – all objects are potentially released into a floating world of signification from the cultural prisons in which they were formerly incarcerated. In this respect, advertising is in Robert Goldman's phrase 'an institutional process in *a political economy of commodity sign-value*'. (1996: 285; italics in original)

This formulation returns his theoretical understanding of advertising to familiar territory. Again, advertising is characterised as a decisive mechanism in the transition to a consumer society, in which the formerly stable and coherent spheres of culture and economy are irredeemably disfigured. This resonates both with accounts like Williamson's (1978) and Goldman's (1992), which attempt to apply the 'post-Althusserian' traditions of cultural analysis to advertising texts and with institutionally focused analyses of advertising's transformative impact. Ultimately, though, Moeran's position is ambiguous. His detailed exposition of practice reveals subtle interconnections between cultural values and commercial decisions that sit awkwardly with his closing theoretical argument.

This is a topic on which Miller is more circumspect. In his focus on articulating an 'organic' model of capitalism he marks out how instrumental accounts of business processes tend to underplay the significance of the 'culture of business' (1997: 319–29). For Miller the fit between business processes and specific local cultures patterns both commercial success and the social impact of business. Underpinning this argument is a commitment to the involvement of both 'cultures of production' and 'cultures of consumption' in commercial processes. Miller invokes a view of culture and business as inevitably, 'organically' interlinked. This is quite at odds with the emphasis prevalent in other work on advertising's transformative impact on culture and economy. Yet his ethnography never really explores questions about how this culturalist approach rests with the theoretical case made against advertising. This is undoubtedly because advertising is not among his primary concerns, whereas the relationship between culture and the economy, notably in his more recent work, is. His distinctive formulation will warrant some further exploration below.

On one level Miller's case for the cultural nature of business processes appears to be supported by Nixon (1996) and Mort's (1996) accounts. Nixon's main concern is with the 'regimes of representation' embodied in imagery of the 'new man'. His analysis deploys a mix of Foucauldian- and Gramscian-inspired frameworks to extend the focus from the text to include a broader range of sites of representation, such as retail interiors and the style press. This emphasis on the significance of institutional practices leads Nixon to argue that underlying the 'cultural' construction of 'new man' imagery are the very commercial calculations of key groups of practitioners (Nixon, 1996: 197–8). This is not, he argues, a new form of economic reductionism, but about the need

to rethink the usual relations of determination that are assumed between economic and cultural practices within the tradition of post-Althusserian cultural analysis, a tradition that continues to broadly frame, in an often unacknowledged way, a good deal of cultural analysis. At the heart of my disagreement has been the ambition to delimit the imbricated and interdependent nature of some of the economic and cultural practices within the sphere of cultural production I have centred upon. (1996: 198)

Mort's account shares a similar theoretical commitment to the interlocking of economic and cultural practices, and positions his account against those which tend towards an over-generalisation of shifts in the relationship between production and consumption practices (1996: 1–12). His 'particularist' concerns are situated against theoretical formulations of the consumer revolution that regard contemporary shifts as a total, epochal break with the past, transfiguring both the realms of economics and of social and cultural life.

This stress on the multiple interconnections between the cultural and the economic in daily practice can be found throughout the practice-based literature. It represents a distinct break with the critical formulation of advertising's unprecedented 'de-differentiation' of the 'domains'. Yet it would be a mistake to suggest that writers on practice share a unified approach to culture, economy and questions of hybridisation. As has been shown, despite his sensitivity to practice, Moeran returns to a position in which advertising devalues or destabilises culture. Miller's nuanced explanation of the organic relations between business and culture leaves its implications for advertising largely undeveloped. Finally, despite Mort and Nixon's respective commitments to particularist modes of analysis, their descriptions of the age of creativity bear traces of the well-worn teleological narrative of what advertising does to culture and economy. Tracking the subtle distinctions between the different authors is further complicated by the fact that, although they all refer to culture and economy, none of them spends much time (at least in these accounts) in qualification or clarification of the terms. This is understandable. As analytical categories, culture and economy are pretty hard to avoid, and a rough baseline conception is widely accepted. It is also to be hoped that advertising can be meaningfully investigated without a sustained reappraisal of what it means to talk about culture or economy. Still, the banality of the terms is a problem when they feature so prominently in diagnoses of the contemporary epoch and advertising's place within it. To be clear about whether such diagnoses can be sustained requires a closer look at different conceptualisations of culture and economy.

culture, economy and the question of increasing hybridity Advertising has been allocated a starring role in the presumed rupture of economic and cultural modes of existence. This role has been theorised in a variety of different ways. In institutionally based accounts, advertising is often the key transformative medium, while in practice-based accounts it is generally viewed less dramatically as an exemplary hybrid practice. In both accounts advertising mixes culture and economy in some way. This emphasis on hybridisation or de-differentiation entails very particular, provisional and sometimes undertheorised ideas about what culture and economy are. The underlying goal here is to explore these and some alternative ways of conceptualising culture and economy, in order to help make the case for an approach to advertising as a material practice necessarily constituted by both cultural and economic dimensions.

Whether the distinctiveness of the contemporary moment resides in the Frankfurt School vision of culture entirely subordinated to economy, or in a later 'post-Fordist' view of culture as organising the economy, it is clear that culture and economy are supposed to be separate domains. If culture and economy are today increasingly mixed together, logically they were once more clearly differentiated. The thesis of increasing hybridisation thus invokes a conceptualisation of culture and economy as normatively distinct, separable, even autonomous. This type of thinking is undoubtedly convenient from an analytical viewpoint – it is much easier to think about all aspects of social life if these categories are kept separate. Yet such a clear delineation has long been questioned by anthropological research, and is increasingly considered theoretically problematic in other branches of social theory.

According to Latour (1993), anthropology has long since developed straightforward methods for dealing with the simultaneously real, natural and cultural character of objects. Authors like Sahlins (1976) and Appadurai (1986) certainly make no bones about the inextricability of the cultural and the economic in material practice. Sahlins rejects economic determinism on the basis that cultural and economic forces are structurally interdependent.

> The very form of social existence of material force is determined by its integration in the cultural system. The force may then be significant – but significance, precisely, is a symbolic quality. ... Culture is organised in the final analysis by the material nature of things and cannot in its own conceptual or sociological differentiations transcend the reality structure manifested in production. (Sahlins, 1976: 206–7)

Sahlins's 'cultural account of production' may seem like a simple reversal of the relation of determinism found in Marxist and post-Althusserian versions of political economy. But as Appadurai argues, Sahlins's work is not simply an attempt to restore the cultural dimension to 'modern' societies conceived by critical literature as economically constituted; it also restores the calculative dimension to 'pre-modern' societies widely caricatured as culturally constituted. In flagging the cultural definition of economic practices and the dissemination of cultural meanings through economic activities in any recorded society, anthropologists like Sahlins and Appadurai raised pressing questions about the usefulness of the theoretical opposition between culture and economy.

These questions were picked up by a range of other theorists who noted that, however compelling it might be in abstract terms, dividing cultural and economic activity in material practice was quite a different matter (Morris, 1988; Rorty, 1994). Whether this practical interdependence is best understood as a generalised characteristic or as a specific product of an epochal implosion has been the subject of some recent scrutiny. Ray and Sayer's discussion, for instance, identifies the dependence of contemporary hybridisation theses on a general distinction between 'cultural' and 'economic' logics, which they concede is difficult to sustain. Nevertheless, they see the continued deployment of culture and economy as separate terms as evidence that their distinction remains politically and theoretically important. A distinction should therefore be maintained between an economic logic based on the external, instrumental calculation of means/ends relations and a cultural logic based on intrinsically meaningful activities, artefacts and relationships. This sort of distinction depends on the well-worn conceptual separation of instrumental and intrinsic value that may seem convincing in the abstract but is extraordinarily difficult to apply in practice. As du Gay and Pryke's (2002: 8–12) contribution to the debate has it, instrumental, economic action is not only the product of socio-cultural relations of training and practice within specific contexts, but itself gives rise to substantive, cultural goals. There is no single, unified 'cultural' logic, but an array of cultural interests and capacities that are the plural creation of particular historically specific religious, legal, aesthetic, economic and educational regimes. For this reason,

> any attempt to instigate categorical distinctions between 'intrinsically' and 'instrumentally' oriented activity in order to support a general normative analysis of economic and cultural life will quickly come up against brute empirical realities that it will not be able to account for or make much reasonable sense of. (du Gay & Pryke, 2002: 11)

This challenge to the general analytic distinction between culture and economy draws not only upon anthropological work but upon a distinct theoretical heritage. Reformulations of the dualistic definition of culture as the other to economy, nature or society often refer to its specific and relatively recent historical and intellectual origins (Hunter, 1988; Turner, 1992; du Gay & Pryke, 2002). Hunter, for example, locates contemporary approaches to culture 'in the shadow of the model of a single general process of contradiction, mediation, and overcoming at whose end lies the "fully developed" human being' (Hunter, 1988: 106). This idea of culture as concerning the true reflection, development and realisation of the nature of 'man', Hunter argues, is the product of a mode of aesthetico-ethical practice instituted by the Romantic tradition and (mis)appropriated by Marxism (cf. Gaukroger, 1986). In opposition, Hunter posits an approach to cultural interests and attributes as defined only in relation to the 'delimited norms and forms of calculation' made available through specific historical institutions of education, economy, politics and so on. This formulation of culture as contingent upon modes of conduct defined by specific institutions resonates with critical engagements with Weber's conception of culture (Turner, 1992; du Gay, 2000; du Gay and Pryke, 2002). Turner's analysis traces the conceptual history of 'culture' against its 'others' but this, he argues, is not what Weber had in mind. 'As long as we talk of the relationship between culture "and" politics, culture "and" economics, between a realm of culture which pertains to human inwardness and a social realm which does not, we will miss the point completely. "Culture" *is not a sphere at all*' (Turner, 1992: 43).

This encompassing view of culture may seem to compromise its value. As noted above, Moeran (1996) argues that 'culture' is now too vague a term to be useful while for Grossberg (1998) such moves equate culture with consciousness or experience, thereby threatening its distinctiveness. But these concerns make sense only from *within* the restrictive conceptual perspectives of the sort posited by Ray and Sayer (1999). It makes little sense to regret the dissolution of culture when it is defined as existing only by and through specific material practices.

A related approach to the conceptualisation of culture and economy has been developed in recent work in the anthropology of science and techniques (AST) (Barry & Slater, 2002; Callon, 1998a, 1998b; Callon et al., 2002; Law, 2002). The domains of culture and economy are understood in this critical trajectory not as ahistorical realities, but as the results of specific processes of configuration. Culture, according to Law, is everywhere, including in what he terms 'economically relevant activity', and there is nothing new in this.

> ... if we are to talk about culture at all, then it certainly doesn't exist in the abstract. It doesn't even simply exist as a set of discourses programmed into the body – although bodies are to be sure, crucial in the performances of culture. Instead, or in addition, culture is located and performed in human and non-human material practices. And these are material practices which extend beyond and implicate not only human beings, subjects and their meanings but also technical, architectural, geographical and corporeal arrangements. (Law, 2002: 24)

Law's aim is to develop an approach to studying material practices that are composed of both cultural and economic elements. This involves the recognition that material practices enact complex interferences between orders and discourses. To understand economically relevant activity it is crucial to explore these interferences. The practices, subjects and cultures of economically relevant activity are 'performed' and thus always multiple, variable and incomplete. This emphasis on the performance of the economic is perhaps the most important contribution of AST to the culture–economy debate. The argument may not be all that new – it certainly draws upon principles developed in structuralist and Foucauldian thought, and elaborated in relation to economic life elsewhere[8] – but it offers a distinctive framework for analysing the material operation of given economic practices that warrants detailed consideration.

As we have seen, what Law terms 'interferences' between cultural and economic activity are recognised as inevitable by many anthropologists. Nonetheless, the 'culturalist' approach to the economy taken by anthropologists like Sahlins has been criticised from within economic sociology for leaving a model of the market which pays insufficient attention to social structuring and the 'reality' of economic life (Zelizer, 1988). This is a reference to the importance, following Granovetter (1985), of giving due empirical weight to the embeddedness of economic behaviour in concrete, ongoing systems of social relations, and to the specific, heterogeneous and plural character of markets. These objectives are taken up and reformulated in Callon's work on economies and markets. He applies the actor–network theory (ANT) framework developed in AST to enable him to map the ways in which economics, broadly defined, formats or 'performs' the economy. The economy, for Callon, does not exist in the abstract as a 'thing' awaiting study and analysis by economists; rather it is the contingent outcome of a process of configuration in which it moves together with economics in a 'mutual performance'. In this sense economics as a discipline configures the economy through shaping the ways in which agencies calculate. This opens up a new direction for the sociology of economic life.

It is not a matter of giving a soul back to a dehumanized agent, nor of rejecting the very idea of his existence. The objective may be to explore the diversity of calculative agencies, forms and distributions, and hence of organized markets. The market is no longer that cold, implacable and impersonal monster which imposes its laws and procedures while extending them ever further. It is a many-sided, diversified, evolving device which the social sciences as well as the actors themselves contribute to reconfigure. (Callon, 1998a: 51)

Here Callon is at odds with much economic sociology. He rejects the preoccupation with uncovering the social context in which economic action is *embedded* (Barry and Slater, 2002). What is exterior to economic action is not a prior social context, precisely because the exterior is itself defined through the framing of market transactions. This is a classic ANT move, where context is characterised as the simultaneous creation of given collective practices (Latour, 1993). Externalities, for Callon, are defined dynamically, not as a context but as a product of the operation that defines the market for any transaction. For this reason Callon's focus is on how, through the process of framing, agents become temporarily and partially disentangled from other networks to enable a transaction to take place. This is not a disembedding of the economic from the cultural, as agent's 'objectives, interests, will and thus identity are caught up in a process of continual reconfiguration, a process that is intimately related to the constant reconfiguration of the network of inter-actions in which he or she is involved' (Callon, 1998b: 253).

Framing aims to extricate agents from this network of interactions, but as the frame can never be hermetically sealed, bi-directional overflows occur as the 'inevitable corollary of the requisite links with the surrounding envi-ronment' (1998b: 255). The work of framing and disentangling is necessary to clear the stage for calculation to take place. Calculativeness, for Callon, is the mainstay of market transactions, and therefore definitive of the eco-nomic itself. To calculate, agents have to have access to the minimum infor-mation necessary to hold preferences, rank them, then reveal and negotiate them to enable transactions to take place.

This definition of calculation is invoked in Callon et al.'s recent work on the 'economy of qualities', a term linked to but not synonymous with the service economy. The economy of qualities is structured around the qualifi-cation of products through supply- and demand-side processes of product singularisation and attachment. Consumers' social networks coalesce with business and marketing strategies to produce a complex socio-technical device that aids consumer efforts to evaluate and 'singularise' products, resulting ultimately in attachment to 'that particular product'. This attach-ment is always under threat as competitors seek to 'detach' attached con-sumers. Detachment involves breaking into the routines of attached consumers to force them to hesitate at the point of purchase and 'requalify' products. Supply-side professionals 'constantly try to destabilise consumers, to extract them from their routines and prompt them to re-evaluate the qual-ities of products' (Callon et al., 2002: 206). To illustrate this process, the authors use the example of an orange juice manufacturer who offered a free Pokemon in an effort to recruit consumers attached to other brands by targeting their children.

The child would predictably detach herself from her father, pull him by the arm, force him to leave the routine he automatically followed, and put him in front of a product which, strictly speaking, he had not seen. A discussion between father and child would follow, which was likely to end in a purchase and, eventually, in attachment to a new brand. (2002: 206)

This perfectly exemplifies the model of singularisation and attachment, invoking as it does both marketing strategies and the weight of the collective network in which consumers are immersed. Unfortunately it reads like a textbook marketing solution, with the same characteristic overemphasis on the predictability and rationality of consumer behaviour. Despite the authors' efforts to instil a sense of the fluid and simultaneous nature of processes of routine attachment and (re)qualification, the model retains an obstinately mechanistic edge. This may, in part, be due to its dependence on a calculative consumer. 'The dynamic of reflexive attachment', Callon et al. insist, 'implies consumers who are calculating, that is, capable of perceiving differences and grading them, and who are accompanied and supported in this evaluation and judgement by suppliers and their intermediaries' (2002: 213).

Despite the attempt to incorporate multiple influences on qualification processes through the notion of a socio-technical device, the risk of providing only an impoverished account of the dynamics of purchase remains. The orange juice manufacturer's strategy may succeed or fail according to a range of factors extrinsic to the qualification of the product. The parental attitude to what marketers call 'pester power', the manufacturer's capacity to negotiate a shelving location prominent enough to secure the child's attention, and the atmosphere in the shop that day, might all conceivably influence purchase, but not necessarily qualification. This amounts to an argument that purchasing does not always involve qualification or calculation in the sense that Callon et al. suggest.

Callon's definition of the economic through the notion of calculativeness is perhaps the most troublesome part of his argument for sociologists and anthropologists concerned with economic life. Both Don Slater's (2002b) and Daniel Miller's (2002) contributions to the debate resist this aspect of his account, although Miller's disagreement is undoubtedly the most serious. As we saw above, Miller's account of advertising emphasises the cultural nature of business processes. In his recent work (1998, 2002) this culturalist emphasis becomes a more explicit argument that the economic and the market exist only as cultural practices. Quite simply, the market is a 'virtualism' – a representation, albeit a particularly powerful one, of economic life. For Miller, Callon's argument that framing defines the market system by creating a space for calculation, is 'upside-down', as:

what lies within the frame is *not* the market system as an actual practice, but on the contrary a ritualised expression of an ideology of the market ... The confusion is that this ritual and ideological system in the case of capitalism is actually called the market. (Miller, 2002: 225)

Miller goes on to make his case, using the example of a car purchase, that successful transactions ultimately depend not on disentanglement, as in Callon's model, but on further entanglement between business practices and the rich mixture of consumer motivations. Disentangled market situations exist only in economists' models, not in actual practice. This is not the place to engage extensively with Miller's critique, but it is worth noting that, as compelling as his account of the rich and entangled nature of market transactions is, the critique of the market as an ideological representation raises more questions than it solves. It is not just the dissolution of everything into a broad category of 'culture' that is at stake, but a return to the limitless, interpretative problematic raised in Chapter 1 of differentiating the 'real' from the 'constructed'. The risk is that, in centring upon the meta-theoretical debate over whether the economy and the calculating agent exist in reality or only as ideological constructs, the more practical insights offered by Callon's perspective are bypassed. As Slater (2002b) argues, the aim may be to reformulate the perspective, in order to retain an analysis of how economic behaviour is formatted without the diverse but still restrictive model of calculation.

This is pertinent in the context of this study because, while the theoretical debate over the precise definition of the economic might rage forever, the notion of performance offers a practical approach to the analysis of advertising processes. For instance, in his discussion of accounting, Peter Miller explains how accounting tools shape the reality they set out to measure. Accountancy tools are 'largely improvised and adapted to the tasks and materials at hand' (Miller, 1998: 190). No general principle defining what should and should not be measured exists; the relevant reality is constantly renegotiated and reconfigured in accounting. Accountants cannot practise or perform calculations without tools, and tools shape meaning. This is a point that emerges with some force in Law's (2002) empirical account of the role of spreadsheets and the Thatcherite culture of 'enterprise' in creating a category of 'real costs'. It has also been productively applied to the study of marketing and advertising practices to uncover the connections between marketing knowledge and the formation of markets and marketing categories (Cochoy, 1998; Slater, 2002a, 2002b).

The advantages of an approach levelled at the performance of material practices rather than at a theoretical analysis of the culture–economy dynamic can also be illustrated by returning to the insights offered by the practice-based literature. One of the most significant of these, it was suggested above, was the identification of the multiple motivations that bear on practice. Practitioners' behaviour emerged as never purely economic, but always underscored by other 'non-economic' motivations. These motivations often relate to the reproduction of occupational roles and the advertising community as a whole. Such 'non-economic' motivations are hard to separate from more instrumental 'calculation', because, utilising Fish's notion of interpretative communities, to be a particular sort of practitioner inevitably involves constructing the task and thereby 'calculating' in particular ways. Thus, what for account managers might appear as a matter of understanding the interpersonal dynamics in a given company, for creative staff may appear to be a question of finding the right expressive platform. One way of looking at these differences is to construe them as 'cultural'. It is arguably the case that they relate to the presence of different 'micro-cultures of production' within advertising agencies (du Gay, 1997; Negus, 1997). But this sense of the intervention of broadly 'cultural' values in advertising practice is only part of the picture. The 'cultural' could be defined, as Ray and Sayer recommend, as that which concerns intrinsic meanings and values, but exactly how this can be distinguished from the economic realm is obscure. It is not as if the economic can be thought of without the mediation of meanings and values. The cultural is not something that intervenes in economic processes; rather it is constitutive of them. To avoid getting drawn into the meta-theoretical terrain of defining the extent of culture and economy, and the boundary between them, the approach advocated here is to focus on the performance of advertising as a *constituent material practice*. This term is intended to signal the impossibility of a purely cultural or purely economic form of business practice. In as far as they exist at all, 'culture' and 'economy' exist in concrete instances of material practice. Thinking of advertising as a constituent material practice offers an alternative to the critical invocation of an idealised past in which culture and economy existed in a purer state. It focuses attention instead on the particular ways in which advertising has been conducted as a multifaceted, diverse and shifting device deployed in the promotion of consumption.

concluding comments   This chapter's main aim has been to address the argument that advertising has acted to transform the relationship between culture and economy. This argument has had an enduring hold on critical thought, and it has appeared in a number of different guises. Attention focused first on accounts that take a broadly institutional perspective on advertising, and uncovered an almost neurotic preoccupation with the contemporary shape of the culture/economy configuration. Theoretical diagnoses range from accounts of culture subjugated to economic imperatives to accounts describing a de-differentiation of the spheres. In all versions the role played by advertising is decisive. More than any other medium, advertising is deemed responsible for the production of consumption, and consumption is the definitive mark of the epoch. Advertising is thereby culpable for the mutation of the culture/economy relation.

The focus turned next to accounts which took the practice of advertising as their starting point. Theoretical work in this vein has featured a less dramatic account of advertising's transformative impact, foregrounding instead the contingent and diverse nature of practice. Advertising practice emerges as neither predominantly cultural nor economic, but a mixture of both. In some accounts this compound nature appears as a function of a broader epochal tendency towards increasing culturalisation. Advertising is thus at times characterised as an exemplary hybrid practice. But writers on practice approach questions of culture, economy and hybridisation in quite different, often implicit and sometimes ambiguous ways. As important and suggestive as this work is, ultimately it reinforces the need to rethink the categories of culture and economy as they have been applied to advertising.

An attempt at this task was made in the final section. A general analytic distinction between culture and economy, it was suggested, was difficult to maintain against evidence about their inextricability in practice. Culture as a bounded, total sphere of intrinsic human value is a specific historical conception, not a transcendent reality. A number of theorists posit a model of culture as a more situated and contingent category, whose limited forms are best considered as existing only through specific historical arrangements, institutions and practices. The anthropology of science and techniques in particular provides productive ways of rethinking how the economic and the cultural are performed in material practice, under particular arrangements and utilising particular socio-technical devices. Advertising practice, it was concluded, could be usefully studied as a constituent entity, neither cultural nor economic in essence but, necessarily, both. The object of study thus becomes the diversity of forms, tools, techniques and rationalities that have historically constituted the device of advertising. A study of these contextualised socio-technical phenomena promises a more sensitive portrayal of the historical development of advertising than is often encountered in critical literature.

notes

1 See du Gay & Pryke (2002); *Economy and Society* (2002) Special Issue: The Technological Economy 31 (2) and Ray & Sayer (1999) for more extended debate of this problematic they raise.

2 See Chapter 2 for a fuller discussion.
3 See for example Negus (1992); McRobbie (1998); Mort (1996); Nixon (1996; 1997; 2003); Soar (2002).
4 See Williams's (1980) seminal essay on advertising as a magic system.
5 Miller's project was conducted at an agency in Trinidad, whilst Moeran conducted a more extensive ethnography of advertising practice in a Japanese agency. Both conducted their fieldwork over the course of a year, but while Moeran worked as a participant observer in one agency, Miller's observationally based research was part of a much broader ethnographic exploration of capitalism in Trinidad.
6 The OBC is similarly sought after in the UK. It commands the highest rates, and in magazines like *Cosmopolitan* is often booked up more than a year in advance by the most prestigious clients.
7 The notion of ESP stands in opposition to the 'traditional' Unique Selling Proposition (USP) approach described in Reeves's (1961) *Reality in Advertising* where adverts seek to stress a 'unique' feature of each product.
8 See Foucault (1980, 1982), Miller & Rose (1990), Allen & du Gay (1994) and du Gay (1996).

the uses of history

introduction History is a quiet, understated but constant element in the edifice of critical explanations of advertising reviewed thus far. In a broad swathe of cultural critique – and not just that directed at advertising – claims about the distinctiveness of the contemporary moment are based upon a largely assumed history. Yet claims about the distinctiveness of the contemporary moment are inherently historical claims. To theorise about ruptures, transgressions and mutations is logically to invoke a different history, but the details of that history are largely absent from critical theory. This chapter takes the relationship between theory and history as its focus, with the particular goal of demonstrating that a 'genealogical' description of advertising is an appropriate, even necessary response, to the prevalence of particular modes of thinking and methods of analysis in existing critiques of advertising.

Two primary factors have swayed the argument in this direction. First, as Morris remarks, the predominant tendency in cultural studies has been to treat the various activities around production as 'known', while those centred around consumption have been understood as 'enigmatic' and worthy of sustained analysis (Morris, 1988: 24). This has certainly been the situation until quite recently in the specific study of advertising, where serious and careful analyses of the advertising text and its consumption far outnumber their equivalents devoted to production practices. The most influential, almost canonical, works in the cultural study of advertising have derived their powerful expositions of advertising's cultural and economic significance almost exclusively from analyses of individual advertising texts (Leymore, 1975; Barthes, 1977; Williamson, 1978; Goldman, 1992; Goldman & Papson, 1996). Although robust attempts have been made to rectify this imbalance through the adoption of a more institutionally focused analysis (Leiss et al., 1986; Wernick, 1991) or through attention to production practices (Moeran, 1996; Mort, 1996; Nixon, 1996, 1997; Miller, 1997), such attempts are not without their problems. There are some indications that the balance may be shifting, but to date few detailed empirical studies of advertising production have been conducted.[1]

Second, critical work has tended to attribute to advertising a very particular historical role. Advertising is conceptualised as a singular mediative institution located between the realm of production and the realm of consumption. This structural position endows advertising with a unique capacity to connect reality with meaning, people with objects, and culture with economy. Further, advertising is understood to transform that which it connects, occasioning substantive and probably irrevocable changes in the nature and organisation of contemporary life. These changes are regarded as the outcome of an ongoing process of evolution in which advertising becomes increasingly persuasive, pervasive and culturally/economically hybridised. Diverse strands of critique share an 'epochalist' concern with marking out distinctions between loosely periodised epochs where the central role of advertising in producing new societal forms, designated by terms like 'postmodernity', 'consumer society' or 'information society', is foregrounded.

This chapter argues that a historically situated and contextualised study of advertising practices can respond both to the deficit in cultural analyses of the economic and to the epochalist bent in existing theory. It is split into three main sections. First, a summary is provided of the critical tendency to theorise advertising in terms of its effects on domains dualistically conceived as reality and meaning, subjects and objects, and culture and economy. Attention then moves on to how this is thought to have been accomplished through gradual and progressive increases in the persuasiveness, pervasiveness and hybridisation of advertising, in line with the changing requirements of epochally defined societies. This historically *theorised* claim tends, almost paradoxically, to be weakly historically *empiricised* – whatever evidence is presented about advertising 'now', evidence about advertising 'then' tends to be scant and decontextualised. This leaves the path clear for a final discussion of the uses of history and its relationship to theoretical problems. Despite the apparent, and convenient, fit between a problematic epochalist tradition in critical discourse and a descriptive, historical method, things are not quite that straightforward because, at best, history offers fair empirical accounts, not general theoretical answers. Despite these limits, the chapter still concludes that a history of practice is worth undertaking, and can offer different ways of thinking about advertising and its contemporary and historical roles in social life.

the dualistic nature of advertising critique   Theoretical approaches to the study of advertising tend to be organised around three central dualisms: meaning and reality, subjects and objects, and culture and economy. These pairs manifest themselves in a variety of different ways in the various branches of critique, but one particular theme dominates; that is, the desire to express the action and effects of advertising on relations between the pairs. Before exploring further some of the specific conceptual problems which arise through the reliance on these oppositions, however, it is worth inserting a note of caution.

First, despite their prevalence, these dualisms do not in any way describe a general conceptual approach to the socio-cultural study of advertising. Rather, critical literature adopts and defines these terms, sometimes explicitly, sometimes implicitly, in a variety of ways. Any discussion, therefore, of their presence in the work of different authors necessarily risks collapsing some of the finer distinctions intended. Nonetheless, the contention remains that a significant degree of commonality exists in the ways that various writers have used dualisms to 'think' advertising. Second, far from being tidy, contained and distinctive analytical categories, these dualisms are characterised by substantial overlaps that make it almost impossible to refer to one term without simultaneously invoking some of the others. So, for example, the notion of meaning might be discussed as an abstract category, but the object that means and its cultural significance are never far behind. With these provisos in mind, the following addresses in turn how each of these dualisms – meaning and reality, subjects and objects, culture and economy – have structured critical discourse.

Meaning and reality   Chapter 1 argued that critical discourse, particularly that in the semiotic tradition, understands advertising fundamentally as a technique of influencing demand through managing the meanings of products. Advertisements attempt to make products *mean* particular things largely through associating them with other, often tenuously related, 'things'. This is one of the most widely remarked features of advertising. Verbs like abducted, dissolved, corrupted, emptied, depleted and cannibalised are deployed to describe the effect this aspect of advertising has upon 'real' meanings. For authors like Barthes (1977), Williamson (1978), Goldman (1992) and Goldman and Papson (1996), adverts manufacture 'false' meanings which act 'ideologically' to conceal the 'real', material base of society.

This base concerns the contest of man's 'real' historical relation to nature, where nature is transformed through labour. The semiotic approach thus invokes a materialist conception of meaning, where the constructed artifice of advertising stands in opposition to 'real' historical meaning.

Even authors like Leiss et al. (1986) and Wernick (1991), who sought to distance themselves from a semiotic deconstruction of advertising's texts, retained a preoccupation with the loss of meaning. So for Wernick, the casualty in a 'dereferentialised' promotional culture is the 'meaningfulness' of language (Wernick, 1991: 189), whilst for Leiss et al. the 'true' meanings of goods are concealed behind the 'elaborate masks' constructed for them by advertising and marketing processes (Leiss et al., 1986: 325). These authors concur that the symbolic processes of advertising are colonising an increasing array of 'real' objects and values. This acceleration is diagnosed as a function of the epoch, whether designated as consumer society, postmodernity or late commodity capitalism. Whatever tag is employed, the sense is one in which the commercial appropriation of the meaning-making process represented by advertising and characteristic of contemporary society marks a decisive break from earlier societies.

These concerns, at least in the first instance, seem entirely reasonable. The integrity of language and cultural symbols surely should be defended against random, commercial appropriation and devaluation. This stance, however, invokes a very particular formulation of the term 'meaning'. If meaning is to be considered so vulnerable to advertising processes it has to be approached as an otherwise relatively stable category with some sort of basis in reality. 'Real' meaning, the proper relationships between meanings and objects, must thus be amenable, in theory at least, to taxonomic classification. This taxonomic or semantic approach is hard to sustain in the face of widespread theoretical emphases on the fluidity of meaning. The meaning of objects, as anthropologists have long insisted, derives from their uses, their forms and their patterns of circulation – it is not an inherent 'essence' but a judgement conferred by others. For these reasons it is proposed that meaning is best understood as comprised of both semantic and pragmatic elements. Use, far from a separate category, is a major factor in the determination of meaning.

This simultaneously semantic and pragmatic conception of meaning suggests a *contingent* nature, whereby meaning is bound up with the context of use and is, of necessity, subject to change. This conception raises awkward questions for critical accounts of the commercial devaluation of meaning. If meaning is not a contingent construct, how does advertising get into it in the first place? If it is a contingent construct, how then does advertising achieve privileged status over all other sources in the determination of meaning? Meaning, its sources and determinations, is a notoriously slippery category that shifts over time, space, context and between users. In these circumstances evaluating the impact of advertising on meaning becomes a speculative and potentially limitless interpretative task.

The dualistic opposition of meaning and the real provides an elegant and powerful conceptual framework for describing the ways in which objects come to take on a symbolic significance which extends beyond their material characteristics. In the specific study of advertising this yields a cogent and persuasive basis from which to articulate concerns about its perceived or potential degenerative effects. The dualism, however, relies upon a reduction and simplification of the multifaceted relations between meaning and reality. Inherent in this formulation is the assumption that somewhere underneath layers of 'semantic artifice' lies the 'real' essence of objects and social relations. It is not merely that this reality, this essence, is always beyond reach, but the very opposition of constructed meaning to the real is a theoretical abstraction. As Fish (1994) argues, in a world where everything is constructed, the constructed is as real as anything else. In other words, meaning is not dualistically opposed to the real; in the absence of an unconstructed reality the constructed meanings that constitute social life are as real as it gets.

Subjects and objects   The logical extension of the critical focus on advertising's effects on meaning/reality is to the subject/object relation. Where advertising has the potential to reconstruct what things *mean* to their users, it necessarily has the potential to alter the nature of the relationship between people and objects. Chapter 2 argued that critical accounts owe a great deal to the Marxist formulation of the types of relation between subjects and objects that arise under capitalist modes of economic organisation. In particular advertising has been accommodated very neatly within the commodity fetishism thesis as a technology centrally concerned with manufacturing exchange-values. This type of explanation structures work by theorists like Horkheimer and Adorno (1973), Ewen (1976), Haug (1986) and Jhally (1987), who see advertising as a process whereby objects under a capitalist system of production are given sensual, aestheticised identities that conceal the 'real' nature of their production. Similar arguments were traced in more recent work by Leiss et al. (1986) and Wernick (1991). For the former, advertising has resulted in a change in the core function of goods from the satisfaction of wants to the communication of meaning (Leiss et al., 1986: 285). In the process social and material characteristics have been masked, creating an ever-increasing 'objectification' not just of goods but of an expanding array of natural and human elements (1986: 324). For Wernick, commodity fetishism does not go far enough. Objects, he argues, are not simply embellished or 'dressed up' in the promotional process, their 'very being' is transformed (Wernick, 1991: 190).

In all these accounts, the advertising process does not simply impact upon the nature of objects, but extends to the nature of human subjects. Haug, for instance, refers to the transformation of the human species, Wernick to the loss of the authentic subject, whilst Leiss et al., in more measured terms, urge caution over the human and social consequences of increasing objectification. Throughout these different accounts, the most elemental property of advertising is conceptualised as *masking* the underlying reality of objects, and it is this ultimately that impacts upon subjects. In distorting the true nature of things, capitalist societies alienate human subjects from the real relations of production and consumption, and produce a transfigured, objectified subject.

Again, this transformative process is characterised as ongoing, cumulative and a function of the contemporary mode of societal organisation, defined as 'market-', 'commodity capitalist-' or 'consumption-' based. Chapter 2 argued that this hypothesis is underpinned by the assumption that the present represents a decline from a past where objects were related to on a more pragmatic basis. Yet as anthropologists have long maintained, there is little evidence to support this view (Sahlins, 1976; Appadurai, 1986; Miller, 1995). Utility, they point out, is not opposed to meaning-making processes, but is itself symbolically defined and constructed across all traceable societies.

These problems with the way critiques of advertising have characterised relations between subjects and objects stem, in part, from overplaying the oppositions between the categories. In the first instance, the contrast between the way people relate to objects *now* and the way they are supposed to have related to them *then* is oversimplified and overdramatised. At a deeper level, however, the contrast between objects and subjects itself, some argue, is overdrawn and essentialised. Appadurai, for example, remarks on the tendency in certain forms of contemporary thought to draw the distinction between people and objects too sharply.

> ... the powerful contemporary tendency is to regard the world of things as inert and mute, set in motion and animated, indeed knowable only by persons and their words ... Yet in many historical societies, things have not been so divorced from the capacity of persons to act and the power of words to communicate. (Appadurai, 1986: 4)

Even if the theoretical view that things have no meanings other than those endowed by human beings cannot be escaped, Appadurai argues, methodologically the need is to follow the trajectories of objects themselves in order to grasp fully their human and social significance. This view has been elaborated in work within the anthropology of science and techniques, which signals the intercalibration of the biographies of people and things, such that neither people nor things are intelligible outside of their relations with each other (Latour, 1993; Callon, 1998a, 1998b; Law, 2002). Rather than dualistically opposed, human beings and objects are inextricably bound up with one another. This position is consistent with the semantic and pragmatic conception of meaning outlined above in foregrounding the manner in which the forms and uses of objects are part of their symbolic meaning. Objects here both construct and are constructed by human activity and meaning-making. This explanation contrasts sharply with the critical picture of advertising as animating the inanimate and symbolically transforming the functional. In the latter, outside of the associated processes of commodification and advertising, objects are stable, inanimate, primarily functional entities, essentially opposed to human subjects.

Culture and economy   If the dualistic opposition between meaning and the real, between subjects and objects, prevalent in critical literature does produce a flattened, two-dimensional picture of advertising's effects, the same has also to be said of the characterisation of the culture/economy relation. Ultimately, for many theorists, the effect of advertising upon meaning and reality, subjects and objects, is reproduced in a transformation of culture and economy. The desire to retheorise the culture/economy relation is not restricted to the critics of advertising. Advertising is accorded a significant, formative role in the shifting culture/economy relation by a number of theorists not directly concerned with its empirical study (Horkheimer and Adorno, 1973; Baudrillard, 1988a, 1988b; Adorno, 1991; Featherstone, 1991; Lash & Urry, 1994). The trajectory of this work shares a preoccupation with the singularity of the configuration of the culture/economy dualism in contemporary life. In some accounts culture is increasingly prone to economic imperatives, whilst in others the distinction between these 'separate domains' is increasingly blurred. In both versions the role played by advertising is decisive. Advertising, more than any other medium, is responsible for the production of consumption, and it is thus centrally implicated in the reconfiguration of the culture/economy relation.

This is a formulation that has been of particular significance in critical work focused on the institution of advertising. Wernick provides probably the most detailed account of the *mutation* of the culture/economy relation through promotional processes, so that the distinctions between the two 'zones' has progressively eroded (Wernick, 1991: 19). In essence, this mutation is the result of advertising's involvement in the manipulation of meaning. The problem, for writers like Jhally (1987), Leiss et al. (1986) and Mattelart (1991) does not reside in the construction of a symbolic dimension to goods per se, as this is regarded as a historical and anthropological constant. Rather, the problem resides in the location of this meaning-making process in a specific, economic regime: that of capitalist commodity production. In societies, defined as prior to, or other than capital- or market-based, meaning 'gets into' objects through a variety of state, religious, community and kinship institutions. It is against the perceived decline of these institutions that advertising's impact on culture and economy is generally judged. The fundamental concern here is that formerly autonomous cultural systems have given way to advertising – as an economic instrument, to determine meaning and ultimately culture, thus accomplishing a hybridisation of culture and economy. Different writers, of course, characterise advertising's intervention in the relation between culture and economy differently, but there is a baseline agreement that, outside the ravages of commodity- or market-based societies, culture and economy exist as separate and autonomous 'spheres'.

This formulation also has some purchase on critical accounts focused on the practices, rather than the institution or products, of advertising. In some accounts of creative practice, for instance, hybridisation or 'culturalisation' figures in an emphasis on practitioners' roles as 'new cultural intermediaries' in producing novel juxtapositions of cultural and economic knowledges (Mort, 1996; Nixon, 1997). On the whole, though, practice-based accounts tend to make less dramatic claims about the effects of advertising upon culture and economy, illustrating instead how different aspects of advertising practice inevitably combine 'cultural' meanings and values with 'economic' calculations (Moeran, 1996; Miller, 1997). This provides an important contribution to a re-conceptualisation of advertising as a constituent practice comprising both cultural and economic elements.

But the recognition of how meanings and values broadly defined as 'cultural' are necessarily involved in the practice of advertising is only part of the picture. The 'cultural' may be conceptualised as the realm of human meanings and values, but if this is the case it is not entirely clear how the 'economic' realm can be differentiated from the cultural. Outside human meanings and values, how can the economic be understood, defined, measured or represented? Culture is not something that sits on top of economic practices and processes, but is *constitutive* of them. For this reason the approach advocated throughout this book is to leave aside the task of defining absolutely what is cultural and what is economic, and to focus instead on a constituent view of material practice. The conceptualisation of culture and economy as discrete and separate domains of activity employs an artificial analytical distinction that is extremely awkward to sustain in instances of material practice. It is in the brute empirical realities of advertising, or any other form of material practice, that the substances of 'culture' and 'economy' are configured and reconfigured. As categories they cannot transcend their definition in specific forms of material practice and institutional ordering.

This may be one reason why the pursuit of decontextualised norms for culture and economy so often results in the kind of disembodied abstractions common in critiques of advertising.

Critical thought, it has been argued, is characterised by a pervasive and excessive dualistic tendency that parodies and artificially reduces areas of diversity within opposed poles (Appadurai, 1986; Latour, 1993). In the critical aim to sharply distinguish different sorts of 'thing', areas of difference are overplayed and areas of similarity ignored. In all three cases the adoption of dualisms to structure and inform critiques of advertising has had precisely this effect, reducing and simplifying what are in practice plural and contingent relations. There is little doubt that these dualisms have provided powerful and elegant ways to think about advertising and its role and effects. But what such oppositions yield in terms of analytical convenience incurs costs beyond the artificial reduction and simplification of complex categories.

One cost of dualistic modes of thinking is a tendency to establish in advance how specific phenomena are to be categorised and understood, rendering certain phenomena known and thus unworthy of further investigation. One instance of this is what Morris (1988) describes as the general legacy of Marxism to cultural studies, in which the sphere of production is deemed 'already' understood. Williamson's (1978: 17) characterisation of advertising as a field of production without originating subjects provides a specific example of this tendency. Advertising, she insists, is not the product or 'speech' of its makers. This effectively dispatches the intentions and activities of advertising producers as an irrelevance, because their role has already been explained theoretically as deriving from the necessity of the relations of production. Thus the need to explore directly and research the practices and activities of those involved in the production of advertising never arises. In this way dualistic modes of thinking helped enable critiques of advertising to continue making assertions in the absence of empirical evidence, describing the industry it claims to study.

Finally, running through all three dualisms is a further dualism in the form of the polar opposition of societies 'then' to societies 'now'. As has been argued throughout, critical work has attributed to advertising a particular, historical role in the transformation of society through the disruption of relations between meaning and reality, between subjects and objects, and ultimately between culture and economy. As should by now be clear, the critical interpretation of how this takes place tends to be general and theoretical, with the distinctions between 'then' and 'now' more often assumed than tightly periodised and empiricised. This reflects the tendency in epochally driven theory to use particular large-scale changes, be they in economic organisation or in consumption practices, to read off, explain or assume a series of smaller-scale changes (Rose, 1996). The problems immanent in such epochal explanations are examined in the next section.

things are not as they once were: the teleology of the epoch   The epochalist tendency in critical literature sees advertising as fully imbricated in shifts from one societal form to the next. Advertising's particular role in these shifts has been variously related at different moments and by different authors to changes in advertising form, institutional context and practice. The general drift of critical literature sees advertising as a medium that has steadily become more persuasive, pervasive and hybridised. To establish the consequences of this it is worth providing, firstly, an overview of the more detailed arguments already presented regarding the forms these 'teleological' tendencies have taken. The focus then shifts to consider the questions raised by these tendencies, and the related inclination to situate changes in advertising within broader changes in societal epoch.

The overarching tendency in socio-cultural analyses understands advertisements to have attained their current form as a function of a gradual, incremental, evolutionary process unfolding throughout the century. Chapter 1 suggested that the facility of advertisements to produce artificial structures of meaning is judged as an ideological capacity advancing in tune with the needs of 'modern capitalist economies'. This argument is taken up more explicitly by the authors featured in Chapter 2, who describe a progressive shift in the format of advertisements, from an informational base at the beginning of the twentieth century to a persuasive base by the end: what has been characterised as a move from an information orientation towards a persuasive lifestyle orientation (Williams, 1980; Dyer, 1982; Pope, 1983; Leiss et al., 1986; Jhally, 1987; Pope, 1991; Myers, 1999) is understood elsewhere as a shift from announcement to advertisement (Falk, 1994), from simple to compound advertisements (Fowles, 1996), or from modern to postmodern discourses (Davidson, 1992; Goldman, 1992; Goldman & Papson, 1996; Kang, 1999).

This teleological tendency also manifests itself in quite distinctive ways in thinking about advertising practice. Some accounts of practice have lit upon advances underpinning the production of more heavily symbol-laden advertising. Thus contemporary forms of advertising practice are seen as emblematic of an underlying structural change, producing a new hybrid form of cultural/economic practice. Advertising is thereby described as a culture industry (Lash & Urry, 1994) staffed by practitioners blending symbolic expertise with economic aims in a 'third wave' creative revolution (Mort, 1996; Nixon, 1997).

The final instance of teleological thinking in critiques of advertising refers to the changing institutional context of advertising. As argued throughout, advertising is assumed to have become an increasingly pervasive medium. Semiotic accounts refer to advertising's role today, as distinct from anything that has gone before. In semiotic critiques, adverts are inescapable to an unprecedented extent (Leymore, 1975; Williamson, 1978; Dyer, 1982; Vestergaard & Schroder, 1985). In institutionally focused accounts, advertising's particular contemporary significance is judged in terms of its increasing presence in everyday environments enabled by the decline of older institutions of socialisation (Leiss et al., 1986; Baudrillard, 1988a; Featherstone, 1991; Wernick, 1991; Lash & Urry, 1994; Fowles, 1996; Myers, 1999). Few of these accounts, however, provide much in the way of evidence to support this everyday proliferation; in most cases it is simply intuitively assumed that it is unprecedented.

Throughout this diverse range of critical work, increases in the persuasiveness, hybridity and pervasiveness of advertising are frequently explained as a function of the epoch. Irrespective of how this epoch is designated – whether in terms of consumption, market organisation, or commodity production – advertising is widely conceived through its role in stimulating demand as one of the defining characteristics of the era. So, in Baudrillard's (1988b), Moeran's or Davidson's accounts of consumer society, in Wernick's notion of promotional culture and in Williamson's, Leiss et al.'s or Goldman's versions of commodity capitalism, it is advertising that enables society to function in a given form. Advertising, by generating demand, altering the relations between people and things, producing a political economy based on sign-values, is understood as a primary constitutive element in the identity of the current epoch.

Advertising is characterised almost as a causal variable in the definition of the epoch, essentially a product of the 'modern' mode of societal organisation. It can be thought of in Turner's terms as one of the 'substantive criteria which … define the point at which the modern age as a whole breaks with the pre-modern' (Turner, 1992: 12). This is precisely how critical interpretations of advertising have characterised its historical development. Advertising in the 'modern' era takes on the functions previously performed by older 'pre-modern' institutional structures, evolving in tandem with the epoch. This theoretical statement, however, is seldom supported by detailed, empirical evidence. As argued in Chapter 2, even those studies of persuasiveness or pervasiveness that do present significant empirical evidence give scant consideration to the institutional, organisational or technical circumstances of production. Such consideration, as argued in subsequent chapters, is essential to an informed understanding of the nature of the promotional appeal being made.

Moreover, the notion of 'period' tends to be very loosely deployed. 'Then' is somehow self-evidently distinct from 'now', but few theorists will be drawn on how advertising has operated in specific historical periods. Wernick, for instance, urges caution against 'too sharp a sense of periodization' and stresses instead the need to think of the move to 'promotional culture' as a 'cumulative tendency' (Wernick, 1991: 185–6). There are obvious, and sound, intellectual reasons for this reluctance. Nevertheless it does contribute to the high level of generality and abstraction at which critical models of advertising tend to function. There can be little objection to the principle that nineteenth-century advertising differs substantially from twentieth-century advertising, and this may bear some relation to the distinctive characteristics of each historical period. The risk, however, is that in relying upon generalised 'epochal' explanations, the more interesting questions about the specific nature, sources and causes of these differences never get asked. The remainder of this section explores some of the reasons why the definition and periodisation of the epoch present such challenges.

Throughout his analysis of the relationship between culture and economic production, Sahlins (1976) is at pains to point out that, in terms of the underlying relation between these two dimensions of human activity, there is little that fundamentally distinguishes the modern from the pre-modern. The primary distinction that he settles on is the contemporary illusion that it is otherwise – that 'modernity' is economically constituted where 'pre-modernity' was culturally constituted. His contention is that societies across time and space are simultaneously culturally and economically constituted. In this Sahlins anticipates the concerns of later theorists of modernity for whom this reflective introspection, this need to contrast the modern with what had gone before or was about to come, is itself perhaps the defining feature of modernity. In Turner's terms 'the distinctiveness of modernity consists not only in the empirically observable emergence of the modern state, a modern understanding of self, modern capitalism, modern science, but in our very need to define the modern epoch' (Turner, 1992: 9).

There are some parallels between Turner's observation and Foucault's suggestion that modernity is not so much a period of history as an 'attitude'. For Foucault the attitude of modernity involves particular ways of thinking, feeling and relating to the world (Foucault, 1984a: 39). This conceptualisation is suggestive for two reasons. First, it provides an explanation of why it has proved so difficult to arrive at a final description of the characteristics of modernity. As Dean (1994) has observed, the substantive features theorists see as comprising modernity are practically inexhaustible, as evidenced by the various definitions advanced in terms of the mode of production, technology, consumption, organisation, knowledge and risk (cf. Dean, 1994; Osborne, 1998). For Turner, this endless theorising of the nature of the epoch is a function of the introspective attitude that defines modernity. In his view the continual reassessment and redefinition of substantive characteristics satisfies the 'caesural' impulse to define the break between the modern and the pre-modern or, in some versions, between the modern and the postmodern. Secondly, the notion of modernity as attitude rather than epoch goes some way towards providing an explanation of why, despite all this reflection, it has proved so difficult to arrive at a more precise historical definition of periods, or to identify more precisely how breaks between epochs can be identified. Regarding modernity as an attitude helps to explain the critical preoccupation with establishing, in the most general and historically flexible terms, how advertising today differs from before.

Further, as both Turner (1992) and Osborne (1998) have argued – and this is an element that is extremely pronounced in discussions of advertising – most theoretical accounts of modernity as an epoch are really critiques of modernity, yearning for a golden age either lost or yet to come. Foucault's conception of modernity as attitude provides, at least for Osborne (1998: 6–8), the possibility of an escape from the 'binary politics' which insist that a position either for or against modernity be taken. For Osborne, the notion of modernity as attitude invites an empirical rather than a theoretical approach.

So long as the concept of modernity is understood in *epochal* terms, that is, attached to a periodization rather than an ethos or attitude, then we will encounter problems at the level of critique. That is because such epochal periodizations lend themselves intrinsically to a logic of dichotomization that establishes the available terms of critique in advance, either for or against. (Osborne, 1998: 19)

What Osborne is getting at is the intrinsic dualism of the concept of the epoch as a historical period. No period can be sustained indefinitely, ultimately the question of the supplement, what comes after, arises; hence the prominence of the 'post' prefix, as in 'post-'modernity or 'post-'industrial society. His point is similar to the one made above regarding the consequences for empirical research of excessively dualistic modes of thinking. The risk of structuring analyses around theoretical dualisms is that of reducing, caricaturing or ultimately rendering invisible concrete historical processes. This risk arises in the tendency of such powerful theoretical narratives to erase awkward historical specificities by rendering them 'already' known, explicable or understood. If we know the 'modern' as the era of the advertising, promotion, or commercial signification of goods, there is little call to explore the substantive nature of these activities in oppositionally defined 'pre-modern' societies. This tendency is what underlies Osborne's assertion that critical, epochal theories of modernity 'overdramatize the characteristics of social change and reduce such change to one or two fundamental elements' (1998: 19). Osborne prefers a lower-level analysis, one that eschews the desire to produce a universal critical model, and directs effort instead only to 'particular kinds of enterprise' (1998: 39).

Adopting some form of lower-level empirical or historical analysis may provide a way out of the critical dilemmas raised by dualistic theory generally, and epochalism in particular. If, as authors like Foucault (1984a), Turner (1992) and Latour (1993) have argued, the concept of modernity as a unified, coherent, historical epoch can be neither described substantively or definitely periodised, this raises questions about its validity as an organising principle for critical approaches to advertising, or any other social phenomena. Moreover, the logic inherent in epochal theory imposes disabling constraints on our capacity to describe and understand the conditions in which the forms or practices of advertising emerged. Advertising is generally thought of as an exclusive possession of the modern epoch – even as definitive of it. It is this type of thinking that underlies the teleological emphases running through many critical accounts of advertising. Advertising in these accounts is increasingly persuasive, hybridised, and pervasive. By extension, this frequently renders advertising increasingly culpable in the negative transformation of social relations underlying many theories of modernity. A more modest, empirical history of the emergence of advertising as a specific promotional form may reveal this to be an over-generalisation of a much more interesting reality. In this respect the aim in the remainder of this book is to conduct, for advertising, something like the effective history envisaged by Dean, whereby

[t]he point is not to seek the universal conditions that make it possible to speak and act, and to enshrine them in foundational moral codes and epistemologies, but to discover what it is possible to think, say and do under various contingent conditions. ... It follows that it is not particularly insightful to characterise historical processes in terms of increasing or decreasing rationality. What emerges is an understanding of plural, non-unified, systems of rationality, possessing no necessary coherence among themselves and having specific and analysable conditions of existence. (Dean, 1994: 57)

With this aim in mind, the final section will explore more fully how history can be used to respond to some of the difficulties raised by existing critical, theoretical approaches to advertising.

the uses of history

Genealogy is grey, meticulous and patiently documentary. (Foucault, 1984b: 76)

The fundamental claim of this chapter is that a genealogical approach to the study of advertising can be used to respond both to the epochal abstraction and to the theoretical bias inherent in much of the critical literature on advertising. The use of history in respect of the former may be apparent, but the two weaknesses are related, albeit indirectly. If epochally driven theory acts to overgeneralise and universalise the complex and plural histories of the field, this is partly attributable to the binary, dualistic logic inherent in such theory. This logic itself both facilitates and is facilitated by a methodological approach to the development of advertising, which overwhelmingly relies on the text as the key material source. Thus the emphatic tendency in critical literature is to read changes in the form of advertisements as an evolution to be read alongside the unfolding of broader processes of modernisation. But to tell the history of advertising solely from the text is to tell a story which is unusually dependent at every stage on the type of hermeneutic, interpretative method that, as argued above, can be so problematic. The potential benefits of a more modest description of advertising practice are a liberation from some of the constraints of dualistic theory, and a more informed understanding of the contingent conditions in which various advertising practices *and* forms – for the two are inextricably linked – emerged.

To this end, this section explores the potential of historical, genealogical analysis to address theoretical problems. It suggests that, despite the apparent neatness of fit between the two, history – as the work of Cousins (1988) and Fish (1994) demonstrates – cannot so easily be imported as the magical solution to the theoretical puzzles of the human and social sciences. Nevertheless, the overall argument of the chapter remains that a historically informed investigation of advertising has a number of more moderate advantages, even if these do not include providing the solutions to ongoing debates within critical theory.

The availability of history as a means of responding to broader critical problems in social theory has seemed intuitively obvious, at least since Foucault's genealogical approach to the emergence of specific institutional phenomena achieved widespread dissemination. As Cousins argues, the sheer historical variety – what he terms the 'excessiveness' – in the forms of any given phenomenon, whether sexuality, language or even advertising, may promise an escape from the limitations imposed by the conceptual categories we labour under. '[H]istorical investigation appears to guarantee the truth of this excess and its product, History, can seem like a new horizon which theoretical work must strive to encompass, and by which it will be measured' (Cousins, 1988: 127). History may thus seem able to address what Cousins terms 'chronocentrism' in the same way that anthropology has been deployed to address 'ethnocentrism'.

History and anthropology can productively reveal both the specificity and contingency of practices often chronocentrically or ethnocentrically understood as universal and transcendental[2] and conversely, the 'universalities' in forms of practice constituted as archetypally 'modern' or 'Western'.[3] As Minson (1985) points out, however, the first function of Foucauldian genealogies is to provide *specific histories*, not to serve as empirical illustrations of theoretical arguments, even where such general implications appear clear. For Foucault, genealogy was a historical method based on the patient accumulation of apparently insignificant details. Its distinction from other forms of 'meta-historical' method resides in a rejection of linear narratives of development and 'indefinite teleologies' (Foucault, 1984b: 77). Genealogy is a form of history that attempts to reveal the historical contingency of objects and the low-level conditions of their emergence; as such, it proffers a challenge to teleological accounts that view historical movement as a singular process of transformation in response to 'universal' forces.

This is the form of analysis favoured by Saunders in his historically rather than conceptually grounded account of the emergence of copyright law. For him, the 'critical politics' of the latter 'post-structuralist' deconstructionist approach becomes a logical game 'caught up in a pressure to be emancipatory (or emancipated)', disabling useful historical description by treating all phenomena 'within some version of the exhaustive antinomy of domination and subversion, blame and praise' (Saunders, 1992: 3–4). This sense also informs Dean's account of 'effective history'. Such a project, he argues, involves recognition of the types of conceptual obstacle imposed by certain forms of theory – particularly those structured around dualistic, binary modes of thinking. These obstacles arise in the form of the requirement for an ethical stance for or against any given phenomenon to be taken. For authors like Minson (1985), Saunders (1992), Dean (1994) and Osborne (1998), working in what might be termed a post-Foucauldian governmentality tradition, the desire to be free from the 'political' for-or-against dynamic of grand theory is pronounced. Underlying this desire is the conviction that empirical, historical work is unduly confined by this dynamic, and by the preference for theoretical models which operate at high levels of generality and abstraction. These are precisely the difficulties that, it was argued above, structure the specific critique of advertising. However, the attempt to set up an effective history of advertising is not intended as a direct response to these difficulties. It might better be understood as a sideways move, or even an exit from the debate.

This movement is motivated by two convictions. First, whatever the explanatory force of epochal and dualistic theory, there remains an array of smaller things, untouched by theory, whose histories are worth knowing for themselves. Investing in an account of these smaller things need not involve a simultaneous investment in a naïve view of history as a straightforward reconstruction of the past. The past is not available as an unproblematic reality to be discovered by assiduous, objective historical method. History, as Dean acknowledges, does not bear reference to a single, uncontested past.

Rather, the history of the past is inevitably motivated by the interests of the present.

> ... history is above all a practice, a practice undertaken in a particular present and for reasons linked to that present. For no matter how much historical writing is about dimensions or aspects of the past, and refers to events, irruptions, discourses and social practices that can be given a particular time-space, it is in fact an activity that is irrevocably linked to its current uses. (Dean, 1994: 14)

Secondly, and closely related to this point, history is not called upon here as a direct solution to the theoretical problems raised in the advertising litera- ture, simply because it cannot act in this way. History, as suggested above, may, in offering up the 'excessive' variety of the past, succeed in challenging or revealing the rigidity of contemporary thinking. As Cousins argues, how- ever, this in itself does not enable it to bypass or resolve theoretical prob- lems, as this would necessitate a yet-to-be-discovered, general objective philosophy of history to act as higher court for the human sciences. The philosophical histories that do exist, Saunders maintains, are not objective, grand sciences but impose their own 'necessity and direction upon the con- tingency of things' (Saunders, 1992: 1).

This problem arises, as Cousins (1988) and later Fish (1994) demon- strated, because historical research itself inevitably involves and deploys the same academic and decision-making practices that are to be found in other branches of the human sciences. Any historical investigation must group objects according to identity and difference; phenomena to be studied have to be classified and their differences established. For Cousins, historical writ- ing is thereby 'caught up in the play of representing differences through iden- tities which differ from each other. This point is not a criticism of historical decision-making, but it underlines the fact that there is a level of irreducible theoretical decision within historical writing' (Cousins, 1988: 128). Fish takes this debate forward, arguing that awareness of the 'symbolic violence' of classification offers little prospect of a new, improved, more liberated form of historical practice. The desire of 'new historicist' writers to escape the practice of classification by becoming more open and classifying less simply, cannot be met. It is impossible, Fish argues, to become more gener- ally open; openness will always be in respect to some specific criteria or fea- ture, and in this sense is really a matter of being 'differently closed' (Fish, 1994: 251). In the end you can't not categorise – you can only categorise differently.

None of this need be taken as a negation of the explanatory reach of historical investigation. The critical view that history is textual, comprised of 'constructed' facts rather than referential 'truths' does not render historical investigation futile or redundant because, as Fish points out, the two practices are completely separate and involve different dispositions. To assert the textuality of history is to make a general, philosophical argument, whereas to conduct positive historical investigation involves exploring a different set of specific historical questions. Moreover, the general belief that facts are constructed does not destabilise the certainty or firmness with which particular facts are known or understood. For even the most basic level of human intellectual or communicative activity to occur, there has to be some level of agreement, however temporary, on the validity of specific facts. This does not have to involve a commitment to the notion that facts exist as absolute, universal truths. Rather it involves a more pragmatic recognition that 'facts' or 'truths' have purchase in relation to the particular contexts, disciplines or other areas of human endeavour in which they are produced. Cousins describes how the task of the law is specifically to uncover the 'legal truth', and this is quite distinct from the discovery of a single, unproblematic, uncontested reality. The same conditions apply to the 'truths' uncovered by historical investigation.

> But to reject any general foundation to historical truth or any general truth of History does itself not undermine a notion of historical truth as such. There is no need to enter a form of scepticism about statements about the past. It is enough to recognise that the justification for truth claims about the past are part of the particular practice of historical investigation. Historical facts are not illusions; we may well say that they are true. But their truth is the finding of a particular mode of instantiation, and one which has particular effects on the type of objects which may enter its canons of verification. (Cousins, 1988: 134–5)

Historical arguments, in the end, are empirical not epistemological (Fish, 1994). This is fundamentally why social theory cannot look to history to resolve theoretical dilemmas. The findings of historical inquiry are the results of a definite practice, with specific conditions of existence and specific consequences. These contingent findings, then, cannot have the status of final, epistemological truths which stand above the claims of social theory, precisely because historical investigation involves uncertainty, provisionality, and abstraction in the same way as do other forms of investigation. Recognising the contingency and specificity of historical facts does not invalidate them; rather, it urges caution in treating such facts as an exhaustive and total picture of the past. This is not a picture which history, or any other method of investigation, can provide.

What history can do is provide a picture of the diversities and discontinuities which constitute any field of production. The exposure of such diversities and discontinuties in specific cases can problematise the more general claims of global theory. It is these awkward specificities in the history of advertising that critical theory has tended to ignore. Historical investigation, whatever its limits as a theoretical solution, is well placed to tell the empirical story of the patchwork of events that fuelled the emergence of contemporary advertising. The excessive variety, sideroads and reversals of this history may yet act as a challenge, if not an answer, to the teleological, evolutionary emphasis inherent in most critical accounts of the industry. The aim of conducting a historical description of advertising practice which does not attempt to squeeze itself into the categories of either epochal or dualistic thinking is simply to provide a more grounded explanation of the historical contingency of advertising institutions, practices and forms. It is to this task that attention now turns.

notes

1 See Nixon (2003).
2 See for example Hirst & Wooley (1982), Saunders (1992), Hunter & Saunders (1995) and Dean (1994) on the variations between different cultures and historical periods on different forms of specification of human beings in different cultures and historical periods.
3 See for example Glennie (1995) on continuties in consumption practices between different historical periods, and Appadurai (1986) on the continuities in the status of objects and commodities between different cultures and different periods.

pervasive institutions and constituent practices

introduction Advertising stands out within critical theory as an object over which there is an unusual amount of agreement. Theorists working across a range of traditions regard advertising not only as a unique device in the articulation of production and consumption, but one which is steadily advancing in sophistication and accomplishment. This teleological conception of advertising emerges in a number of guises. Advertisements are considered more persuasive, more adept at fusing economic/commercial and aesthetic/cultural objectives, and definitely harder to avoid. Advertising pervades contemporary society to an unprecedented extent and serves as an exemplary hybrid practice, undertaken by 'new cultural intermediaries' working in a hybrid 'culture industry'. This chapter takes up critical claims of this sort through an exploration of the institutions and practices of advertising in historical context.

The motivation behind this strategy is straightforward. Regardless of the variety and detail of studies of contemporary institutions, assertions about their profound differences from whatever has gone before tend to be based more on theoretical presupposition than on historical description. This bypassing of historical context may be one reason why theorists see a little too much novelty in the advertising of their own ages. But history does not provide answers in any straightforward sense. Making direct comparisons of the role of advertising relative to criteria like pervasiveness or hybridity at different historical moments is no simple matter. Problems arise because historical comparisons cannot really compare like with like.

Differences in the various institutional arrangements, technologies, media, techniques and practices that have, historically, constituted advertising production make simple comparison untenable, because the categories differ so much over time. There is no exact historical equivalent of television, or contemporary equivalent of the nineteenth-century religious newspaper. Nor is there a direct link between the work of a nineteenth-century 'all-rounder' or of a late twentieth-century art director. There might be similarities in the way different institutions and practitioners perform, but that is not quite the same thing. Institutions and occupations involved in the business of advertising in the nineteenth century have specialised, rationalised, professionalised, diversified or disappeared entirely from view. They have not survived unaltered. Historical comparisons must therefore make adjustments, allowances, classifications and categorisations in the criteria they examine. It is, as Fish and Cousins have insisted, impossible to conduct historical investigation without doing so.

Nevertheless, historical description can still provide an important counterbalance to the claims made in critical theory about advertising's increasing pervasiveness and hybridisation. These claims are historical in scope but seldom in evidence – often differences with the past are simply assumed. Where evidence does appear, it is usually in the form of quantitative measures of advertising volumes (Pope, 1983; Leiss et al., 1986) or cultural industry workers (Featherstone, 1991). Such measures of course have their value, but they invariably side-step and reduce detailed contextual differences which are material to any assessment of the pervasiveness or hybridisation of advertising. These features, it is argued, are contingent upon the specific institutions, arrangements and practices that prevailed at given historical moments.

This chapter begins with a discussion of the institutional context of advertising. The term 'institutional context' is used here to refer to the relations between advertising practitioners or agencies, the media, and the businesses that advertise. It is the ideal place to address the extent to which advertising penetrates everyday life, because it directs attention to the points of contact – whether newspapers, magazines, billboards or other locations – between advertising and its audience. The aim is to recreate a sense of how advertising made its presence felt in a variety of different settings, rather than to offer a comprehensive history. The sheer diversity and scope of arrangements and actors involved in the early development of the institutional field bear witness to its integral role in nineteenth-century economic life. This also emerges when attention turns to outdoor environments. Contrary to expectations, and notwithstanding technological limitations, advertising and corporate promotion saturated nineteenth-century outdoor environments of both large urban centres and, more surprisingly, rural locations.

The next part of the chapter reviews the historical practice of advertising. The underlying aim is to reconsider the critical argument that the contemporary era bears witness to a unique juxtaposition of the cultural and the economic. Two main problems are raised with this argument. The first of these is that what would often be construed as intrinsically valuable 'cultural' knowledge was evidently important to historical practitioners. Instances of practitioners deploying specific 'cultural', or what might be described more accurately as 'aesthetic', knowledge of literature, the arts and music can be traced at least as far back as the early nineteenth century. The second problem is with the way culture is defined. If, as was argued in Chapter 3, culture is defined not as a separate and bounded 'sphere' but as constitutive of material practice, then the presence of 'aesthetic' knowledge in historical practice is a relatively minor issue. Much more troublesome is evidence emerging from a discussion of the development of the functional specialisms – account management, media buying and research – that demonstrates some of the specific ways in which culture can be viewed as constituting all aspects of material advertising practice.

pervasive institutions
The diversity of the institutional field

> The early agencies then developed primarily as buyers in bulk of media space that they then divided into smaller pieces and retailed. ... As the agencies developed new skills, such as copywriting and artwork and expertise in the arts of advertising, they also began to sell these as a service to the advertiser. ... Industry gradually adjusted its marketing practices to the novel situation created by consumer culture and by and large it was the agencies who taught them how to do it. (Leiss et al., 1986: 124–5)

This section offers a picture of the early institutional development of the advertising agency that is at odds with a frequently articulated theme in critical explanations. This well-rehearsed theme refers to the 'evolution' of the advertising agent from the newspaper agent, in response to the developing needs of consumption-based societies (Hower, 1939; Turner, 1952; Williams, 1980; Dyer, 1982; Leiss et al., 1986; Fowles, 1996). Yet the early history of the advertising field reveals a range and diversity of arrangements that moved in an uneven, contradictory and haphazard pattern towards the prevailing agency model of the twentieth century. The contemporary advertising agency did emerge as the result of historical circumstances, but circumstances that were far more local and specific to the field than many critical narratives have allowed.

On the basis of evidence derived from London trade directories, the first UK advertising agency has been identified as Tayler and Newton in 1786, followed by Whites in 1800, and then in rapid succession in 1812 by Reynells, Lawson and Barker, and Deacon's (Chipchase, 1977, HATa; Nevett, 1977).[1] These early agencies were clearly very closely linked to the press, but these links went further than the sale of advertising space. Lawson and Barker (later Charles Barker), for instance, was first established when James Lawson was the printer of *The Times* (Derriman, HATa). The firm initially planned to receive advertisements for *The Times* in return for access to their news services, which could then be distributed to the regions in the form of *London Letters* (Derriman, HATa). Between 1812 and 1843 Lawson and Barker acted variously as parliamentary correspondents, gathering the news and distributing it to subscribers, as the City editorial office of *The Times*, as the distributors of other newspapers and as advertising agents who would place advertising in any newspaper requested (Charles Barker Letters Book 1825–1847, MS 20011, CBa). Barker's were not alone in this. Firms like Whites, Deacon's and Newton's in the UK, and Volney Palmer in the US, placed advertising in any requested paper, and carried out a broad range of services, from advice on the suitability of specific media to the form of advertisements, as early as the 1830s and 1840s.

The first agencies were also linked to an array of other sorts of enterprise. The Streets agency, for example, served as stationers and booksellers, (Chipchase, HATa) while Deacon's acted simultaneously as a coffeehouse. Agencies often appear to have developed opportunistically, out of the employment connections of their founders. James White, for instance, is reputed to have taken up business as an agent on the basis of his experience placing advertisements for his old school, Christ's Hospital, where he worked initially as a clerk (Crowsley, c.1952, HATa). This diversity in service provision was not unusual. Newspapers and advertising agents throughout the nineteenth century received advertisements from a range of intermediaries, including newsagents, coffeehouses, hotels, printers, stockbrokers, dentists, even undertakers (Nevett, 1982; SL 04/27, Sells Box, HATa).

The initial development of many advertising agencies seems to have owed more to local commercial connections than to a developed business philosophy responding to broader changes in the economy and consumption patterns. The first agencies do not seem to have been connected to the 'birth' of a consumer society (cf. McKendrick et al., 1982). The most heavily advertised consumer goods at this point were products like patent medicines, blacking, razor strops and maccasar oil, whose advertising tended to be handled by their own manufacturers ('Puffs', 1855). Agencies like Charles Barker and Whites meanwhile placed advertising primarily for institutions like banks, insurance companies, recruiting companies, shipping companies, auction houses and, by the middle of the century, the railway companies (Charles Barker Letters Book 1825–1847 MS 20011, CBa; RF Whites Box, HATa).

The significance of local, commercial links to the development and growth of early advertising agencies continued throughout the nineteenth century. This mixture of connections, rather than a more tightly defined business project, emerges in the initial commercial activities of agencies. Benson's, one of the first agencies to develop a reputation for 'creativity', and a major player through much of the twentieth century,[2] was founded in 1893 by Samuel Benson at the suggestion of his former employer, St John Johnson, the founder of Bovril. Similarly, T.B. Browne, the largest agency at the end of the nineteenth century, was initially set up as a result of Thomas Browne's work placing advertising for his employer Horniman's Tea and their client Cadbury. In the US many of the best known agencies – George Rowell, Pettengill and Co. and Lord & Thomas – were also part-owners of the proprietary medicine firms they advertised (Hower, 1939; Rowsome, 1959; Hopkins, 1990). These foundational connections were extremely varied, and clearly influenced the type of services that agencies offered. One of the first US agencies, Volney Palmer, was linked to the *Mirror* in New Jersey, a paper published by Palmer's father and for which he solicited advertising, a service he also provided for the *Miner's Journal* (Hower, 1939: 13). The connection to the *Miner's Journal* must have been particularly productive, because Palmer also listed amongst his services the sale of wood and coal. Similarly, the founders of two of the most famous US agencies, N.W. Ayer and James Walter Thomson (JWT), started their agencies on the back of experience selling space in religious periodicals. Meanwhile, Samson Clark, a former member of Regent Street Polytechnic, established his agency in 1896 after being granted the agency to manage the advertising for the *Polytechnic Magazine* (Samson Clark Box, HATa).

The importance of these connections in patterning the work of agencies can be surmised from a closer look at Clark's business. In addition to the *Polytechnic Magazine* Clark took on the management of the advertising space in the *Gynaecological Journal*. He saw in this business 'the possible nucleus of an advertising agency', but it clearly took some time before it held its own financially, and for a time he combined this work with selling insurance (Letter 20-5-1896, Letters Book 1896–7, Samson Clark Box, HATa). According to his letters book, Clark wanted to concentrate on the advertising side of the business. To achieve this he had to obtain an account with major newspapers, a task which involved demonstrating credit-worthiness, usually assessed on the basis of premises, size of business, number of clients, and so on. Clarks were clearly having some difficulty with this, as suggested in their correspondence with the *Globe*.

So far from the Polytechnic Magazine being our only client, we may point out that we have already opened accounts with Messrs Maple & Co, Dr Lunn, Ragged School Union, Lyons & Co. in fact some fifty clients altogether, in addition to which we have the sole agency for 3 or 4 small magazines. (Letter 5-1-1897, Letters Book 1896–7, Samson Clark Box, HATa)

Samson Clark's control over the advertising space in these small magazines was the core of his business. This is salient because it illustrates how varied the services offered by different firms around the same period could be. Far from following a linear pattern of evolution, advertising agencies developed in unpredictable patterns in response to particular circumstances and occupational connections. To make this clear it is worth exploring Clark's business practices more closely. In the following letter Clark explains why he would like to take on the exclusive agency for the magazine *Cosmopolis*.

We should be very happy to take up the work for *Cosmopolis* provided ... we should be your sole agents for the paper as such. The reason for this as you shall readily understand is that if more than one agent applies to an advertising firm for advertisements for one magazine it prejudices both the paper and the agents as it lays both under suspicion, the agents that they are pushing for a special commission and the magazine that it is in dire need of extraordinary pushing. (Letter 1-6-1896, Letters Book 1896–9, Samson Clark box, HATa)

According to the letters book Clark received a 10–15% commission for the exclusive management of advertising space, most of which they rebated to the client, retaining 5% for themselves. Now, despite being the subject of intense and enduring debate, the commission system in advertising agencies has persisted in one form or another at least since 1819.[3] The system involved agencies being paid a percentage, usually around 10% to 15%, on the media space they purchased, which they then deducted as their fee before billing their client. The system has been hugely controversial for a variety of reasons, primary amongst these being that if agency profits derive from the volume of media purchased from the publications which grant them the highest level of commission, the structural tendency may not be in the client's best interests.[4] In other words, it might be in the best financial interests of the agency to push the client towards unnecessary volumes of advertising in unsuitable publications. In addition, agencies that retained the full 15% as recompense for the level of service rendered were potentially vulnerable to the rate-cutting of agencies, providing a lesser level of service. This was one of the key controversies of the 1880–1920 period, which Dunbar (1979: 19) describes as 'a period of chaos' in the institutional development of agency practices. Samson Clark was one of the agencies trading on a rate-cutting basis.

> As to the charges. My own experience is that the work taken altogether is worth 5%, but I am almost certain that if I undertook your work on these terms, I should show a much better net result to you than the prices you are now paying. (Letter 7-1-1897, Letters Book 1896–9, Samson Clark Box, HATa)

Samson Clark's business methods then included 'splitting' the publisher's commission with his clients, and 'farming' periodical space. The term 'farming' refers to the practice of taking on the whole advertising space in particular journals and selling it on to clients or other agencies. Both commission splitting and farming were viewed as dubious practices by the 'full-service' agencies[5] of the 1920s and 1930s, but at the end of the nineteenth century their use was widespread by many major agencies, including T.B. Browne, Sells, JWT and George Rowell. Clark's practices were not, then, unusual, but they were increasingly unpopular among agencies like Benson's in the UK and Ayer in the US, who were working to establish the 'full-service' advertising agency model. A 1902 publicity document outlines Benson's terms.

> Mr Benson has no personal interest in any publication; he does not prepare schemes in competition with other agents, nor does he divide his commission with clients, the nature and amount of work put in by himself and his staff requiring the retention of the full ten per cent allowed by the press. (Pigott, 1975)

It is significant that these two different approaches to advertising practice – farming and commission-splitting, and 'full-service' – developed in agencies with very different connections. Benson's agency held the Bovril account, one of the major consumer goods advertised in this period, and by 1902 had a client list including Rowntree, Brown & Polson, Virol, H. Samuel, Ivory Soap and Colman's Starch. Benson's client orientation was undoubtedly shaped by the foundational connections between his business and major advertising clients. In contrast, Samson Clark began in a much smaller way with his control over the advertising space in the *Polytechnic Magazine*. Clark's links to publications clearly figured in his initial attempts to form an agency based on cheap advertising space, rather than client service. The nature of the advertising process was thus circumscribed in these agencies by the character of their links to other institutions.

Of particular interest here is the extent to which these agencies operated along quite different lines. Derrick (1907) estimated that of the 339 firms listed as Advertisement Agents in the 1906 Post Office Directory, only 36 of these qualified as 'full-service' agents. This indicates the coexistence of competing models of how advertising service should be managed. Benson and Samson Clark represent two approaches, but there were many other variants. T.B. Browne, for instance, combined farming space in *People's Friend* and *Answers* with a higher level of advisory service. Other firms, in what was known as the 'country list' racket, retained as little as 1% or 2% commission for space bought wholesale from local publications, and of dubious value to any save local advertisers (Dunbar, 1979). In addition there were agencies like Spottiswoode, W.H. Smith and Caxton that were basically offshoots of printing, publishing or stationery firms, and at least initially offered a fairly limited level of service provision (Field, 1959; Spottiswoode's Box, HATa). There were 'dummy' agencies, like Steele's, set up with a skeleton staff to enable manufacturing firms who produced their own advertising in-house to claim the agency commission from the media (Steele's correspondence, Spottiswoode's Box, HATa). There were also large firms like Lever Bros who conducted their own advertising, and were able to claim the agency commission direct from the media on the basis of the volume of advertising they placed.

This variety of institutional forms and practices is simply bypassed by many writers, who suggest a sort of inevitability in the evolution of the full-service agent. Yet, as Pope's analysis of the economic position faced by US advertising agencies in this period indicates, the underlying forces fuelling the institutional development of advertising along 'full-service agency' lines are far from self-evident (Pope, 1983: 144–50). In many respects, he argues, it would have made more sense for the advertising function to have been internalised by firms.

> ... the very conditions ... leading to internalization and integration of functions – complexity, uncertainty, and opportunism – bedevilled advertisers. Yet between the 1890s and the 1920s, independent agencies became the suppliers of advertising services to virtually all important national advertisers. (1983: 147)

The reason for this, Pope submits, lies in the commission system. In the US the commission system, thanks to an 'alliance of convenience' between agencies and publishers, was relatively settled and widely adopted by the 1890s (1983: 153). The system that resulted from this alliance, and in particular from the efforts of trade organisations like the *American Association of Advertising Agencies,* granted commission only to established, independent agencies, and standardised the rate at 15%. It took a little longer for a comparable system to be established in the UK, but from the turn of the century organisations like the *Incorporated Society of Advertising Agencies* (ISAA) and the *Association of British Advertising Agents* (ABAA), the precursors of the Insititute for Practitioners in Advertising (IPA), tried to set up a similar arrangement, finally resulting in the *Times Agreement* in 1921, which granted 10% commission only to recognised agents (Dunbar, 1979).

Pope's argument is persuasive. The development of the full-service agency in the UK may have lagged behind that of its US counterpart, but it is clear that the *Times Agreement,* and the system of agency recognition administered by the *Newspaper Publishers Association* (NPA), the *Newspaper Society* and the *Institute for Practitioners in Advertising* (IPA) that resulted from it, played a major role in the adoption of full-service as the primary system of advertising production. The degree to which recognition was central to agency viability by the post-World-War-Two period is clear in the strength of feeling expressed in the following correspondence on the subject retained by the advertisement manager of *The Times*, George Pope.

The Newspaper Society have written us that as we did not invest a minimum of £5000 display advertising in newspapers in membership of the Society ... our name will be deleted from the Register of Recognised Advertising Agents ... this is obviously grossly unfair. (Letter from Howat's to NPA, 23-12-52, Agencies Box, HATa)

This high-handed treatment is reminiscent of the policy of the country which Britain decided must be defeated if FREEDOM was to continue here. I feel confident that you will use your influence to get our name restored to the list of Recognised Advertising Agents ... (Letter from Howat's to George Pope, *The Times*, 2-4-53, Agencies Box, HATa)

It was very nice of you to spare your valuable time on Friday to talk about the position of my little business in relation re recognition [but] I shall never be happy associated with a body whose policy is to exploit little men because they are little and whose whole attitude seems to invite corruption and intrigue. ... I am a bona fide agent and I have given my clients and publishers a square deal. *I am morally entitled to any commission but it is withheld.* (Letter from Humphrey-Lloyd to George Pope, *The Times*, 2-5-54, Agencies Box, HATa)

Underlying the writers' concerns in these letters is the awareness that agency recognition was, by then, a prerequisite for functioning as a provider of advertising services. Not only was it difficult for unrecognised agents to compete with agents who received the agency commission from the publishers but, in addition, certain advertising accounts – particularly large accounts and government contracts – were open only to registered agents. The precise criteria by which recognition was granted varied between the first *Times Agreement* and subsequent agreements, but minimally the criteria addressed such things as company capital, ownership structure, the maintenance of offices, agreed levels of advertising volume and, crucially, membership of the IPA (1933 NPA/Newspaper Society agreement, Spottiswoode's Box, HATa). Both the IPA and its predecessor the ABAA explicitly sought to promote the professionalisation of the industry, partly through rationalisation of provision along full-service agency lines. The service agency was one that could offer 'advice and assistance in the selection of advertising media, the preparation of adverts and the conduct of advertising and selling' (IPA, 1956: 26). This model was also favoured under the terms of the *Joint Recognition Agreement*, which stipulated that agencies receiving commission had to be recognised by the NPA, the Newspaper Society, the Periodical Publishers Association and the IPA. There can be little doubt that this formalising of commission in the recognition agreements between the publishers and advertising trade associations worked in favour of the rationalisation of institutions involved in the provision of advertising along full-service agency lines.

The salience of these specific institutional arrangements in shaping the form taken by the advertising industry in the twentieth century is widely underplayed in the evolutionary thrust of critical work on advertising. What this discussion has endeavoured to show is that the development of the advertising industry towards its contemporary form was not an inevitable outcome of the epochal shift towards a 'consumer' society. The conduct of advertising agents was governed far more by the specific arrangements within the field of production, their contacts, client bases and employment histories, and the internal regulative framework of the industry, than by their capacity to divine the forthcoming market opportunities of a burgeoning consumer society. In this sense advertising agents did not act as 'rational economic calculators' able to sense and respond to scarcely formulated market needs; rather, their eyes were focused more immediately on the institutional field in which they operated (Bourdieu, 1993: 141). The nature of this field was also far more elaborate and diverse than many accounts of the development of the industry have suggested. Newspaper agents were only part of an institutional history that also comprised coffee-houses, local newspapers, publishers and printers, stationers and booksellers, as well as other firms, agents and contractors. It was through this array of intermediaries that advertising found its way into the environments of everyday life. The range of institutions involved in the advertising process begins to suggest the extent to which, in its pre-specialised, pre-rationalised form, advertising nevertheless acted as a pervasive medium. But a stronger sense of this can be gained through a consideration of its material impact on outdoor environments.

The historical clutter of advertising

> Advertising strategies such as hyperreal encoding, reflexivity and the use of hyper-signifiers have been motivated by intertwined crises in the political economy of sign value. Advertisers not only confronted disaffected, alienated viewers armed to foil ads with their remote control zappers, they also faced the problem of differentiating their commodity signs from the clutter of formulaic advertising. (Goldman & Papson, 1994: 24)

The place of advertising within the 'crises in the political economy of sign value' has been extensively debated (Baudrillard, 1988a, 1988b, Featherstone, 1991; Jameson, 1984; Wernick, 1991; Goldman & Papson, 1994, 1996; Lash & Urry, 1994). Inherent in these critical assessments is a sense of a vast overproduction of signs and symbols: advertising seems to have gone too far cluttering the environment and assaulting the senses with brand images and commodity signs. Undoubtedly, advertising's precise impact on the sensory environment is historically peerless. At no other time has there been a technological infrastructure with an equivalent capacity to reach into domestic environments with quite such a volatile range of audiovisual stimuli. The question here is whether the specific form of technological mediation utilised by advertising really defines its pervasiveness. Advertising is a remarkably adaptable institution that has, over time, made ingenious use of a diverse and eclectic range of technologies to ensure that its message is seen and heard. Its achievement in this area, to the point of widespread public irritation, is recorded both in commentary and legislation designed to suppress it, and in some of the devices and media deployed. The following are extracts from mid-nineteenth-century critical essays, and are typical of the types of comment which appeared frequently in both mainstream press organs like *The Times* and satirical publications like *Punch*.

> The newspaper press is the greatest lying and puffing machine in the world! Then comes the walls with their barefaced falsehoods, and the shopwindows with their gilded lies. The railway carriages too, are hung with the paper tricks of trade in every variety of form ... publicity is all the go whether we deal in pills, punch or paletots. (Burn, 1855: 113–14)

> These articles are put into our hands by men who sow handbills in the street with the hope of a harvest of green corn, they meet our view in the omnibus and on the railway; on a dead wall, or in lively conversation; for even our drawing rooms are not free from their intrusion. In short we never know when or where we may be puffed upon. ('Puffs', 1855: 12)

These descriptions provide a revealing insight into how ubiquitous and inescapable advertising messages could be. Advertising is on the walls, the streets, on bridges, on public transport, and even gets into remote locations and private, domestic spaces. These accounts may seem exaggerated, but other historical evidence offers a similar account of advertising clutter and saturation on both sides of the Atlantic (Schlesinger, 1853; Smith, 1853; Young, 1961). According to Pyne's 1808 comments 'within six hours, by means of printed bills, the inhabitants of a great city can be advertised of a thousand things necessary to be publically known' (Nevett, 1982: 53). The extent of advertising's presence in outdoor environments also emerges in public opposition to the nuisance of billposting. This opposition was serious enough to produce a series of legislative efforts, beginning with the 1817 Metropolitan Paving Act and the 1839 Metropolitan Police Act, to curb street advertising (Elliot, 1962). The popularity of poster media was partly a response to the stringently regulative environment of press advertising, which was subject to draconian restrictions on display, as well as heavy stamp and advertisement duties, until 1855.[6] Yet even without these restrictions poster advertising had its own attractions as a medium. Just like today's billboard advertising, it had greater reach and permanence than press advertising, which lasts only as long as any given issue. Moreover it could create a much greater visual impact. Even by the early nineteenth century, technical capabilities allowed large poster displays of up to 36-sheet size, which could be printed with large woodcut letters and illustrations (Nevett, 1982). Poster sites at this time were unlicensed, competition for sites and space was fierce, and oversticking and the defacing of private property was common. Public awareness of advertisement sticking can also be gauged by the level of comment it attracted (*Punch's Almanac*, Vol. 11, 1846; Schelsinger, 1853; Smith, 1853). Sampson describes editorial discussion in the 'sporting papers' over whether the mythical status of a self-proclaimed

'Champion Billposter' depended on his ability to paste bills or to 'beat and thrash all rivals' (Sampson, 1874: 26). Billstickers were also immortalised in one of the most popular music-hall songs of the early nineteenth century. Indeed, music-hall performances frequently overlapped with advertising, as performers would routinely 'puff the goods and establishments of particular tradesman' within their acts (*Punch's Almanac*, Vol. 10: 63, 1846).

> I'm Sammy Slap the billsticker and you must all agree, sirs,
> I stick to business like a trump while business sticks to me, sirs,
> There's some folks call me plasterer, but they deserve a banging,
> Cause yer see, genteelly speaking, that my trade is paper hanging,
> With my paste, paste, paste!
> All the world is puffing,
> So I'll paste, paste, paste!
> (Sampson, 1874: 26)

By the end of the nineteenth century, poster sites increasingly came under the jurisdiction of advertisement contractors who had purchased the exclusive right to particular hoardings. This, allied with an active stance on the enforcement of anti-billposting legislation, resulted in a new, more ordered system of billposting, as can be seen in Figure 5.1.

Given the practice, employed from around the 1830s, of using gas lanterns to illuminate posters and premises, and from the 1870s of using displays animated by magic lanterns, the sense is of quite a hectic visual environment, with advertising playing a dominant role. Some of the strategies employed sound eerily familiar, as in Sweet's description of tube advertising.

> Each night in January 1876, a team of men would unroll an enormous curtain and suspend it from the side of a house adjoining the western entrance of Charing Cross; upon this curtain a series of slides would then be projected from a powerful lantern mounted on a kiosk by the station gates. This initiative by the Metropolitan and District Railway company threw up scenes of London's most popular tourist attractions ... accompanied by notices of the nearest tube stop.
> (Sweet, 2001: 43–4)

However crucial, posters were not the only way advertising and promotion made its presence felt in public environments; numerous other mechanisms, some familiar, some bizarre, were also deployed. Schlesinger describes a profligate use of gas to display shop interiors at night in busy thoroughfares.

Figure 5.1

Railway
Station
Advertising
1874
(Source:
extract from
print in
Sampson,
1874)

Figure 5.2
Fashions for
Advertisers
1846
(Source:
Punch's
Almanac,
Vol. 10: 236,
Jan.–Jun.
1846)

A practice has lately sprung up among advertisers of sending out persons 'made up' in such a style as to represent the article it is intended to advertise. We have seen a series of men converted into gigantic hats, and we have observed other contrivances of equal ingenuity. We think, however, the principle might be still further carried out.

> 'Moses and Son,' the great tailors and outfitters … have lighted up the side-fronts of their branch establishment. All round the outer walls of the house, which is filled with coats, vest; and trousers, to the roof, and which exhibits three separate side fronts towards three separate streets, there are many thousands of gas-flames, forming branches, foliage, and arabesques, and sending forth so dazzling a blaze … What do they make this illumination for? … this is our time to attract the idlers. Up, boys, and at them! light the lamps! A heavy expense this, burning all that gas for ever so many hours; but it pays, somehow. Boldness carries the prize, and faint heart never won fair customers. (Schlesinger, 1853: 17)

Placard bearers were also extensively used in the nineteenth century to provide street advertising. Men, women and children in smart, brightly coloured costumes carrying boards announcing drapers, pens, whisky, accommodation, exhibitions and other services and events were a common urban sight in the 1820s. In post-Civil War America, individuals often worked in groups, sometimes sporting letters or phrases that linked up to spell out product names or slogans (Young, 1961). Alternatively, as satirised by *Punch* in Figure 5.2, placard bearers were got up to resemble the object advertised.

These human peripatetic advertisements could also take more bizarre forms. 'Obtrusive demonstrations' were commonplace in London, creating a regiment of foot, with placarded banners; sometimes one of cavalry, with bill-plastered vehicles and bands of music; sometimes it is a phalanx of bottled humanity, crawling about in labelled triangular phials of wood, corked with woful faces; and sometimes it is all these together, and a great deal more besides. (Smith, 1853: 279)

This description refers to the use of mobile 'advertising machines' in a variety of shapes – globes, pyramids and mosques shepherded by 'hindoos' and 'arabs' were especially popular – to create what Hall (1997) terms 'a spectacle of the other' (Schlesinger, 1853; Smith, 1853; Young, 1961). The last state lottery, in 1826, was announced by placard-bearers on horseback and by huge horse drawn vans (see Figure 5.3). The vans appear to have caused mayhem traversing London, to the 'terror of the horses and wonder of the yokels' (Sampson, 1874). *The Times* noted in 1846, 'the bottom of Cheapside is nearly choked in consequence of the snail pace of one of these nuisances – a van – with a large globe on the top, and a man blowing a trumpet sitting beside the driver' (Nevett, 1982: 59).

Numerous similar complaints finally resulted in their abolition under the terms of the London Hackney Carriage Act in 1853. By this time their function had in any case begun to be overtaken by the omnibuses that carried advertising from the 1840s onwards.

Then, as now, much outdoor advertising was adapted to suit busy urban environments. Other forms travelled further afield. Advertising clock cabinets appeared in public houses; flagstones were stencilled; envelopes, notepaper, sails and bathing machines in coastal resorts, railway embankments and even copper coins carried advertising; tradecards, stickers and handbills were posted through doors and distributed on the streets, in shops, on buses, and even dropped by balloons from the air (Schlesinger, 1853; Smith, 1853; Sampson, 1874; Sweet, 2001). According to contemporary commentators like Smith and various *Times* correspondents, the country provided no respite from advertising.

You wander out into the country, but the puffs have gone thither before you, turn in what direction you may; and the green covert, the shady lane, the barks of columned beeches and speckled birches, of gnarled oaks and rugged elms – no longer the mysterious haunts of nymphs and dryads, who have been driven far away by the omnivorous demon of the shop – are all invaded by Puff, and subdued to the office of his ministering spirits. Puff, in short, is the monster megatherium of modern society. (Smith, 1853: 278)

Figure 5.3

An 1826
Advertising
Van
(Source:
Sampson,
1874)

Advertisements are turning England into a sordid and disorderly spectacle from sea to sea ... Fields and hillsides are being covered with unwonted crops of hoardings. The sky is defaced by unheavenly signs. (Richard & Sumner in *The Times,* 22 November 1892, in Sweet, 2001)

These and other responses, like an 1846 cartoon showing Marble Arch converted into an advertising station (*Punch's Almanac,* Vol. 11: 186), or another in 1886 suggesting that the moon would be improved by a touch of advertising, reflect a real sense that nothing is sacred (www.victorianlondon. org). In Young's account of advertising in nineteenth-century America it is the use of odd locations such as rocks, trees and country barns, as well as shops, bars, offices and public transport, which made it seem inescapable. Added to this, the use of a stunning array of merchandise to carry advertising, and the cross-merchandising of tie-ins with well-known books and plays, is well documented (Sweet, 2001). By such means nineteenth-century advertising messages were disseminated within and well beyond the confines of major urban centres.

Corporate promotion and advertising also drew heavily on the design and architecture of premises, and their reproduction as images of the corporation. Corporate culture, at least since the Great Exhibition of 1851, seemed intent on impressing its importance on the outside world through architectural and promotional messages about scale, prestige, permanence and solidity. These messages were designed into the fabric of buildings and endlessly reworked as images on a range of materials from packaging to stationery, promotional leaflets and merchandise. Buildings were situated, selected, designed, adapted and adorned with their capacity to communicate the right sort of messages in mind. The emphasis was generally upon scale and grandeur, though stress was also placed on location, to create positive historical and professional associations.

Scale was clearly a key consideration when one of JWT's clients, Theron Pond, decided in 1875 to adorn the 'huge red brick edifice' of the Pond's Extract factory building with what was then 'the largest advertising clock in the world' (Box 3, Account files, JWTa). JWT itself took a similar approach to corporate promotion, as evidenced in their regular promotional publication *The Thompson Red Book on Advertising*. The 1899 issue describes the company's offices in some detail and features numerous pictures of company buildings and views of New York and Chicago. Words like 'famous', 'commodious', and 'historic' are used, and the emphasis is on the location of the JWT in the heart of the newspaper district alongside the Sun, the Pulitzer and the Tribune Buildings. Drawings and descriptions of the building were almost always featured on promotional material, indicating something of the importance attached to architecture as a way of communicating corporate significance. This is also clear in director Howard Kohl's description of the installation in 1906 of a huge sign.

Mr Thompson had installed the biggest sign in New York city, running around two sides of the building on the fifth floor where his offices were ... reading, or if you will, shouting: Advertising – J Walter Thompson. (Kohl, 1956, Dawkins Papers, JWTa)

This was a common corporate strategy. Mather and Crowther's offices, opened in 1894, were described at the time as having 'no fewer than fifty-two windows, each setting forth a suitable legend in gold, which with the immense sign in gilt wood letters running the full length of the building, forms one of the most striking

Figure 5.4

JWT

headquarters

in 1899

(Source: *The*

Thompson

Red Book on

Advertising,

1899)

of London's business landmarks' (Pigott, 1975: 10). From the 1880s through to the 1920s, Sell's Advertising Agency also used its premises as a promotional medium (see Figure 5.5). 'The finest building in Fleet Street' and 'At the Sign of the Sundial' were phrases designed to draw attention to the historical, literary and press connections of the agency, and they appeared on numerous publicity

SELL'S GIVE PRACTICAL AID TO ADVERTISERS ::

SELL'S

SELL'S EST? 1869 ADVERTISING OFFICES

SELL'S OFFICES—"The Finest Building in Fleet Street."
ENQUIRIES should be addressed to Mr. Sell (Marked Private), SELL'S ADVERTISING OFFICES, 168 & 167 Fleet Street, London, E.C. :: :: :: ::
T. A.: "SELL, LONDON." Tel. No. 5811 HOLBORN (5 lines).

Figure 5.5

Sell's Building, 1908 (Source: The Propelling Power, SL43 Colour Promotional Leaflet, 1908, HATa)

documents and publications throughout this period (Sell's Box, HATa). The attempt to associate the landmark status of the building with the importance of the business was explicit, and the firm used expensive promotional material with colour reproductions of the building as early as 1908 to get this point across.

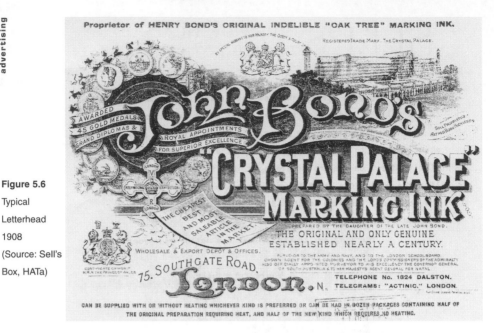

These messages about corporate size, solidity and permanence were not reserved for use on special promotional items; they were also a routine feature of letterheads and smaller items of office stationery. Letters held in the advertising archives from both clients and agencies feature an array of incredibly elaborate and ornate headings (HATa; JWTa). Figure 5.6 is a perfect example of the style. John Bond's letterhead displays 18 medals, a Great Exhibition insignia and two royal crests. The legend boasts the company's 45 gold medals, diplomas and royal appointments and, in the top right-hand corner, is the Crystal Palace itself, which the company adopted as a trademark.

Ornate illustrations like this were featured on the most mundane items of office stationery, including memoranda, bills and receipts. Turton (1982) describes how the department store D.H. Evans took every opportunity to advertise to its customers on even the smallest items of stationery. Paper bags, boxes, receipts and parcel labels all featured intricate illustrations of the store and its departments. While retailers tended to use illustrations to describe their department stores, manufacturing firms often used them to describe the quality of their merchandise. One firm that was particularly attached to this promotional strategy was Colman's of Norwich.

Like many manufacturing companies, Colman's made great play in their advertising of awards, medals and certificates given to them at the large International Exhibitions held in Europe between 1851 and 1900. The financial and commercial success of the 1851 Great Exhibition staged in Crystal Palace, Hyde Park, London convinced business houses that they could derive profit from the attendant publicity. (Colman's publicity document, 1977, HATa)

Colman's strategy was not unusual. Many manufacturing firms got extensive promotional mileage out of medals and awards, which would be featured prominently on packaging and office stationery. Advertising agencies also participated in the exhibition culture. There were several advertising exhibitions in the UK in this period, and medals awarded in these exhibitions were often made a feature in newsletters, annual reports and promotional material (Sell's box, HATa).

Buildings, exhibitions, awards and medals were all used as part of the corporate, promotional culture. Exhibitions and medals were sought after for the prestige and status they could bestow, whilst company buildings that could convey similar associations were selected, designed and adorned with the company name and trademark symbols. Both awards and buildings were endlessly reworked on stationery and promotional materials as icons signifying the scale and permanence of the enterprise. There was nothing particularly new in this. McKendrick (1982: 118–22) outlines Josiah Wedgwood's careful design of his factory, Etruria, and London showrooms, to meet promotional objectives. This promotional use of premises was also adopted by Matthew Boulton and Josiah Spode (Robinson, 1963; McKendrick, 1982). What was specific to the late nineteenth century was the particular concentration on the scale and grandeur of buildings and the exhibition system. Vast factories and grand corporate headquarters topped with large signs in gilt lettering, flags and other emblems were a ubiquitous part of late-nineteenth-century economic life. The symbols and images of this corporate promotional culture were very different from those circulating in contemporary societies, but they undoubtedly had a profound effect on the environment. This style of promotional message appears to have been abandoned gradually, as companies began to tailor more differentiated and specialised corporate identities. As Reginald Browne remarks of T.B. Brownes' premises in the 1920s,

[t]he entrance hall and front ground floor rooms were ... 'Edwardian' mahogany panelling. Excellent of its kind ... but in a period when 'modern' meant black glass and chromium plating, it gave the impression of the solidity and conservatism of a bank instead of the liveliness, creativity and modernity required for the image of an up-to-date advertising agency. (Agencies Box, HATa)

Browne links this 'stodgy and old fashioned' image to the increasing failure of the agency to compete with the 'creative' agencies of the period like Crawfords and J. Walter Thompson. By the 1920s corporate advertising changed and the specific nineteenth-century style – the elaborate letterheadings, gilt lettering and iconic use of grand buildings – was gradually discarded.

During this period, then, promotion was not restricted to the obvious and overt media of press, billboards and street advertising. Factories, buildings, stationery, packaging and other routine forms of corporate paraphernalia were all adapted to promotional purposes. Promotion and advertising are mutable forms, adjusting to whatever media are available. The nineteenth century did not have the audio-visual technologies which defined the field in the twentieth century, but this did not in any way prevent advertising from saturating the environment by other means. Against the critical tide that has emphasised advertising clutter as a predominantly late-twentieth-century phenomenon, evidence suggests that advertising impacted in substantial and sometimes troublesome ways on nineteenth-century environments. In its street presence in poster, pavement, mobile display, on placards and novelty media, and in the published comment and regulative legislation it attracted, the overwhelming sense is of advertising as an intrusive, pervasive device. This evidence makes sense only if the idea of pervasiveness is detached from the contemporary technologies and quantitative measures with which it is generally associated, and reconsidered as contingent upon specific historical conditions. The next section adopts a similar approach, to suggest that the 'hybrid' or 'culturalised' nature of contemporary practice has to be assessed against a more detailed knowledge of the techniques, devices and arrangements that constituted historical practice.

the constituent nature of advertising practice
The aesthetic dimension of historical advertising production

Too many copy writers think in terms of big places like New York and of cultured people of the sort with which they associate and too little about simple people who after all make up the great masses. (Charles Hoyt agency training manual, 1926, HOYTa)

[A]n in-house survey of New York copywriters conducted for J. Walter Thompson in 1936 … found that not one copywriter belonged to a lodge or civic club; only one in five went to church except on rare occasions; half never went to Coney Island or any other popular public resort and the others only once or twice a year; more than half had never lived within the national average income of $1580 per year, and half did not know anyone who ever had. While 5 per cent of American homes had servants, 66 percent of J. Walter Thompson homes did. The profile was affluent, metropolitan, secular and (superficially) sophisticated, and this was typical of the most prominent agencies with the largest accounts. (Lears, 1994: 197)

The possession and use of specific forms of aesthetic knowledge by those who have historically been employed in the construction of advertisements is the main focus of this section. This is intended as a response to the characterisation of contemporary advertising producers as a distinct grouping of 'new cultural intermediaries' embodying a very particular mix of aesthetic and stylistic sensibilities. As *new* cultural intermediaries, advertising creatives are deeply implicated in the epochal shift to an increasingly culturalised economy. Their task is understood to involve reference to their own stocks of 'cultural capital', as they attempt to manage the sign values of the products they advertise. Accounts of advertisers as an occupational group have, in this vein, tended to emphasise their atypicality: their status as a predominantly young, well-resourced, well-educated and fashionable, urban elite (Mort, 1996; Nixon, 1997; Thornton, 1999). The only challenge offered here to this characterisation is to the emphasis on the new – these types of competences have their historical equivalents in the lives of much earlier generations of advertising producers.

The importance of such competences may be surmised in the fragments of evidence that remain about the lives of some of the people who circulated around the earliest advertising agencies. One of these, R.F. White, an agency which survived in one form or another into the 1980s, was founded in 1800 by James White. White was a writer and a key player in London's literary scene. He was a friend of the essayist Charles Lamb, and there are a number of references in Lamb's correspondence to attempts to promote White's book (RFW 2/3, Whites Box, HATa). Lamb himself also had occasional involvement in advertising production. As his sister Mary wrote in 1809, '... White has prevailed upon him to write some more lottery puffs' (RFW 1/6/1, Whites Box, HATa).[7] Another individual who shared links to both advertising and the literary and artistic circles of nineteenth-century London was Thomas Alsager. Alsager was City correspondent of *The Times* from 1817, but in the very different institutional arrangements of the period this involved his being situated at the offices of Lawson and Barker. Founded in 1812, Lawson and Barker devoted their business to advertising in the 1820s. At this stage, however, the firm was carrying out a variety of different operations, including City and parliamentary news gathering and news and newspaper distribution, as well as placing advertisements in *The Times* and a variety of other newspapers (Charles Barker Letters Book 1825–1847 MS 20011, CBa). Alsager's life and connections are relatively well documented in *The History of The Times, Vol 1*.

He was versatile and held a prominent position in two arts: finance and music ... he was a frequent visitor to Leigh Hunt during his imprisonment. Hunt had much affection for him and dedicated a sonnet to his name ... Lamb was fond of him and chronicles his sayings and doings in letters to their friend Wordsworth. ... On December 24th, 1832, Beethoven's Mass in D was given at Alsager's for the first time in England. (ibid.: 415)

This is suggestive of the types of social milieu some early advertising figures existed in. Charles Lamb had connections to both Whites and Barkers, which were among only a handful of agencies in operation at the time. Lamb and White were both also contacts of Josiah Wedgwood and the poet Robert Southey (Stuart, 1889; Crowsley, c.1951, Whites Box, HATa). These connections are unremarkable when viewed in the context of the much less clearly demarcated relations that existed at the time between agencies, manufacturers, newspapers, publishers and literary figures. Newspapers like *The Times* and Daniel Stuart's *Morning Post* had extremely close connections to advertising institutions. *The Times* had particularly close links to Barkers and another firm, Streets. Streets had been involved in the book and stationery trade since the 1760s, but by the early 1800s it was hiring out copies of *The Times* and acting as an advertising broker to it and other newspapers (Chipchase, c.1977, Streets File, HATa). The range of activities that these early agencies were involved in, then, frequently embraced literary work, publishing, the book trade, journalism, and news agency. This network is of some consequence, because it undoubtedly patterned the lives and conduct of early practitioners.

This can be gleaned from letters published in the *Gentlemen's Magazine* between June and August 1838 regarding the relationship between Stuart, the proprietor of the *Morning Post,* and Samuel Coleridge. These letters refer to Coleridge's claim that his 'literary department' – comprising Robert Southey, William Wordsworth and Charles Lamb – had made the fortune of the paper but received scant financial reward for it. Stuart refuted this claim, arguing that Coleridge exaggerated his and his fellow writers' contributions; the fortune of the paper, according to Stuart, owed more to its policy of attracting 'numerous and varied' advertisements (July, 1838). Regardless of whether Coleridge's or Stuart's version of events is preferred, what the lengthy exchange on the matter does make clear is the extent of connections, both socially and occupationally, between writers like Coleridge, newspaper proprietors like Stuart, and advertisers like Wedgwood and Christie the auctioneer.

These connections emerge in other correspondence between Southey, Wordsworth, Coleridge and Stuart. When Coleridge set up his own periodical, the *Friend*, he produced 'rude sketches of short advertisements' for Stuart to check and place in the *Morning Post* (Stuart, 1889: 450). Southey also refers to the importance of advertising in another letter to Stuart: 'One newspaper will do more for a book than two reviews. I thank you for the lift you have given Esprilla, and will write to make Longman follow it up by advertising which they certainly do not do enough' (Southey to Stuart, November 27, 1807, in Stuart, 1889). These links between early advertising practitioners and the book trade were a matter of some concern to critics like Macaulay and the pseudonymous author Master Trimmer, who lamented the links between literary circles, advertising and publishing. Book reviews, according to the latter, were 'nothing now but vehicles for the puffing of trash books' (Trimmer, 1826: 4). For Macaulay the 'shameful' artifice of book advertising had become so widespread by the 1820s that it was endangering the literary character (Macaulay, 1830: 196). Macaulay's irritation was not just with the vulgarity of puffing; at least as important was the convoluted network of interests which linked authors, book publishers and periodical publishers and enabled their 'despicable ingenuity'.

> The publisher is often the publisher of some periodical work. In this periodical the first flourish of trumpets is sounded. The peal is then echoed and re-echoed by all the other periodical works over which the publisher or the author, or the author's coterie has any influence. The newspapers are for a fortnight filled with puffs of all the various kinds which Sheridan recounted, – direct, oblique and collusive. (1830: 197)

These connections between advertising, the press and the book trade led to the construction of an elaborate promotional machine where the notoriety of authors could be carefully constructed and managed in what would appear to be an independent editorial (see Macaulay, 1830). Moreover, this extension of editorial puffing into a system of hype has to be understood as simultaneously the product of the publisher's economic calculations *and* its immersion in a journalistic mode of cultural production.

This was a very different field of production from that typical of contemporary advertising. The organisation of advertising production was much less tightly defined or specialised than it was to become. Whilst precisely who did what is likely to remain obscure, it is highly probable that, in spite of the arrival on the scene of the first advertising agencies, whoever considered themselves to have an interest in producing advertising – retailers, manufacturers, entrepreneurs, publishers, journalists and other writers – continued to do so. Many of the people who had an involvement in advertising production in this period also had recognisable forms of aesthetic knowledge. Although the exact division of labour is unknown, it is clear that the staff of agencies like Barkers and Whites had connections to literary, artistic and musical circles, while figures like Lamb, Southey and Coleridge were involved in some way in the production of advertising. These sorts of aesthetic competencies and connections continued to be important and became the subject of more formal mechanisms for development amongst the specialist creatives employed in the developing 'full-service' advertising agency of the late nineteenth century. Such agencies began to employ artists and copywriters towards the end of the nineteenth century, although their use did not become widespread throughout the industry until the 1910s and

1920s. As their occupational roles became more established, certain features of both the types of practices employed and the types of people who would be recruited began to emerge.

One creative practice that emerged early on was the pooling of ideas and images for copy and layout. Hower (1939) describes how the Ayer agency in the 1890s began to run competitions to generate more ideas for copy, and systematically built up collections of copy. From the 1890s onwards, agencies like Sell's, Benson's, Crawford's, JWT and Ayer kept scrapbooks or guardbooks. These books were often used to record advertisements and campaigns produced internally, and any press coverage of agency work. Most agencies kept advertisements for competing products, as well as their own. JWT's archive contains many samples of competitors' advertising, and the account files bear witness to the material import of this work in situating new campaigns. These early creatives, like those in the contemporary industry, worked with their eyes closely fixed both on the competition and on the broader artistic community.

That creatives would benefit from both an understanding of commercial priorities and a developed aesthetic repertoire was recognised quite early in some agencies. JWT, Ayer, and Calkins and Holden in the US (Lears, 1994; Bogart, 1995), and Crawford's, Sell's and Benson's in the UK, made systematic efforts to engineer and maintain links with external artistic communities. Earnest Elmo Calkins of Calkins and Holden, for example, campaigned to improve the artistic standards of advertising, and hosted a series of exhibitions promoting art in advertising (Bogart, 1995). In JWT, newsletters from the 1920s and 1930s reviewed current art exhibits and would feature articles from commissioned artists and photographers like Edward Steichen (JWTa). The firm also ran its own internal gallery, as did Ayer in the same period. In 1927, art directors Ross Shattuck of JWT and Charles Coiner of Ayer held a joint exhibition of their paintings (Lears, 1994). The emerging sense of the occupational milieu of creatives at least in these agencies is one of immersion in a very particular taste culture, as in the following description of Paul Darrow's experiences in Ayer's art department in the 1920s and 1930s.

From the beginning Ayer was a stimulating place to work. What was the mystique? I am sure to a large part it was the people with whom I worked. Real published authors in the copy department. Granville Toogood from an old Philadelphia family who was as interested in black jazz as I was – and got me on the list of Rittenhouse Square's favourite bootlegger. Dick Powell, Mark Goodrich, Jerry Mangione, John Pullen and Charlie Fisher who had studied cooking while on the Paris trip taught me to make a real French omelette. In the art department Paul Froelich, some of whose rich watercolours for Switzerland Cheese, Fostoria etc. had first lured me to Ayer. Leon Karp who taught me a great deal about painting and the real meaning of the French Impressionists. (Paul Darrow, n.d., AYERa)

These links were also reflected in the policies of agencies like Ayer and JWT towards commissioning established artists to produce advertising. Such policies had precedents in English and French poster advertising in the nineteenth century, which had featured work by artists like Millais, Frith, Beardsley, Cheret and Lautrec. In the 1920s to 1940s Ayer commissioned freelance advertising work from artists like Salvador Dali, Andre Derain, Raoul Duffy, Marie Lawrencin, Pablo Picasso, Pierre Roy and Ignacio (Clarence Jordan memoirs, AYERa).

Some of these advertising commissions were from the realm of what Bourdieu might label 'legitimate culture' (1984) or what Horkheimer and Adorno (1973) might call 'serious, autonomous art'. Their presence in advertising is an indication of the complicated relations that exist between advertising, art worlds and commercial practices. At one level, advertising practitioners sought to legitimate advertising with 'legitimate' art. At another level, art was an intrinsic element in the everyday work of people like Ayer's art director Paul Darrow. At the operational level, artistic and commercial motivations coexisted in the decision to use particular types of artwork. In practice the choice of a specific artist often grew out of working practices and connections, and was closely articulated to the commercial aims of the campaign.

Figure 5.7, for instance, shows an advertising photograph by Edward Steichen for JWT's Jergen's Lotion account. The design was one of the first 'realist' photographs used in an advertising campaign, and Steichen was already a well-known photographer/artist by the time it was commisioned (Steichen, 1962). The decision to use this style of photography was closely linked to a marketing decision to resituate the lotion as a product for care of the hands. This was a decision which was itself rooted in other contextual factors. The market for facial skin care – the 'complexion' as advertisers redefined it around this time – had been successfully captured by companies like Pond's. Jergen's therefore needed to 'redefine' its product and its market. A 1923 market research investigation suggested some consumers preferred to use the lotion on the hands, and this led JWT to identify a new market: 'women of the middle class who do their own housework' (Account Files, Box 1, JWTa). The choice of Edward Steichen was calculated as a way of getting this new message across through using 'sincere, dramatic and beautiful' photographs of familiar tasks (Account Files, Box 1, JWTa). What the Jergen's Lotion campaign illustrates is how closely artistic and commercial aspirations were interweaved. Steichen's willingness to take on the commission was a function of the level of reimbursement and dissemination it afforded. JWT's decision to use Steichen reflected the opinion that the dramatic impact of his photography would be an effective commercial tool to reposition the product.

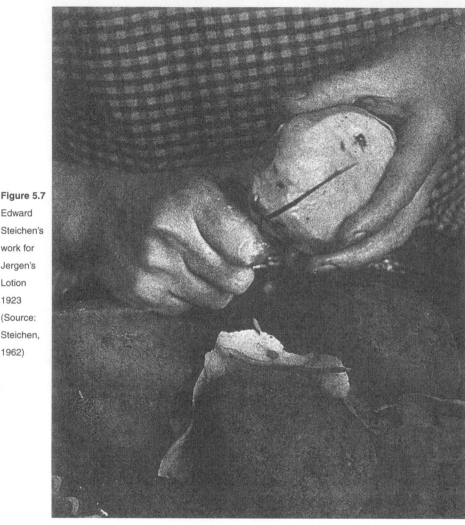

Figure 5.7
Edward
Steichen's
work for
Jergen's
Lotion
1923
(Source:
Steichen,
1962)

If advertising art was closely linked to external art-worlds, parallel links were also in play between advertising copy and external literary culture. The stereotype of the copywriter with unrequited literary ambitions arose for good reason. The files of agencies are full of staff who went on to publish novels, poetry and biography.[8] Dorothy Sayers worked for the agency Benson's in the 1920s in a copy department known at the time as the 'literary room' (Pigott, 1975; Benson's Centenary document, Agencies Box, HATa, a term also favoured by US agencies like Charles Austin Bates and Ayer. The privileged role of literary influences in Ayer also emerges in Weir's recollection of the management of copywriting.

Fry never interfered with Copy in any way. You had a free hand and he saw to it that people were recruited for the dept. who were not just copywriters who had done well in another agency but people who had written books, plays. He got genuine writers ... poets ... Jim Daley, Granny Toogood ... many others. (Walter Weir: Ayer copywriter 1928–34, AYERa)

As agencies began to switch from using freelance writers to in-house copywriters, they made frequent references to the status of copywriting as a specialist type of writing. Numerous treatises were published on how to write advertising and 'star' copywriters like JWT's James Webb Young and Helen Lansdowne Resor, Benson's Oswald Greene and Dorothy Sayers, and Ayers' Granville Toogood began to emerge. In an article on the challenge of copywriting JWT used Aldous Huxley's description of advertisements as 'one of the most interesting and difficult of modern literary forms' (JWT Junior Newsletter, February 1936). This specialism was in large part considered to arise from the need to combine literary skills with commercial objectives. Copywriters had to consider 'the amount of space needed to tell the story, the positions of copy, the kind of headline, the prominence of logotype, the appeal the copy should carry for breaking down resistance or building up active demand' (Stanley Resor, JWT Junior Newsletter, February 1936).

The creative work of the first specialist copywriters and art directors might be defined as *constituent* practices, in that they seem, necessarily, to combine cultural and economic knowledge. The significance of this constituent mix is also illustrated in the relationship between agencies and women copywriters around the same period. As agencies became formalised, a range of practical principles began to emerge. One of these was that advertising should cultivate the 'feminine point of view'. This must have posed a bit of a challenge, as by the end of the nineteenth century women appear to have had limited representation in advertising production.[9] Ernest Norris, a former employee of the agency Sells, describes a system of organisation which circumvented this difficulty by having senior clerks – a position analogous to that of account executive – specialise in the type of account to which they were best suited.

Skilbeck loved opera ... was a knowledgeable collector of old china and works of art. ... He was a bachelor and lived with a friend ... The friend had a housekeeper, but Skilbeck seemed to do the cooking and quite frequently prepared meals such as peeling apples etc. in the office. ... Skilbeck dealt with the more feminine accounts, such as the London Corset Co., the London Glove Co. and one or two stores. (Norris, 1967, Sell's Box, HATa)

It is clear that Skilbeck's cultural and lifestyle choices are thought to equip him to handle the feminine viewpoint. Around the same period other agencies began to take the more radical step of employing women to represent women. One of the foremost of these was J. Walter Thomson (JWT), which soon developed a reputation as a company 'where a bright young lady could go far' (Hodgins, 1947: 205). This reputation may be partly related to the prominence in the firm of its best known woman copywriter, Helen Lansdowne Resor, who became, alongside Charles Raymond and Stanley Resor, part-owner of JWT in 1916. Her role in the firm after her marriage in 1917 is a little obscure; she did not officially occupy an executive position, yet she was clearly involved in its management.

> ... throughout her JWT career she always remained subservient in name to Mr Resor, although her contribution was undeniable. That she never took credit ... Mrs Resor would always quote Mr Resor. Most staff members believed that what she said was usually her own idea but she always gave him credit. (Resor's Folder, Bernstein Files, Box 4, JWTa)

The peculiarity of Helen Resor's position as a respected advertising professional and major stock-holder with no formal executive position, but an operational interest in daily management, is undoubtedly a function of her status as a woman and the wife of the boss. Paradoxically, Helen Resor is credited as being responsible for JWT's claim to gender equality in its employment policy, whilst the role she herself played in the agency was systematically underplayed in public.[10] There are numerous reasons for this public disavowal, from JWT's stance against employing relatives to social attitudes to working wives, but of particular interest is the way that JWT defined the role of women in the agency. A hint of this can be gleaned from a 1929 internal training speech in which Stanley Resor explains that the 'desire to emulate is stronger in women than in men. Lombrosco, the celebrated psychologist, explains it in terms of woman's ability to excite her imagination with external objects. It enables her to become princess or movie queen by using the cold cream or toilet soap they recommend' (Resor's Folder, Bernstein Files, Box 4, JWTa).

The employment of women at JWT in this period was specifically calculated to enable their advertising to 'speak' to the mysterious psychology of female consumers. That it was their 'unerring woman knowledge' or 'woman experience' which was judged to be of significance emerges in the organisation of the agency and in the way in which female expertise was defined.[11] A 1919 Organisation Chart shows both the Planning and Editorial

Production departments split into women's and men's sections (Standardisation Committee, JWTa). These divisions represented both the nature of the product and the gender of staff, as female copywriters worked in a separate department focusing on 'feminine' products. Within this system women's expertise was defined strictly in relation to their knowledge of other women. As an account history of a disagreement between a female copywriter who recommended a strategy based around glamour and a male copywriter who favoured price proudly reported, 'the woman won, as they usually do in our shop on questions about products women use exclusively' (Cheseborough Ponds Folder, Account Files, Box 3, JWTa). Similarly Helen Resor is reported as having told a representative of Levers,

Mr Countway, you can not be content to sell Lux for woollens. The women of America are going to put more and more money into fine fabrics: silks, satins, lace. That is the growing field and the field you should concentrate on. (Resor file, Box 3, Dawkins Papers, Officers and Staff series, JWTa)

Here again, Helen Resor's contribution is defined in relation to her superior understanding of women and their foibles. Yet women like Helen Resor and her co-worker Ruth Waldo, who went on to become the first female Vice-President (as general head of feminine copy), and Dorothy Dignam of N.W. Ayer, can be considered subordinate only in relation to their male colleagues. These 'elegantly frocked, superlatively salaried executive[s]' (Abbott, 1920: 43) were nevertheless amongst the top 5% of earners, and occupied an elite position in their industry. JWT's women copywriters of this era were renowned for their couture, particularly 'their stylish hats' (Resor file, Box 3, Dawkins Papers, Officers and Staff series, JWTa; Butler, 1985: 11). When Dorothy Dignam went on a research visit to 'keep house' in Europe it was reported not only in the trade press but also in the *Chicago Tribune* (7/8/28). Professional women in advertising in the inter-war period were a privileged group, who appear to have been distinguished by their adoption of specific dress codes and a social status akin to that of 'society' figures. The 'taste culture' and 'unerring woman knowledge' they represented played a major role in defining their commercial value to agencies.

Entrepreneurs, writers, agents, journalists, publishers, the first specialised creatives and women copywriters all brought particular sorts of aesthetic knowledge and competence to the production of advertisements. In early full-service agencies these types of knowledge were explicitly sought and nurtured as an effective way of achieving commercial goals. These groups could reasonably be categorised as cultural intermediaries deploying 'cultural capital', but the long-standing use of 'culture' to meet economic goals is only one aspect of the problem, with arguments about increasing culturalisation or hybridisation. The next part of the chapter describes how the functional specialisms – account management, media buying and research – can be understood as constituent practices in which the economic and the cultural necessarily coincide.

The functional specialisms as constituent practices As argued in Chapter 3, this book is informed by the view that 'culture' and 'economy' should be understood not as domains or spheres, but as dimensions of material practices. In line with this conception advertising is defined as a constituent activity, where the cultural and the economic are performed through practices that involve human beings, meanings and values, but also technical devices, techniques and technologies. The aim is thus to uncover some of the ways in which both these dimensions of practice were enacted through specific, technical and organisational arrangements in the developing field of advertising, as even the most mundane of activities comprise devices in the 'performance' of 'culture' and 'economy'.

The main functional specialisms, in addition to creative work in contemporary advertising, are account management, media planning and research. Account management involves managing the link to the client; the media department plans, places and buys space and time in the various media deployed in a campaign; the research department provides research information on markets, products, and consumers. These specialisms represent the general approach to the structural organisation of work that persisted in many agencies by the 1930s, and were a function of industry-wide moves to formalise and professionalise the conduct of advertising.[12] The first difficulty in tracking the development of the functional specialisms concerns the dissimilarity of the formal organisational structure adopted by agencies at particular moments in their history. Account executives, for instance, were not always account executives, and this change is not simply one of designation. In Norris's memoir of his working life at the agency Sell's, beginning in 1911, the four key senior personnel were described as Senior Clerks (Norris, Sell's Box, HATa). Their positions were, in some respects, similar to contemporary account executives, but there were also substantial differences, as these clerks had a much broader role than client management. As Reginald Browne, the grandson of the founder of T.B. Browne, the UK's largest agency in 1900, remembers it:

> There was no Creative Department ... 'Copy' and the form of the advertisement should be made entirely the concern of the man in the agency who knew the Product and the Client best – namely the Contact Man as he was then called. In addition to his other responsibilities, the Contact Man had therefore to be 'Creative'. He had to be capable of determining the selling points of the product, conceiving the best method of presenting them in an attractive manner, and of himself finding headlines, writing the copy, and in most cases giving the Art Studio a rough idea of the layout. (Browne, c.1975: 4–5)

The involvement of contact men in the production of copy was likely to have been pragmatic. Between 1870 and 1920 agencies had very different policies regarding their primary functions, and although some agencies were involved in the production of advertisements at least as early as 1870, it took many other agencies much longer to undertake production formally as one of their services. As described in Charles Raymond's memoir of agency life in this period,

> Mr Daniel M Lord of Lord and Thomas, told me years afterwards, that when an advertiser first asked him if he would not write and fix up an advertisement for him, he was aghast, and rather resented the idea he should be asked to do the advertiser's work for him. (Charles E. Raymond, 1923: 9–10, Officers and Staff series, Box 1, JWTa)

The involvement of clerks, managers and contact men in the preparation of copy and layouts was a particular phase in the development of 'full-service' agencies at a time when copy production was not widely regarded as a specialist occupation. It was a task that a variety of people – advertisers, newspaper journalists, freelance writers and agency staff – dabbled in. This appears to have been the case in a number of agencies with surviving records of the period. Ayer's historian, Ralph Hower, describes the appointment of its first copywriter around 1891, yet the agency had been preparing copy for clients since 1880 (Hower, 1939: 94, 317). Similarly James Walter Thompson himself is credited with involvement in the preparation of famous advertising campaigns for Eastman Kodak, the Prudential and Cream of Wheat in the 1890s. In spite of this he felt the core business of advertising was space-buying, and he resented the increasing emphasis on planning, research and copy preparation in the early part of the twentieth century. It is unsurprising then that during his era the copy department in the New York office, at its height, consisted of only one writer and two artists (1928,

C.E. Raymond file, Officers and Staff series Box 1, JWTa). 'All-rounders' were the key to production in this period.

> When he joined JWT, Mr Kohl relates, the degree of specialisation was undreamed of. Key men in the organisation were 15–18 advertising allrounders. Known as solicitors, these men brought in the accounts, serviced them, wrote the copy, organised the artwork – even supervised production. (Howard Kohl, Dawkins Papers, Officers and Staff series, Box 2 JWTa)

The work of these all-rounders cannot be easily classified as solely 'cultural' or 'economic', but in practice blended together meanings, values and calculation. This emerges more explicitly in a close exploration of the everyday business practices of Henry Sell of the London-based agency Sell's. Sell's main concern in the bulk of his surviving correspondence appears to have been liasing with clients and finding new business. This aspect of agency business is deeply immersed in what Moeran (1996: 48–9) describes as 'human chemistry'. The significance of this commerce in human relations in winning and maintaining business emerges quite clearly in Sell's correspondence. In one letter John Maddocks, a contact who had been asked by Sell to help him win business from Bovril, responds:

> I dare not say any more to Bovril people than I did or they will think I am getting a commission for doing so – If you get the Advertising it will be on account of what I said and advised Mr X (*indecipherable*). We had a long talk in which he made certain complaints about you and other agents and then came my personal experience of you &c. &c. – which aided in his having a different opinion of you. You will therefore see it would do more harm than good my writing him. (SL 04/83: 1890, Sell's Box, HATa)

It is clear from this that Maddocks is acting informally to try and secure the clients' good opinion of Sell, and that this involves a delicate balance. If Maddocks overplays his recommendation of Sell, this will render the 'economic' basis to the transaction apparent, and devalue the 'cultural' calculation of its worth.

These intricate entanglements between the 'cultural' and the 'economic' in the management of client relations also emerge in a memo from Jim Nance of General Motors to Howard Henderson of JWT regarding an unsuccessful presentation.

... your fellows just didn't have anyone that could make a speech. Do you know what I mean? In other words, you didn't have anyone who dished it out with any conviction ... there's something to the human emotions too – dishing it out to them [executives] is no different to dishing it out to salesmen ... I wouldn't want them [JWT management] to feel that the General Motors Corporation decided on an advertising agency too much on the way they presented their story but that's part of the agency business. (1935, Howard Henderson file, Bernstein Company History Files, Biographical File Series, Box 4, JWTa)

The memo provides a remarkable insight into some of the technical arrangements used in presentations, and into how decisions about the allocation of accounts were made. Although Nance is keen to avoid giving the impression that the decision was made on the strength of the style of the presentation, it is clear that JWT's presentation did not meet General Motors' expectations. Nance's memo goes on to explain that General Motors felt that JWT's market analysis was weak, that the JWT team 'didn't come in with any charts, their material was poorly gotten up'. This was a significant failing, Nance explains, because 'our organisation are just accustomed to talking that way'.

The salient point here is the extent to which this 'economic' judgement was a function of the tools JWT deployed to represent their analysis. Marketing charts are tools that shape or 'perform' the economic – they do not simply measure an economic 'reality' (Cochoy, 1998; Miller, 1998; Law, 2002). Marketing tools, as part of the discipline of marketing, define the practices and objects that constitute markets. This does not reduce to an argument that the market is socially constructed, but instead marks the ways in which specific marketing practices incorporate both economic 'science' and more cultural forms of managerial knowledge (Cochoy, 1998). JWT's failure to win the account is thus neither a cultural nor an economic failure, but the result of differences between it and General Motors in both these dimensions of practice.

These illustrations of the constitutive interconnections between the economic and the cultural in the technical and organisational infrastructure of advertising are also evident in the development of media planning. Media planning is a function that was carried out even in the earliest agencies. Agents like Barkers and Newtons, in the early nineteenth century, accepted advertising for any newspaper and provided a vital link to the volatile and rapidly changing newspaper industry by publishing lists of provincial newspapers (Letters Book 1825–1847 MS 20011, CBa). By 1833 Barkers were describing themselves as agents of *advertisers* like the London and

Westminster Bank, and offering to keep books of advertisements placed with their prices and locations, and to check on all insertions (26/12/1833 Letter to London Westminster Bank, Charles Barker Letters Book 1825–1847 MS 20011, CBa).

Newspaper directories published by agencies throughout the nineteenth and early twentieth centuries offer a useful insight into the development of media planning. By the 1840s press directories were published by agents like Lewis and Lowe, whose list dates from 1844, and Charles Mitchell, who published his first *Newspaper Press Directory* in 1846 (Linton, 1979: 29). In the 1860s the agency Streets began publishing the *Indian and Colonial Mercantile Directory*, and in 1885 Sell's published the first edition of its *Dictionary of the World's Press*. These and similar publications were updated regularly, often annually, and were an integral technical device in the practice of media planning. An indication of the types of use to which they were put can be gleaned from the style of entries. *The Times*, for instance, is described in Mitchell's first edition as:

> Daily, Price 5d. Established January 1 1788. ADVOCACY. High Church – Mercantile – Anti-New Poor Law – Anti-Corn Law. This the leading journal of Europe, has for the field of its circulation, emphatically, the WORLD, and its influence is coextensive with civilisation ... *twenty thousand* impressions ... (Mitchell, 1846, in Linton, 1979)

This engagement with the politics, religion, class and geography of newspapers and their readerships was a common feature of directories. Directories were devices that aided in the performance of media planning by making a form of order out of the complex and chaotic range of publications that carried advertising. Particular sorts of information about the press were ordered in particular ways, creating some possibilities and excluding others. This helped constitute and reinforce the cultural meanings attached to newspapers like *The Times*, and in doing so helped define the economic value and price of advertising space in an irregular and haphazard market. Space rates set by newspapers in the UK and the US were negotiable and subject to large, capricious discounts (Nevett, 1977; Linton, 1979; Streets, n.d.). Often, 'the agent's column would be located alongside local advertising paying five and even ten times as much' (Raymond, 1923: 18; JWTa). This anomalous system persisted because the absence of reliable circulation data made it extremely difficult for a uniform method of assessing the value of the space to be developed.[13] These circumstances were ideal for the development of a media specialism based on knowledge enshrined in the various, competing agency press directories to thrive, and by the end of the century media expertise was widely regarded as the core of advertising business, as in the following 1890s definition.[14]

The businessman has an article he believes the multitude want, the question is how shall we apprise them of it in the smallest possible time, and in the least expensive manner? ... He knows the newspaper is the efficient means but which and when and how and where and last but not least what will it cost? are correlative questions which require knowledge and experience, and are not easily or quickly answered. This is the legitimate province of the advertising agent, and can be acquired only by special training and years of patience, industry, experience and skill. (Dodds in Raymond, 1923: 10–11)

This view of space-buying is at odds with the view of it described above as a basic service in an advertising system based around information rather than persuasion. Space-buying, viewed in this light, is a material practice that requires the exercise of both cultural judgement and economic calculation. Culture is not the context in which economic reality is embedded; rather, categories such as price are simultaneously economically and culturally constituted. This emerges in specific instances of media-buying practice. Early agencies placed advertising not simply according to the status of the publication, but also according to beliefs about the nature and habits of their readership and the degree of fit between them and the advertised product. Browne describes how the selection of media in this period was based entirely on the familiarity agency space-buyers acquired through continual study of editorial content and advertisements in different newspapers (Browne, c.1975). In 1897, for example, the agency Samson Clark advised Ogden's Tobacco to advertise a promotional competition in the half-penny papers 'because we believe they are read more by the class of people who would be likely to take advantage of the advertisement' (Letter 25/11/1897, Samson Clark Box, HATa).

The selection of media, moreover, was only one aspect of agency service. Also important were decisions about how advertising should be placed within the media. In an estimate of advertising space costs sent out by Sells in 1888, for instance, papers are selected on the basis of their willingness to accept 'large display types' or 'blocks' and to position advertisements next to or surrounded by 'reading matter' (SL40, Sell's Box, HATa). This reflects the judgements practitioners made about how to secure maximum impact. The preference for blocks and display reflects their eye-catching capacity, but the desire to secure particular positions indicates a more subtle system of judgements about the value readers attached to different positions. This is evident in the following complaint sent by Samson Clark to *Ladies Field* in 1898.

> We received copy of *Ladies Field* yesterday and were not a little disgusted to find that three of the orders which we placed with you have been placed contrary to instructions. Messrs Debenham and Freebody's quarter page was to face matter on the right hand page but it is on the left hand page in no position at all. Messrs Hampton and Sons half page was ordered for a right hand position, and if possible to face the last page of matter, it is on the left hand page and is under a very heavy advertisement of Fry's. Messr's Langley small advertisement was ordered specifically to go over Court and Society News – you have put it with the other small advertisements in no position at all! What are we to say to our clients? (Letter 18/3/1898, Samson Clark Box, HATa)

Media planning involves intricate decisions about reading practices and patterns of mental association between the nature of 'matter', competing advertisements and the advertisement placed. These decisions involve judgements which are neither cultural nor economic in nature, but integrally both. Thus the economic value of space cannot be calculated outside its cultural value.

This inextricability of cultural and economic elements is repeated again in instances of research practice. Research is the newest of the functional specialisms. It is of particular interest as the immediate, historical predecessor of account planning, a methodological variant formulated in the 1960s to improve the articulation of research information with campaign production. By incorporating the consumer's voice into creative strategy, planning has been accorded a central role in informing the production of a new generation of emotionally articulate advertisements (Nixon, 1996). For Lash and Urry, account planning is an exemplary hybrid practice 'emblematic of the implosion of the economic, advertising as a business service, into the cultural, advertising as a "communications" or a "culture" industry' (Lash & Urry, 1994: 141). Yet it is a function that can be traced in different forms at much earlier moments in the history of advertising practice.

The aims and methods employed in the earliest traceable research efforts varied enormously, but it is clear that by the mid nineteenth century at least some clients and agencies had begun to recognise the value of using research to inform advertising. N.W. Ayer, for instance, undertook a market survey for a threshing machine manufacturer in 1879 (Hower, 1939) while in 1891 JWT surveyed the face cream market for Ponds and in 1894 produced a campaign for Pabst Brewing Company based around a historical study of brewing (Account Files, JWTa). In 1903 JWT began testing consumer reactions to various advertising layouts by comparing the coupon responses to different advertisements placed for the same product (Raymond, 1923; JWTa). This method of tracking the responses to advertisements placed in different publications through coded coupons was attempted as far back as the 1850s (Nevett, 1982: 52). The extent to which it was employed in this period is difficult to gauge, but by the early twentieth century it had become a cornerstone of the technique of 'scientific advertising' advanced by practitioners like Claud Hopkins in his work at the agency Lord & Thomas (Hopkins, 1990). Scientific advertising, according to Hopkins, was 'based on fixed principles and according to fundamental laws. I learned those laws through thirty-six years of traced advertising. Through conducting campaigns on some hundreds of different lines. Through comparing, on some lines through keyed returns, thousands of pieces of copy' (1990: 179). The approach emphatically stresses the importance of measuring advertising effectiveness and quantifying results. Hopkins believed that advertisements should be simple, sincere and provident: 'brilliant writing', persuasiveness and humour should be avoided at all costs (1990: 181–3).

Hopkins's views were extremely influential, but they were far from the only principles guiding advertising production in this period. Other far less 'scientific' approaches to mapping the consumer were also adopted. One such practice was the distribution of products to staff members. At T.B. Browne's, for example, whenever more information about the qualities and uses of a product was sought it was distributed amongst appropriate staff members to provide a 'not scientific but practical' sample (Browne, c.1975: 4). This practice continued long after more extensive research methods became available. In 1923 JWT used this approach in one of the first stages of a two-year programme to launch *Teba*, a new Ponds shampoo.

Samples of the first three experimental formulas for Pond's Liquid Castile Shampoo were distributed amongst members of our office, along with questionnaires on which they were asked to give their reactions to their sample ... Criticisms in these questionnaires were studied carefully and new formulas were worked out and new experiments made. (Cheseborough-Ponds file, 1923–6, Account Files, Box 3, JWTa)

This type of information gathering might be supposed to have been superseded by the development of more formal, economistic research instruments. Ethnographic studies of contemporary practitioners, however, continue to stress the centrality of practitioners' own idiosyncratic consumption habits and cultural references to the production process (Mort, 1996: 99–102; Nixon, 1997: 215; Thornton, 1999).

Using agency staff as 'sovereign' consumers was not the only method agencies used to gather qualitative information about products. By the First World War agencies like JWT and Ayer also sent staff out to work in department stores, replacing regular sales staff when they went on leave. There are numerous references to feedback derived in this way in JWT's account files for clients like Cheseborough-Ponds and the Andrew Jergen's Company. These researchers were most often women, 'our girls', who would work as demonstrators to gather research information on products. Women, again, were selected for this work specifically because of their perceived familiarity with the intimate knowledge, habits and desires of other women. An insight into the form this research information could take can be gleaned from the following.

> Miss Ashland acted as a Jergen's demonstrator and had some very interesting experiences. For instance we asked what really sold Violet Soap, and she said, 'Well, the coloured people come in, just one whiff of it and they cannot resist. (Cheseborough-Ponds file, 1923–6, Account Files, Box 3, JWTa)

Despite their sometimes idiosyncratic nature, staff reactions to products and experiences of consumers were regarded, institutionally, as of some consequence, and they fed back into the production process in a variety of ways. At the start of the twentieth century, the likelihood was that any research activity was undertaken by 'advertising all-rounders' who would also be involved in copy and layout production. By end of the First World War, larger agencies had begun to employ specialist researchers who would participate in 'account groups' with account executives and creative staff. Even after research as a functional specialism had become more established in the late 1920s, however, agencies still stressed the value of sending copywriters out to 'regain their touch' by selling the product or observing its use (Marchand, 1985: 74). It was such 'hands-on' consumer mapping which sent Ayer's copywriter Dorothy Dignam to Europe to study housekeeping and to work in department stores.

The significance of such informal research knowledge in advertising practice is a little hard to judge. Agencies, unsurprisingly, have tended to emphasise their use of more formal research surveys, and therefore date the beginning of research activity to the 1920s, when the techniques used began to resemble more closely those which became standard practice in the industry after 1945. Certainly by this time JWT, one of the main proponents of research, was using surveys and market investigation on an extensive and systematic basis. Between November 1922 and September 1923 JWT conducted 11 separate dealer and consumer investigations in the New York area for Woodbury's soap alone (Andrew Jergen's Company, Roll 45, Market Research microfilms, JWTa) while in the UK the company reputedly conducted 79,000 interviews for Ponds between 1923 and 1930 (Treasure, 1976). JWT's 1959 account history omits mention of staff trials and selling experience for Ponds, and describes how,

From 1912–38, Pond's research in human behaviour was largely one-time quantitative consumer surveys. The earliest of these now on record was June 1927. It represented for the time a very advanced study of consumer purchasing behaviour, and included these research techniques which in recent years have been more fully developed.

1. **What people do**: how they use cosmetics
2. **Why people do what they do**: reason for using or not using cosmetic brands
3. **People's awareness of and reaction to advertising**

(Cheseborough-Ponds file, 1959, Account Files, Box 3, JWTa)

Even a cursory glance at these 'very advanced' studies reveals the extent to which they were immersed in the meanings and values of the economically and culturally homogenous occupational group which produced them. Segmentation on the basis of race, for instance, was routinely used. Research for the Cheek-Neal Company, makers of Maxwell House, split areas up according to 'the total number of families, number of native white families, number of negroes and foreign born' (Account Files, Box 3, JWTa). This information enabled surveys for companies like Jergen's to focus only on white families (Account Files, Box 1, JWTa). Consumer profiling on the basis of class was equally skewed. Product research for Arbuckle Brothers' coffee lines in 1912–13, for example, remarked that 'it is impossible to make each one of a line of products called by the same name, as strong as you can make a product which has a name of its own … Consumers of the lower class can not be made to remember more than one name' (Account Files, Box 2, JWTa). Similarly, a media plan for Cutex manicure products in 1926 was informed by the view that lower-class interest in hand care was 'wholly negligible', although this was not a matter that the research investigation had actually addressed (Account Files, Box 3, JWTa). The imprint of the mainly female research interviewers' values on their findings is also strongly suggested in the interview summaries.

Interview no. 22 Young Irish girl with black hair and blue eyes – slovenly and very friendly … The place has a rather frousy look … She tried Woodbury's and stopped … From the tone of her replies it is easy to deduce that price is a factor.

Interview no. 52 Sickly, slovenly young woman with whisps of hair flying around her face and most of her front teeth missing. Stupid, preoccupied and overwrought. The house so new it smells of fresh timber and paint but it is already dirty and uninhabitable. This woman uses Ivory and Palmolive … (Andrew Jergen's Company, Roll 45, Market Research microfilms, JWTa)

These research instruments and findings fit well with Cochoy's argument that the discipline of marketing *disciplines* markets through 'inventing special human and conceptual frames for market knowledge and practice' (Cochoy, 1998: 194). This again is an illustration of the inadequacy of the increasing hybridisation thesis as a description of the historical development of advertising practice. It is not simply that this early advertising research could be construed as cultural in the sense invoked by Lash and Urry (1994), Mort (1996) and Nixon (1997) – that its specific aim was to bring the 'cultural' voice of consumers into the advertising process. This restricts culture to the representational domain. The more substantial difficulty is that research practice, as with media planning, account management and all other forms of material practice, is unthinkable outside its cultural constitution.

In a range of different ways, the non-creative functional specialisms – account management, media planning and research – illustrate the irreducibility of working practices to the economic or the cultural. In each specialism, aspects of everyday work are contingent upon the exercise of judgements which are simultaneously economic and cultural. The contention is thus that the economic and the cultural should be understood as elements that *together* constitute practice. This questions the value of thinking in terms of increasing hybridity or 'culturalisation' as advertising's past simply does not, on close examination, conform to its idealisation as an era where culture was sealed off from the economics of daily business.

concluding remarks: conditions and contingency

High speed civilisation … Speed – pressure – complexity – they epitomize American life today. … Once get this picture, and you begin to realize the size of the job confronting an advertiser. These people are busy! They're not interested in him or his product. 'They don't want to read it.' (J. Walter Thomson News Bulletin, November 1922, JWTa)

Each generation wonders if advertising has not reached its zenith. (Presbrey, 1929: 259)

Inattentive, savvy consumers and an accelerated pace of life. If critical theory is to be believed, these are the unique challenges faced by contemporary advertisers. Yet the comments above predate the use of broadcast technologies as media for advertising. Nor are these the first stirrings of frustration amongst 'modern' advertisers at the difficulty of cutting through the clutter of competitors' announcements. Published comment on advertising over-exposure, as well as strategies for cutting through the clutter, can be traced as far back as the eighteenth century.[15] This unlikely-seeming phenomenon arises because the properties of advertising can only ever be judged in relation to their historical context. Recognition of advertising's contingent character unsettles the presentist critical preoccupation with increasing pervasiveness, and acts as a crucial reminder of what is lost when advertising is disentangled from its material, historical context.

These losses are clear when attention turns to questions about the hybridity of contemporary advertising as a practice based around the novel juxtaposition of economic objectives and cultural knowledge. As intuitively appealing as such claims are when confronted with successive generations of advertising's innovative blending of styles and techniques associated with other genres, there is a real cost in generalising too broadly from specific developments. Contemporary advertisers may use new techniques and devices to combine different aesthetic references with instrumental calculations, but however significant such innovations are the underlying form of combination is long-established. Aesthetic knowledge circulated amongst the personnel surrounding the advertising business as far back as the early nineteenth century, while by the early twentieth century agencies explicitly sought to nurture aesthetic competences among their creative staff through mechanisms like art commissioning, agency galleries and policies of recruiting literary talent.

Historical precedents, however, are only part of the trouble if the cultural and economic are defined as existing only through material practices, devices and arrangements. Understood in this way, each of the three functional specialisms in advertising practice – account management, media planning and research – can be understood as constituent sorts of practice, where the cultural and the economic coincide in even the most mundane of everyday activities. The precise form of these interactions depends not on the inevitable teleological drive of the epoch, but on specific conditions prevailing within the field in given places at given times. Technical, organisational and institutional arrangements in the field configure and are configured by advertising practices. Recognition of the contingency of advertising practice on given historical conditions can act as a valuable counterbalance to the critical tendency to generalise too broadly from shifts in institutional forms and practices.

notes

1 This is in opposition to the dating of the first 'proper' agencies to the late nineteenth century in Turner, 1952; Pope 1983; Leiss et al., 1986; and Lears, 1994.

2   Benson's traded until 1965, when a merger produced Ogilvy, Benson and Mather (Pigott, 1975). Ogilvy and Mather finally dropped the Benson name in the early 1980s.

3   Dunbar (1979) provides one of the most informative discussions of its development in the UK from 1819. See also Nevett (1982) and Pope (1983) for a discussion of its pros and cons.

4   The agent and MP Charles Higham, for example, vigorously opposed the commission system throughout his professional life. His agency published house advertising condemning rate cutting, and he was the author of numerous articles and speeches on the subject (Higham File, Agencies Box, HATa). Other, often larger agencies, were content for the system to be retained, but pressed for it to be granted only to 'recognised', independent agencies.

5   Full-service was the term adopted by agencies that sought to provide a complete advertising service including research, art and copy layout as well as space-buying. Maxwell's 1904 *Modern Advertising* outlines this 'full-service' model in some detail.

6   See Chapter 6.

7   Puffs and puffing were terms used to describe advertising in the eighteenth and nineteenth centuries; see also Chapter 6.

8   Dylan Thomas, Helen Woodward, William Woodward, James Webb Young and Dorothy Sayers are examples.

9   The precise extent of their role in agencies prior to 1910 is difficult to judge. They were certainly not unknown, and some of the most prominent women in twentieth-century advertising began work at the turn of the century. The weight of evidence, however, is that women played a marginal role in primarily administrative positions.

10 In 1947 two of JWT's 43 vice-presidents were women, whilst of a total of 1,348 staff in the US, 70 were women in creative positions (Hodgins, 1947: 101). From the 1920s JWT employed women primarily in copywriting and research positions. Marchand (1985: 32–5) estimates that around one in ten advertising staff were women, but in creative positions the figure may have been closer to one in five.

11 Harriet Abbot, widely understood to be a pseudonym of Helen Resor, offers this explanation of advertising in a 1920 article.

12 The claim to provide an essential 'professional' service is a familiar theme in the trade literature of this period. J. Walter Thompson: 1899 *Red Book*; Sell's: 1908 *The Propelling Power;* Spottiswoode's 1909: *The Triangle,* are amongst numerous examples.

13 In the US the Audit Bureau of Circulations was established in 1914, whilst the British Audit Bureau of Circulations was not set up until 1933. Prior to this newspapers published their own data, but its reliability was extremely variable.

14 Curiously, a similar logic of market pluralisation has been used to explain the phenomenon of specialist 'media-buying' agencies which occurred in the late 1980s (cf. Lash & Urry, 1994: 141; Nixon, 1996: 110–14).

15 See Chapter 6 for examples of Addison's and Johnson's writings on the subject.

persuasive products

Early advertising concentrated principally on the use value of products. As selling techniques became more sophisticated, and as the need for new markets became more pressing, advertisements began to stress the 'psychological utility' of their products. ... Escalating emphasis on the symbolic properties or psychological utility of goods represents a qualitative change in the commodity form. (Goldman, 1992: 17–18)

introduction   The desire to capture the unique and distinctive features of contemporary advertising has a powerful hold on critical writing. This desire is part of a conviction that contemporary advertisements have a particular potency, a capacity to persuade and manipulate surpassing anything to be found in the past. It percolates through the work of a range of critical writers who, whatever their other differences, agree that contemporary advertisements are more persuasive than hitherto. This concern with 'increasing persuasiveness' takes a number of different forms. As discussed in Chapter 2, writers on advertising have focused on different elements as definitive of the potency of the contemporary form. The ways in which these elements are defined vary, but concern generally revolves around the persuasive punch of three main elements of advertisements: the use of images, the use of persuasive rhetoric or 'copy' appeals, and the development of emotional or psychological types of appeal. These elements have all been deployed to signal the distinctiveness of contemporary advertisements, and, more seriously, as evidence of the qualitatively different role that advertising plays in an epochally designated 'consumer' society.

Contemporary critical theorists, however, are not the first group to have been struck by the distinctiveness, the apparent sophistication and power, of the advertising product of their era. For many historians, regardless of when they were writing, 'earlier' advertising functioned simply to 'inform', but did not generally attempt to 'persuade' people of the desirability of what was on offer.[1] This anomaly arises from the way persuasiveness is defined. Although images, rhetoric and emotions have been identified as key elements of persuasiveness, they are not synonymous with it. Persuasiveness is a relative judgement levelled at the effects of advertisements or their capacity to make a difference. It is generally made in relation to a context, often historical, of other advertisements, but it is seldom, if ever, made in relation to the historical conditions of production. This is unfortunate because, if crude comparisons of the impact of a 1980s Levi's television commercial over a 1780s draper's tradecard are to be avoided, the conditions of production are of course germane to questions of persuasiveness. The approach advocated here is therefore intended to recognise persuasiveness not as a function of any given element or combination of elements but as a historically contingent judgement.

The chapter considers the use of 'persuasive' elements in advertising – images, rhetoric and emotions – as far as possible within the historical context of their production, to try to establish that critical teleologies of advertising's ongoing evolution are not unproblematically borne out by the evidence of historical advertising product. Reconstructing the context of production is a useful counterbalance to the trend towards decontextualised interpretation. It allows weight to be given to how advertisements are shaped by the variety of institutional, organisational and technical methods used in different social, political and economic circumstances to produce them. As timely as this historical reconstruction is, however, it provides only a partial and fragmentary insight. The passage of time has severely restricted access to the circumstances surrounding the production of advertisements – a medium long regarded as ephemeral and seldom archived.[2] Moreover, the extent of change that has occurred over the three centuries under consideration is such that caution is needed about what, precisely, is being studied. What qualified as an advertisement in the seventeenth century may not today, and it is therefore worth beginning with some discussion of the different forms advertising has taken historically. The remaining three sections focus in turn on the three elements of appeal – images, rhetoric and emotion – most frequently considered definitive of 'modern' persuasive advertising. The aim in each of these sections is to uncover how advertisements were configured by specific circumstances of production.

puffs, advertisements and campaigns: definitions of advertising product   Advertising product has been defined and understood in a range of different ways. The terms 'puff', 'advertisement', and 'campaign', among others, have been deployed at various times and in various contexts to describe the products of advertising, and each has its own distinctive associations. The term advertisement, for instance, can be traced at least as far back as the seventeenth century. Historians differ over the precise dates and status of the first printed advertisements, but the first press advertisement can be fairly reliably traced to the 1620s.[3] These early texts, however, were not defined as 'advertisements' in the contemporary sense of the term. Sheppard's *Mercurius Mastix* in 1652, for example, highlights the absence of an agreed term by referring to advertisements as a 'quaint device in their trading' while the *Daily Courant* in 1702 referred to advertisements simply as 'impertinences' and refused to accept them (Elliot, 1962: 102, 44).

The contemporary sense of the term 'advertising' can be traced to late-sixteenth-century attempts to establish bureaus or registry offices 'whereby ready helps will be offered to supply the wants of everyone without prejudice to any' (Hartlib, quoted in George, 1926: 572). These offices were variously described as centres of 'adresse', 'intelligence', 'discoveries', 'encounters', and 'advice'. The term 'advertise' is from the French, meaning to inform, warn or announce, but its specific association with commercial promotional activity appears to have been a gradual process. In the 1600s 'advertisement' – as evidenced by the publication of numerous notices of absconding servants, missing spouses and stolen property under the title 'advertisement' – was roughly synonymous with 'announcement' or 'notice'.[4] By the 1700s it was deployed in newspapers like the *London Post Man* to refer specifically to particular types of advertisement – for instance publishers' notices (Presbrey, 1929: 65).

The term 'puff', in contrast, was deployed from the beginning of the eighteenth century in reference to promotional messages. 'Puff', 'puffery' and 'puffing' were in common usage throughout the eighteenth and nineteenth centuries, and clearly meant to convey a boosting or inflation of the reputation. The terms 'blasts', 'bubbles' and 'bubblemongering' were also used, but tended to have more fraudulent connotations. For Elliot, the 'puff' refers to a more engaging and subtle form of publicity than 'the blatant Advertisement' (Elliot, 1962: 117); but Henry Fielding is clear about its aims: 'the Institution of Rhetoric, or the Art of Persuasion … is but another word for *Puffing*'. (1741). This sense of the puff as a persuasive, rhetorical form also emerges in McKendrick's discussion of the promotional activities of the razor strop manufacturer George Packwood. He recounts how 'puffing' was, by the late eighteenth century, in sufficient circulation to have produced a whole new descriptive vocabulary (McKendrick, 1982: 148–9). In Sheridan's play *The Critic*, the character 'Mr Puff' introduces himself as 'a professor in the art of puffing, at your service – or anybody else's … Yes, sir, puffing is of various sorts: the principals are, the puff direct, the puff preliminary, the puff collateral, the puff collusive and the puff oblique or puff by implication' (McKendrick, 1982: 148). By the late nineteenth century, however, the term 'puffing' was less used and often associated only with marginal forms of advertising, such as the practice of disguising paid advertisements as editorial matter (Rowell, 1870; Fowler, 1889).

'Advertisement' and 'puff', then, have both had various meanings at particular historical moments. These meanings reflect the specific contexts of use and this is clear in the adoption of the term 'campaign'. The 'campaign' (also the name of the UK industry's principal trade publication), rather than the individual advertisement has, since the early twentieth century, been the core focus of most industry activity. The term was adopted during the period when advertising agencies began to assume the specialist forms and functions of the 'full-service agency'. The idea of the campaign reflects the developing industry's determination to shift the emphasis away from 'brilliant individuals' (Sharpe, 1964: 3) towards a more planned, professional system of production. 'Advertisements had to be made part of planned campaigns, and the campaigns had to be integrated into a coherent and appropriate marketing strategy. Inspiration and intuition were not enough' (Pope, 1983: 140).

By 1910 the term 'campaign' appeared in the promotional documents of a number of US and UK agencies in reference to a style of planned, client service.[5] The military connotations of the term were certainly part of its appeal. By the end of the nineteenth century, the diverse and eclectic field of advertising production had begun to consolidate and rationalise along the lines of the 'full-service agency' model. The term 'campaign' enters the vocabulary at this point as a way of signalling the precise and strategic nature of advertising. Hower, N.W. Ayer's historian remarks that,

> Like real weapons in actual warfare, advertising is used both in offensive and defensive movements … [C]ampaigns … have actively attempted to prevent the substitution of other products or brands or else to combat some idea … Ayer plans have called for advertising which has been ostensibly competitive or institutional in character but which has been intended to a large extent at least, to foster pride or bolster working morale among the clients' own staff of employees. Or the purpose may be to impress investors in a company's stock rather than to interest consumers in its product. (Hower, 1939: 268–70)

This brief overview of the terms used to denote advertising products hints at the extent and variety of the roles individual advertisements have played within specific historical contexts. The first press announcements of books for sale in the 1620s, the elaborate puffs of the eighteenth century, and the agency campaigns of the twentieth century, whilst sharing broadly similar promotional aims, are housed in fundamentally different systems of production.

These systems range from the long-term collective effort of an array of well-resourced institutional actors to the idiosyncratic efforts of entrepreneurial manufacturers. This variety in both the structure and motivations of different systems of production is such that some caution should be exercised in comparing their outputs. In many respects historical comparisons of advertising products refer to quite different and distinct entities. The best hope of understanding the aims, intentions and strategies of diverse historical products is offered by placing them within the context of their production. It is to the task of describing how the visual, rhetorical and emotional elements of advertisements were shaped by this context that the remainder of this chapter is devoted

the image: display, illustration and the visual appeal

Just because it fits so snugly and comfortably, our thick cloak of symbols seems to be a natural part of our being. The consumer society constructed this field of symbols and implanted it at the centre of marketplace activity, causing a profound transformation in social life. (Leiss et al., 1986: 285)

Images did not become a regular and prominent feature of printed advertising until well into the nineteenth century. The scarcity of images in surviving printed advertising prior to 1850 has been read as an implicit sign of their superfluity in a promotional logic based on information. As a corollary, the proliferation of images throughout the twentieth century has for many theorists helped define a contemporary 'epoch' (Berger, 1972; Featherstone, 1991; Lash & Urry, 1994) in which image-based advertising achieves unprecedented persuasive potency (Leiss et al., 1986; Wernick, 1991; Fowles, 1996). But the use of the images in the full range of advertising and promotional media has a more extensive, and, indeed more interesting history than is implied in these accounts. Behind the absence, and presence, of images in advertising media is a set of brute empirical circumstances that have gone largely unremarked in critical, epochal writing. These circumstances indelibly imprinted the use, and disuse, of images and, are therefore essential to any robust historical assessment of the changing role of advertising. The aim in what follows is to uncover how some of these circumstances shaped the use of images in the two primary forms of pre-1900 advertising media – press and poster advertising.

Press advertising   Even a brief glance through the newspapers and periodicals of the eighteenth and nineteenth centuries reveals that the image was not a well-developed element of press advertising. In many sectors of the press, as late as the early twentieth century, display was limited, and illustrations, where they appeared at all, were small and crudely drawn. The underdevelopment of images in press advertising, however, had some very specific and identifiable causes. These causes had little to do with the state of the promotional imagination or the adequacy of less persuasive messages. Rather, they derived from a range of politico-economic, technological and local institutional forces which marked out a convoluted path for image-based advertising, subject to significant local variations in different places, times and institutional sectors.

The most basic elements of the visual, imagistic appeal of printed advertisements are display, layout and typography. Their role in visual appeal is often overlooked, especially by critics speaking from a platform where the manipulation of audio-visual media provides for a more spectacular range of effects. Yet display, layout and typography have been relentlessly and artfully manipulated throughout the history of press advertising, to secure maximum impact. These efforts generated a degree of controversy that is almost incomprehensible by contemporary standards, but is quite sensible in the historical context of production.

Even the earliest surviving press advertisements deployed typographic effects. The most common of these was the drop capitalisation of all or part of the first word over two lines of type. This technique was used in newssheets produced from the 1670s, and remained popular throughout the eighteenth and nineteenth centuries. A range of other techniques, including the use of asterisks, pointing hands and some small woodcut illustrations, were also widely deployed to mark the advertisement. These mundane devices may seem unlikely to register much impact, but Addison's 1710 comments suggest otherwise.

> The great art in writing advertisements, is the finding out a proper method to catch the reader's eye ... Asterisks and hands were formerly of great use for this purpose. Of late years the NB has been much in fashion, as also little cuts and figures ... I must not here omit the blind Italian character, which being scarce legible, always fixes and detains the eye, and gives the curious reader something like the satisfaction of prying into a secret. (Addison, *The Tatler*, 14/9/1710: 1)

Addison's tone is of course pointed, and his object is to reveal himself alert to the tricks of advertisers; but his description, especially of italic type – 'the blind Italian' – reveals something of the impression made by type effects when they were still a relative novelty. Display and typographic effects such as these continued throughout much of the eighteenth and nineteenth centuries to be the primary method of securing a visual impact in mainstream British press advertising. Yet, for a period, this was not the case in many sectors of the American press. Advertisements for patent, or more properly 'proprietary', medicines appeared in American newspapers from the early eighteenth century. Helfland (2003) records the appearance of an advertisement for Daffy's Elixir Salutis in the *Boston News-Letter* in 1708, while Philadelphia's first newspaper, the *American Weekly Mercury* ran proprietary medicine advertisements through the 1720s. In the eighteenth century individuals like Benjamin Franklin, Gerardus Duyckinck and John Zenger introduced a range of visual methods for enhancing the impact of these advertisements. When Franklin's *Pennsylvania Gazette* opened in 1729 he introduced major changes in the layout of advertising (Presbrey, 1929). From the 1730s he used white space, headings, different type effects and small illustrations or emblematic 'cuts', which soon developed into larger illustrated advertisements tailored for individual advertisers.

The sign of the golden spectacles advertised one of Philadelphia's leading opticians. The sign of the blue hand told the story of a reliable glove and clothing cleaner. He also created ornamental borders for clothing shops and other retail outlets, as well as cuts of scythes and sickles, clock faces, books, horses and symbols that instantly informed the reader about the general contents of the advertisement. (Fleming, 1976: 27)

Similarly, Duyckinck altered display techniques with the introduction of elaborate ornamental borders of the type common in late-nineteenth-century press advertising. Zenger meanwhile published an advertisement in a 1743 edition of the *New York Weekly Journal* that took up half a page and was the first to break column rules.

It might be reasonably assumed that these innovations would continue and disseminate in the forthcoming years, but future development was in fact very uneven. While in many eighteenth-century American papers a variety of display techniques and small illustrations were used, in the UK this was rare except in some provincial and farming newspapers (Presbrey, 1929; Elliot, 1962; Fleming, 1976). By the 1820s even crude woodcut illustrations and display techniques had become increasingly scarce in the mainstream press in both countries, due to a combination of politico-economic, institutional, and technological forces.

In the UK a major disincentive to the development of image-based advertising came in the form of stamp duty. Stamp duty was levied in the UK between 1712 and 1855 on every printed sheet of paper, and it effectively limited papers to a single sheet folded once. In addition, each advertisement placed was subject to a flat rate tax of one shilling in 1712, which had more than tripled by 1797 (Nevett, 1982). The combination of duties meant that newspapers could not effectively offset the stamp duty by including more advertising. The result was that space was the scarcest resource, and newspapers were forced to adopt small typefaces and increase the number of columns per page. The situation across the Atlantic, meanwhile, was quite different. Stamp duty was introduced there in 1765, only to be repealed, after intensive opposition, less than six months later (Presbrey, 1929). As a result, paper was less expensive, and newspapers like the *Pennsylvania Gazette* had eight rather than four printed sides. In addition, entrepreneurial proprietors like Franklin and Zengler saw display and illustrated advertising as a way of funding their publications and attracting readers. The result was that illustration in the US press had developed into a 'fairly robust hard sell' by the early nineteenth century (Fleming, 1976).

But things did not continue in this vein. A national paper shortage, combined with a shift in institutional approaches to press advertising, imposed serious restrictions on display advertising. In many of the most prestigious American newspapers a regulation known as 'agate only', requiring strict typographic uniformity, was in force by the 1840s. The 'agate only' rule was particularly associated with the *New York Herald* under proprietor James Bennett, who permitted only small, classified agate type and drop capitalisation. Although it was not universally adopted – trade and some regional papers tended to have more liberal policies – many popular papers enforced heavy restrictions on display and banned illustrations entirely. Restrictions in the UK were less codified than Bennett's but proprietorial policy still effectively banned large and display advertisements. As newspaper publisher Daniel Stuart recounts 'When a very long advertisement of a column or two came, I charged enormously high, that it might be taken away without the parties being able to say it was refused admission' (Stuart, 1838a, *Gentleman's Magazine*, July 1838: 26).

A number of factors underlay this prejudice. Advertisements that featured illustrations or went over the column rule posed a serious technical challenge to newspaper compositors. Printing in the early nineteenth century was still conducted on a wooden hand-press, and this restricted the size of print that could be handled. Furthermore, the predominant method of printing illustrations from woodcuts was ill suited to the type of ink and paper in use, and the end result, after much trouble, was often unusable (Presbrey, 1929). But perhaps still more important was the attitude of newspaper editors and publishers to advertisements. Whilst this had softened since the *Daily Courant*'s 1702 reference to advertisements as 'impertinences', relations between the two remained ambivalent. For many publishers, the view that advertising was vulgar, dishonest and of dubious value was hard to reconcile with its growing financial importance to the business of publishing. Despite the economic contribution that advertising could make, many nineteenth-century newspapers and periodicals, like John and Leigh Hunt's *Examiner*, refused advertisements on the basis that they would lower the dignity of the paper (Sala, quoted in Sell's, 1891). And, even where publishers had a less censorious approach, they tended to prefer many small to a few large advertisements, in the belief that more advertisements would attract more readers. Again, this is captured in Daniel Stuart's policy:

> Besides; numerous and varied advertisements interest numerous and varied readers ... Advertisements act and react. They attract readers, promote circulation, and circulation attracts advertisements ... I would not drive away the short miscellaneous advertisements by allowing space to be monopolised by any one class. (Stuart, 1838a, *Gentleman's Magazine*, July 1838: 25–6)

Although refused by many of the more prestigious national dailies, illustrated advertisements were quite common in Britain's regional press in the first decades of the nineteenth century. Some of these illustrations suggest a robust comprehension of the persuasive potency of images. Figures 6.1 and 6.2 are examples of advertisements for competing versions of blacking, one of the most widely advertised products of the era. Figure 6.1 is drawn from an 1820 edition of the *Gloucester Journal* (Lysons, BL) and advertises Turner's Blacking. Figure 6.2 is from around the same time and depicts a very similar style of advertisement for Warren's Blacking.

Both these advertisements appeared extremely widely in the press, on handbills and posters, as well as being stamped directly on walls and pavements, and provoked much satirical comment (Warreniana, c.1830; 'Puffs', 1855). The illustrations rely upon a strikingly similar device, and this is more likely a consequence of what was already a very self-referential medium than a coincidence. George Cruikshank's drawing for Warren's Blacking is superior in execution, and still aroused comment years later: '... all but minors of the present generation must remember George Cruikshank's exquisite woodcut of the astonished cat viewing herself in the polished hessian, which made the fortune of Warren' (Anonymous, 1855, *Quarterly Review*, 1855: 212). These examples, however, are not really exceptional. There are numerous others in this style, particularly for blacking products and the lotteries, with the emphasis on draughtsmanship and humour (Lysons, BL). Cruikshank (1792–1878) is well known as a prolific illustrator, caricaturist and political satirist, but he was also responsible for many illustrated advertisements for products including lotteries and theatrical 'curiosities', and was far from the only illustrator of advertising. In 1855 illustrated advertisements were

Figure 6.1

1820 Turner's

Blacking

advertisement

(Source:

Lyson's collec-

tion, c103k11

vol. 4, BL)

The Cat and the Boot;

Or, an Improvement upon Mirrors.

AS I one morning shaving sat,
  For dinner-time preparing,
A dreadful howling from the cat
  Set all the room a staring!
Suddenly I turn'd—beheld a scene
  I could not but delight in;
For in my boots, so bright and clean,
  The Cat her face was fighting.
Bright was the boot—its surface fair,
  In lustre nothing lacking;
I never saw one half so clear,
  Except by WARREN's *Blacking.*
(WARREN! that name shall last as long
  As beaux and belles shall dash on,
Immortalis'd in every song
  That chaunts the praise of fashion.
For, oh! without his *Blacking,* all
  Attempts we may abolish
To raise upon our Boots at all
  The least of jet or polish.)
Surpris'd, its brilliancy I view'd
  With silent admiration;
The glass that on the table stood
  Wax'd dimly in its station.
I took the Boot, the glass displac'd,
  For soon I was aware,
The latter only was disgrac'd
  Whene'er the Boot was near.
And quickly found that I could shave
  Much better by its bloom,
Than any mirror that I have
  Within my drawing-room.
And since that time, I've often smil'd
  To think how puss was frighten'd
When at the Boot she tugg'd and toil'd,
  By WARREN's *Blacking* brighten'd.

This Easy-shining & Brilliant BLACKING,
PREPARED BY

Robert Warren

30, Strand, London;

AND SOLD IN EVERY TOWN IN THE KINGDOM.

In Bottles, Pots, and Tin Boxes, 6*d.*—12*d.*—and 18*d.* each.

☞ *Be particular to enquire for*
WARREN'S, 30, Strand.
ALL OTHERS ARE COUNTERFEIT.

Figure 6.2

Warren's Blacking advertisement drawn by Cruikshank (Source: Elliot, 1962) described as 'by far the most effective of their class, as they call in the aid of another sense to express meaning' (Anonymous, *Quarterly Review*, 1855: 212). Nevertheless, illustrations disappeared entirely from the daily press by the 1850s under an institutional regime that made it 'fatal' for daily newspapers that 'twenty years ago admitted illustrations' to continue to do so (Anonymous, *Quarterly Review*, 1855: 212).

This situation was the result of the combined effects of institutional policies, paper shortages, technological constraints and, in the UK, the stamp duty. These constraints produced some remarkably inventive responses from advertisers. Auctioneers and book publishers, for instance would routinely hold back until they could 'come out with a swarm of advertisements in a double sheet to astonish their readers' (Stuart, 1838b: 25). This developed into a practice of beginning each agate type insertion with the same drop capitalised word, giving the entire column a distinctive patterned appearance. By the middle of the century American advertisers began to employ a range of stunts, as in Figure 6.3, to evade the restrictions.

After his attempt to place display advertising in the *New York Herald* was refused, Robert Bonner, the publisher of the literary periodical the *New York Ledger*, placed 93 identical advertisements which filled a column (Presbrey, 1929). The impact this had surprised even Bonner, and encouraged him to continue experimenting using an acrostic to spell out L-E-D-G-E-R, with a drop capital across six columns. Bonner's efforts acted almost immediately to relax display restrictions in the US. In the UK the process was much slower. By the end of the century British dailies had begun to admit bold type and allow advertisements to run across more than one column. Display advertising and illustrations were becoming more common, but were still only reluctantly admitted by many newspapers. A glimpse of how tentative the attitude to illustrated advertisements remained is provided in the following letter, sent by the agency Samson Clark in 1898 to a prospective client.

With regard to blocks the *Daily Mail* do not guarantee to accept them, but we have no doubt that we can get them through should you desire it. They however, charge 50% extra for the spaces where blocks are used, and they must appear either on pages 7 or 8. Should they appear on page 7, the ordinary price is £1 per inch and the 50% extra would bring it to 30/-. We may mention that we can contrive very effective advertising without the use of a block, although not of course to compare with block advertisements as far as a catching and striking appearance is concerned. (Letter to Lonsdale Bros, 1898, Samson Clark Box, HATa)

The *Daily Mail* was one of the more populist papers and while it actively sought advertising revenue it still harboured serious reservations about illustrated

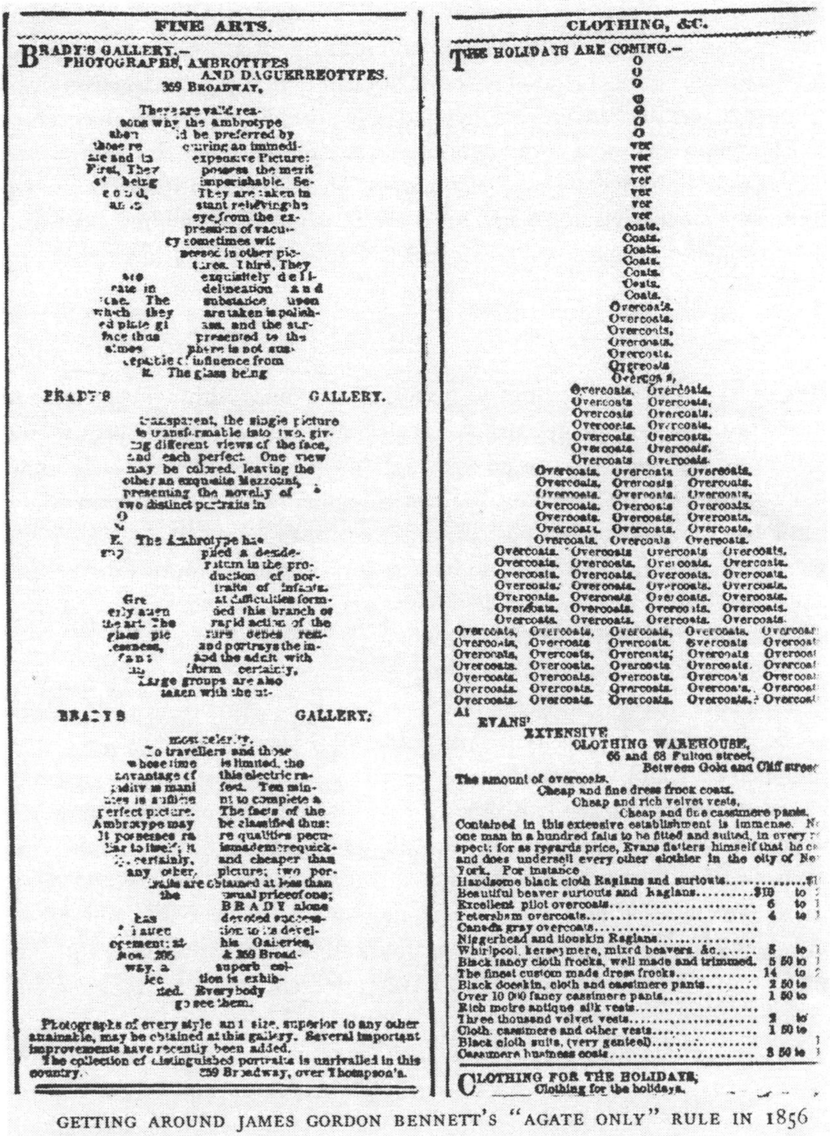

FINE ARTS.

BRADY'S GALLERY.—
PHOTOGRAPHS, AMBROTYPES
AND DAGUERREOTYPES.
359 BROADWAY,

There are valid reasons why the ambrotype should be preferred by those requiring an immediate and inexpensive Picture: First, They possess the merit of being imperishable. Second, They are taken in an instant relieving the eye from the expression of vacuity sometimes witnessed in other pictures. Third, They are exquisitely delineated and the substance upon which they are taken is polished plate glass, and the surface thus presented to the ... influence from it. The glass being

BRADY'S GALLERY.

transparent, the single picture is transformable into two, giving different views of the face, and each perfect. One view may be colored, leaving the other an exquisite Mezzotint, presenting the novelty of two distinct portraits in one. The Ambrotype has supplied a desideratum in the production of portraits of infants. Greatly aided this branch of the art. The rapid action of the glass plate defies restlessness, and portrays the infant and the adult with uniform certainty. Large groups are also taken with the ut-

BRADY'S GALLERY.

most celerity. To travellers and those whose time is limited, the advantage of this electric rapidity is manifest. Ten minutes is sufficient to complete a perfect picture. The facts of the Ambrotype may be classified thus: It possesses rare qualities peculiar to itself; it is made more quickly, certainly, and cheaper than any other picture; two portraits are obtained at less than the usual price of one; BRADY alone has devoted success... attention to its development at his Galleries, Nos. 205 & 359 Broadway, a superb collection is exhibited. Everybody go see them.

Photographs of every style and size, superior to any other attainable, may be obtained at this gallery. Several important improvements have recently been added.
The collection of distinguished portraits is unrivalled in this country. 359 Broadway, over Thompson's.

CLOTHING, &C.

THE HOLIDAYS ARE COMING.—
O O O O O O O O O
ver ver ver ver ver ver ver ver
coats. Coats. Coats. Coats. Coats. Coats. Coats.
Overcoats. Overcoats. Overcoats. ...
At
EVANS'
EXTENSIVE
CLOTHING WAREHOUSE,
66 and 68 Fulton street,
Between Gold and Cliff street.

The amount of overcoats,
Cheap and fine dress frock coats,
Cheap and rich velvet vests,
Cheap and fine cassimere pants,
Contained in this extensive establishment is immense. No one man in a hundred fails to be fitted and suited, in every respect: for as regards price, Evans flatters himself that he can and does undersell every other clothier in the city of New York. For instance

Handsome black cloth Raglans and surtouts		
Beautiful beaver surtouts and Raglans	$10	to
Excellent pilot overcoats	6	to
Petersham overcoats	4	to
Canada gray overcoats		
Niggerhead and Ilooskin Raglans		
Whirlpool, kerseymere, mixed beavers, &c.	5	to
Black fancy cloth frocks, well made and trimmed	5 50	to
The finest custom made dress frocks	14	to
Black doeskin, cloth and cassimere pants	2 50	to
Over 10 000 fancy cassimere pants	1 50	to
Rich moire antique silk vests		
Three thousand velvet vests	2	to
Cloth, cassimere and other vests	1 50	to
Black cloth suits, (very genteel)		
Cassimere business coats	3 50	to

CLOTHING FOR THE HOLIDAYS;
Clothing for the holidays.

GETTING AROUND JAMES GORDON BENNETT'S "AGATE ONLY" RULE IN 1856

Stunts by advertisers in their efforts to obtain display and novelty. This probably was the origin the built-up type which later became a characteristic of the New York Herald.

Figure 6.3 Advertising stunts to evade restrictions on display (Source: Presbrey, 1929)

advertisements. In this context the judicious use of typography could still make an impression, as in H.G. Wells's description of the 'alluring, button-holing, let-me-just-tell-you-quite-soberly-something-you-ought-to-know style of newspaper advertisement, with every now and then a convulsive jump of some attractive phrase into capitals' (Wells, 1923: 132). Wells's comments, like Addison's, serve as a reminder that the impact made by mundane type effects is contingent upon the media environment in which they appear. Even within the draconian limits imposed by the institutional, technical and politico-economic framework in which press advertising was conducted, certain advertisers devised effective visual techniques. These efforts reveal a marked awareness of the persuasive potency of the image and, at times, an inventive and irrepressible visual imagination. The accomplishments of this visual imagination are best recorded in those forms of advertising and promotional media less circumscribed by statute, policy and technology.

Broadsides, posters and other forms of promotion   Although poster and other forms of advertising largely escaped the statutory and institutional regulations imposed on press advertising, they were still subject to the limits imposed by print and reproduction technologies. These limits prevented the distribution of large, colour posters on any scale until well into the nineteenth century. In spite of these constraints, careful reconstruction of how posters and other, often forgotten, media were used suggests the existence of a vibrant, colourful, noisy, even spectacular promotional environment.

The earliest forms of advertising poster appeared towards the end of the fifteenth century, and were known as broadsides. Broadsides were single sheets printed on one side only, and sold by printers, at fairs, and by street vendors for a penny or less. They were used for a variety of purposes, including the distribution of ballads. Broadside ballads were a popular folk music idiom but they were also, simultaneously, a news and promotional medium featuring an eclectic mix of traditional narratives, political and social events, scandal and advertising. They were often kept as declarations of allegiance, souvenirs of great events, and decorations for home, workplace and pub (Anderson, 1991).[6] They appear to have varied enormously over time and according to purpose, but whilst some were printed only in black ink, the use of two colours, a range of typefaces, fancy borders and small woodcut illustrations was also common. Some were hand-coloured and featured intricately detailed illustrations covering the whole of the sheet, an example of which can be seen in Figure 6.4.

It is difficult to say much with any certainty about advertising broadsides as, given the uses to which they were put – as outdoor posters, pricelists and wrapping paper – relatively few have survived. Certainly, illustrated broadsides like that shown in Figure 6.4 were not unheard of – archive collections of broadsides include many examples featuring artwork by well-known figures like Hogarth and George Cruikshank.[7] But most of these were for special events, spectacles and curiosities like balloon flights, the exhibition of exotic animals, new inventions, theatrical events and exhibitions. Illustrated broadsides were also used to advertise luxuries like mineral water,

Figure 6.4
Advertisement
for the 1769
Shakespeare
Jubilee cele-
brations
(Source:
Daniel, c.1860,
c61, BL)

toy and china shops, and auction sales, but it is unlikely that, prior to the boom in poster printing in the 1830s, they featured much in the promotion of more everyday goods and services (see Anderson, 1991).

Illustrations were, however, very much a part of another promotional medium. Tradecards were distributed in hundreds of thousands each year from the seventeenth century (Walsh, 2000). They were from the outset an illustrated, generally monochrome medium, engraved on wood or copper (John Johnson Collection Exhibition, 2001). Early engraved tradecards employed simple, almost heraldic illustrations of the shop sign, often

Figure 6.5

Duesbury & Co.

Manufacturers of

Derby & Chelsea

Porcelain

Tradecard, 1799

(Source: John

Johnson

Collection

Exhibition 2001)

confined within a border and separated from the text (John Johnson Collection Exhibition, 2001). Letterpress tradecards were also produced, although these tended not to be illustrated and were often reserved for poorer trades and provincial areas where competition was less severe, and the shop would in any case be more easily identifiable than in urban areas. The depiction of shop signs on tradecards gradually gave way to engraved illustrations of products, tradesmen at work, manufacturing processes and premises. From the 1730s the style of the card often reflected that of fashions in furniture; trade signs and other illustrations were contained within baroque and rococo cartouches, whilst by the end of the century the vogue for the elegant neo-classical Adam style was reflected in trade cards (see Figure 6.5). Tradecards were an elegant visual promotional medium 'designed to do more than inform. The objective of a trade card was to attract custom and, especially, the patronage of the wealthy. Even chimney sweeps and nightmen (collectors of night-soil) often produced stylish illustrated cards' (John Johnson Collection Exhibition, 2001).

Notwithstanding their accomplishment, there is evidence that neither tradecards nor broadsides were deployed as 'stand-alone' promotion, but were integrated with a range of other devices. A short example may help to reinforce this point. Figure 6.6 shows an advertisement for an exhibition of a panoramic view. The Lyson's collection in the British Library (BL) contains numerous similar advertisements of famous battles like Waterloo and Badajoz, and cities like Rome and St Petersburg. These views were extremely popular[8] and were promoted by broadsides produced in a specially adapted style but even these were only a small part of the promotional effort. The

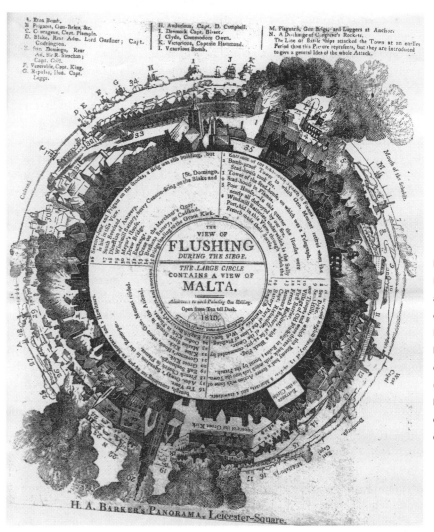

Figure 6.6
Panorama
advertisement
of the
Flushing of
Malta
exhibition
(Source:
Lyson's
collection,
c103k11, BL)

Lysons collection also contains samples of illustrated handbills, tradecards and tickets. Scene paintings published in the press depict street banners, flags, bunting, posters and other sorts of display, giving an overwhelming sense of a chaotic visual spectacle produced through a combination of different promotional techniques.

This is precisely the type of promotional mix famously adopted by Phineas Barnum, often considered one of the earliest proponents of persuasive promotion. Barnum used sandwich-board carriers, handbills, posters and street banners, in addition to newspapers, to promote his attractions (Presbrey, 1929). Like other eighteenth- and nineteenth-century promoters of

169

special events, Barnum overcame technical limits by using multiple forms of promotion to enhance and exaggerate the visual spectacle. The popularity of this type of promotion is unsurprising in a historical context where fairs and carnivals had long been the preferred means of stimulating marketplace activity. Fairs, as a letter published in 1758 makes clear, 'at their first institution were intended for the more ready disposal of all kinds of merchandise' (Bartholomew Faire, BL). The provision of a stimulating visual environment was central to the promotional strategy of market fairs, which aimed to mix the exotic and bizarre, entertainment and commerce, to enhance the consumption of goods produced by entrepreneurs like Wedgwood and Matthew Boulton, as well as those imported from overseas (Lears, 1994).

The compulsion to create 'a grand stir', moreover, was not reserved solely for occasions such as fairs, but was a central promotional strategy, particularly in urban areas. The use of an array of unusual, often forgotten media, including glass pillars, horse-drawn mobile displays, human-occupied pyramids and paper balloons in London is well documented.[9] The visual impact of promotional media was also heightened in London by an extravagant use of gaslight to illuminate both advertising posters and window displays in busy thoroughfares (Schlesinger, 1853). Many of these promotional devices were restricted to major urban environments, but advertising's appearance on rocks, barns, trees, shops, hotels, offices and on public transportation, as well as on a vast range of corporate paraphernalia, ensured its visual impact stretched beyond the city.

The use of an array of promotional devices, from markets, exhibitions, publicity, signs, tradecards, press advertising to every form of bill and poster, leaves little doubt of the existence of well-developed strategies for visual promotion in the eighteenth and nineteenth centuries. These strategies were adapted to suit what was technically and technologically achievable. In this sense, while broadsides and tradecards did carry visual messages they were not, at least until the mid nineteenth century, the most important visual medium. Rather, they were one of a number of elements in a mix which also featured press advertising, handbills, mobile displays, placard-bearers and street banners. Their role as a specialist medium for image-based advertising developed in tandem with changes in the technological and institutional system of advertising production.

In the early nineteenth century posters and broadsides were an extremely popular promotional tool, but the majority of these were text- rather than illustration-based. By the middle of the century, advancing technical capabilities allowed 36-sheet size posters on which woodcut letters and illustrations could be used (see Nevett, 1982; Anderson, 1991). Coupled with the problems with display advertising in the press, these advances began to make conditions favourable for posters to develop as a specialised image-based medium. Technical advances in the reproduction of illustrated colour posters continued throughout the century, and by the 1870s lithographic and printing techniques had reached a stage where production costs were low enough to facilitate large-scale commercial use. This signalled the beginning of a period when the role of the full-colour poster as a medium for advertising became the subject of intense development and scrutiny.

From the 1860s France had led the field in exploiting the visual potential of the poster, exemplified by the work of Cheret and Toulouse-Lautrec. The quality of French commercial posters in this period signalled the beginning of a boom in poster exhibiting and collecting, which was to contribute to ongoing debates about the relationship between art and commerce. In the UK in the 1870s, Frederick Walker's 'The Woman in White' and the work of James Pryde and William Nicholson – the 'Beggarstaff Brothers' – for Rowntrees Cocoa, were some of the first examples of poster advertisements which aimed to appeal through the quality of the artwork. The situation reached a head with Thomas Barratt's purchase in 1886 of the Royal Academy artist Sir John Millais's painting 'Bubbles', for use as an advertisement for Pears Soap. This was followed rapidly by William Lever's purchase in 1889 of another academic painting, 'The New Frock' by William Frith, to promote Sunlight Soap. Frith apparently took even less kindly to this appropriation of his painting than Millais, and complained publically in the *Magazine of Art*, the *Daily Telegraph* and the *Pall Mall Gazette*. Frith regarded the work of artists as unconnected in essence and function to the task of advertisers. Articulating a view that probably characterised most of the artistic establishment, he complained that the use of art for an overtly commercial purpose degraded and devalued the original. In response to this, both Lever and his advertising agent Henry Sell replied to the *Pall Mall Gazette* (Sell's Guardbook, 1891, HATa).

Pictures have been used for advertising ever since advertising was known, and the very fact that in the latter half of the nineteenth century advertisers are seeking the works of our best artists, making thereby their advertisements more attractive, is a change that many lovers of art will consider an advance on the old style of advertising. Surely the use of a picture in this way cannot detract from the reputation of the artist but rather the reverse ... (W. Lever, 10/7/1890, Letter to the *Pall Mall Gazette*, Sell's Guardbook, 1891, HATa)

When a thing of beauty can be produced in the best style of the engraver's art, and distributed throughout the country in millions, it must give pleasure to a vast number of people who never have the opportunity of going to the Academy. It is a pretty picture, whether under the name of the 'New Frock' or the name of 'So Clean.' (H. Sell, 10/7/1890, Letter to the *Pall Mall Gazette,* Sell's Guardbook, 1891, HATa)

This debate had a long history even then, and continued in various guises throughout the twentieth century.[10] It reached a peak of intensity in the late nineteenth century, as a direct result of the use of academic art in advertising posters being made possible by technical advances in chromolithography. William Lever's use of Frith's painting was described as an 'aesthetic experiment' that he did not expect could address the fundamental problems and challenges of advertising (Sharpe, 1964: 6). But the use of academic art in advertising was more than an experiment. It was also a calculated move to reconfigure the status and respectability of advertising. Advertising's status had never been assured, and the street advertising of the first half of the century had done little to improve its reputation. As Lever's and Sell's comments suggest, the purchase of art for advertising purposes was calculated to be 'culturally' uplifting. Such aesthetic improvements to the visual environment and to public taste, it was thought, would lend dignity to an industry keen to professionalise and shake off its crass associations, including the carnivalesque techniques referred to above. Through technological advances, commercial and academic art began to make carnival, as a form of mainstream promotion, obsolete.

What all this recommends is that the use of images in promotion be considered within the context of technical and institutional possibility. Prior to the nineteenth century there were severe constraints on the technical reproducibility of the printed image. When these constraints were overcome printed images clearly did proliferate, and technological advances have continued to alter the range of possibilities and media available for image-based promotion. Yet caution is still needed in how this proliferation is interpreted. As the evidence above suggests, broadsides, tradecards, handbills, carnivals and posters have all, at various historical moments, been used to carry intricate, elaborate and sometimes spectacular visual messages. In the absence of technologies for cheap, mass reproduction of images, pre-twentieth-century traders nevertheless succeeded in combining a variety of techniques to produce a spectacular visual environment, with the express intention of stimulating demand. Under shifting, at times draconian, technical, institutional and politico-economic conditions, images and visual devices were relentlessly and inventively deployed as promotional mechanisms as far back as the seventeenth century. Thus, while the 'thick cloak of symbols' may seem to define contemporary 'consumer societies', image-based promotion is really not the exclusive property of the present.

the words: rhetorical strategies of advertising copy
The capacity to persuade rather than simply inform is one of the primary distinctions drawn between contemporary and historical forms of advertising.

Historical advertising is judged more 'innocent' than its contemporary counterpart on the basis of having an apparently more simple, informative function (see Barnard, 1995). Stripped of their context, the rhetorical strategies of persuasion in historical advertising copy may appear innocent, but this is less clear when an effort is made to reinsert them within their historical context. This section aims to trace the connections between specific styles of advertising copy and their systems of production. It begins with a review of some eighteenth-century discussions of the persuasive, rhetorical force of advertising, before moving on to consider some examples of different historical styles of copy.

One of the first detailed discussions of advertising's rhetorical power appears in the writings of Henry Fielding. Fielding wrote a number of satirical articles in the 1740s on the issue of puffing in the book trade, and for political propaganda (*The Champion*, 1740–3). What these articles convey is Fielding's awareness of the variety of purposes to which 'puffing' could be put. For Fielding, puffing, the 'art of persuasion', could be deployed to many ends, and was a central aspect of human behaviour. Writing as Gustavus Puffendorf, he defended puffing against the wave of satirical comment in the press.

An uncommon inveteracy to *Puffs,* of all sorts … [such that] Every Man who has not forgot to blush trembles to publish the least hint advantageous to himself, for fear of being served up as part of your next Evening's Entertainment … [yet] It is the practice of the whole Species … That 'tis the foremost Idea in either sex to conceal every defect both of Body and Mind with all possible caution, and display every Perfection, real or imaginary, to all possible advantage which renders the whole of life one continued *Puff.* (Fielding, 1741)

There is more than a hint in this of the conception of promotion as an all-encompassing process, which more recent critical writers have directly associated with the commodity culture of 'late capitalism'. Authors like Haug (1986) and Wernick (1991) lament the degenerative effects of advertising on the authentic nature of subjects and objects, in a 'de-referentialised' culture compromised by the instrumentalisation of symbolic values in the promotional process. Yet for Fielding promotion – even self-promotion – is a core 'practice of the species', part of the 'grand science of life'. The following example of eighteenth-century advertising copy seems to follow Fielding's philosophy.

The highest compounded Spirit of Lavender, the most glorious, if the expression may be used, enlivening scent and flavour that can possibly be, which so raptures the spirits, delights the gusts, and gives such airs to the countenance, as are not to be imagined but by those that have tried it. The meanest sort of thing is admired by most gentlemen and ladies; but this far more, as by far it exceeds it, to the gaining among all a more than common esteem. It is sold in neat flint bottles, fit for the pocket, only at the Golden Key in Wharton's Court, near Holborn Bars, for three shillings and six pence, with directions. (Advertisement c.1709 quoted in Addison, 1710)

This style of lyrical exaggeration was fairly typical of press advertising at the time, and much care was clearly taken in the wording. The advertisement features a determined attempt to articulate the product's capacity to lend 'airs to the countenance'. It could accordingly be read as an appeal to the 'continual audience-oriented, self-staging' which Wernick – among others – treats as a symptom of the expansionism of late-twentieth-century promotional culture (Wernick, 1991: 193). This form of persuasive, rhetorical appeal is not one that contemporary critics generally associate with eighteenth-century advertising, but critics of the time were less sanguine. Samuel Johnson addressed the question of advertising's persuasiveness in an essay best known for its claim that 'advertising is now so near perfection, that it is not easy to propose any improvement' (Johnson, 1759). The essay clearly fits within the genre of advertising parody that Fielding referred to, but it nevertheless provides some important clues to how advertising was perceived.[11] In the following extract, Johnson laments the associations established in advertisements between products and unrelated cultural objects.

It has been remarked by the severer judges, that the salutary sorrow of tragic scenes is too soon effaced by the merriment of the epilogue: the same inconvenience arises from the improper disposition of advertisements. The noblest objects may be so associated as to be made ridiculous. The camel and dromedary themselves might have lost much of their dignity between the true flower of mustard and the original Daffy's elixir; and I could not but feel some indignation when I found this illustrious Indian warrior immediately succeeded by a fresh parcel of Dublin butter. (Johnson, 1759)

Such associations or 'associative transfers' are treated in much of the critical literature as one of the primary offences of contemporary advertising, feeding the dissolution of authentic culture (Williamson, 1978; Wernick, 1991; Goldman, 1992). Advertising's skills in this area nevertheless inform Johnson's opinion about its advancement, and prompt him to wonder whether the puffs of his own era did not 'play too wantonly with our passions?' (op. cit., 1759).

Further evidence that the wording of eighteenth- and early-nineteenth-century advertisements was carefully motivated emerges in the styles of verbal appeal dominant in press advertising. McKendrick (1982) has described an array of verbal techniques, including puns, slogans, verse, parody and narrative, in common use during this period.[12] The popularity of these techniques may well be an indirect consequence of the technical and regulative difficulties associated with display advertising. Certainly, the absence of images in press advertising was compensated for by evocative and picturesque 'purple' prose, and a literary culture of 'puffing' was fostered. The following advertisement, which has been attributed to Charles Lamb, is typical of this style (RFW 1/6/1; Whites Box, HATa).

A seasonable hint – Christmas gifts, of inumerable descriptions, will now pervade the whole kingdom. It is submitted whether any present is capable of being attended with so much good to a dutiful son, an amiable daughter, an industrious apprentice or to a faithful servant, as that of a SHARE of a LOTTERY TICKET, in a scheme in which the smallest share may gain near two thousand pounds. (*Bells Weekly Messenger*, 22 December 1806)

George Packwood, Charles Wright, Moses and George Robins were identified as leading figures in this style, of which Robins's description of an estate for sale – 'but there are two drawbacks to the property, the litter of rose leaves and the noise of the nightingales!' – is typical (Anon., 1855: 211). The prevalence of the literary style can also be judged from the commentary it attracted. Numerous critical discussions of advertising, ranging in tone from outrage to parody, appeared in the first half of the nineteenth century. The 'art and mystery' of this 'commercial magic' (Montgomery, 1828: 3) and 'the ingenuity (not to say impudence) of the soothing but delusive generalisations' (Burn, 1855: 190) did not go unremarked. Explicit parodies of the literary approach were common, with pseudonymous offerings by 'Herbert Dryasdust' in *Punch* (1842), 'Warreniana' (c.1830, BL) and Master Trimmer (1826). Warreniana casts the notorious advertiser of blacking, Robert Warren, in a duel with the devil.

> The sneer of a friend to your puffs you may fix
> But if what is worse you assert that your Styx
> Surpasses my blacking (t'was clear he was vexed)
> By Jove! You will ne'er stick at anything next
> I have dandies at Paine's and Almack's
> Despite Day and Martin those emulous quacks
> And they all in one spirit of concert agree
> That my blacking is better than any black sea

Satirical responses are an indication that literary advertisements were understood not as simple information but as beguiling inducements that an unsuspecting public – especially women, 'the amiable and gentile wives and daughters' (Smith, 1853: 279) – had to be protected from. They may now appear crude, but florid language and rhyme were devices that articulated well with the environment in which they were used. Rhymes are memorable, and provide an efficient way of ensuring recall – a core function of all advertising.

Nevertheless, by the third quarter of the century this style of copy had given way to new trends, including topical copy, competitions, gimmicks and bizarre, extravagant claims. Editorial styles of copy had been used throughout the century, particularly in the book trade, but these became increasingly popular and aimed either to disguise advertising as editorial matter or to establish topical connections. Rowell (1870: 14) describes Charles Knox's advertising as always connected 'with some topic or event which is the conversation of the hour. [For example] "… *Although Queen Isabella has lost her crown the crown of Knox's hats never come out, as everyone who purchases them at the corner of Broadway and Fulton will testify".*'

These changing vogues in literary and topical copy make sense in the context of the specific occupational arrangements adopted in practice. As described in Chapter 5, the early part of the century saw writers and poets preparing advertising copy, by later in the century this role was often taken on by newspaper people. Neither trend was settled or universal; nor were occupational groups characterised by the degree of specialisation typical today, making it unremarkable for newspaper proprietors, advertising agents, poets, shopkeepers or manufacturer to write copy. Nonetheless, it seems likely that the involvement of particular occupational groups in a self-referential medium did help to produce and reproduce particular styles in advertising copy, with well-known advertisements spawning many imitators in a similar style.

This is also evident in the shifts in copy style that took place in the last quarter of the century. By this time one of the more significant changes in the organisation of advertising production – the establishment of the full-service agency system – was well underway. This had a far-reaching impact on forms of written appeal. As mentioned above, the developing institutional structure was characterised by a desire to formalise and professionalise the production of advertising. In the moves to redefine advertising as a systematic, scientific and professional activity, agency control of copy preparation, exemplified in the notion of the 'campaign', became increasingly attractive. This was to make the sober style of 'reason-why' copy one of the most popular rhetorical devices by the turn of the century (see Presbrey, 1929). As the name suggests, 'reason-why' was built around the principle of providing a reason for purchase. It essentially involves the same principle as Rosser Reeve's Unique Selling Proposition (USP), which became the orthodoxy of the 1960s. Although generally considered an invention of the late nineteenth century, many earlier advertisements make a 'reason-why' appeal in articulating a specific argument for purchase. The new 'reason-why' might be distinguished not so much by the style of appeal itself, but by its use as part of a more standardised system of trade practices and knowledge. Around this time articles and books began to appear debating advertising and copy technique (Gentle, 1870; Rowell 1870; Fowler, 1889; Maxwell, 1904). This new body of literature was part of the move to a more formalised agency system, and helped disseminate ideas about effective practice. The appeal of reason-why was enhanced by the success of John Power's work in the 1870s and 1880s. Powers wrote clear, economical and sincere reason-based copy on a freelance basis for department stores like Wanamaker's. Against the tide of florid, extravagant copy claims, Power's advertisements stood out.

The tidy housekeeper banishes flies; but one persistent buzzer sticks. The fly fan keeps him off while you dine or doze in peace. It IS a luxury! Winds like a clock, goes an hour and a half and costs $3.00 – best machine $4.00; the latter with nickeled base, $6.50; with decorated-china base, $7.50. It is worth a hundred dollars; send it back if it isn't. (Powers, c.1884 quoted in Presbrey, 1929: 308)

The growth in the trade literature provided an opportunity for the 'Powers method' to be spread by writer-practitioners like George Rowell, and it began to be widely adopted in both the US and the UK. In his history of Lever's advertising agency Lintas, Sharpe (1964) describes how copy like William Lever's and Sydney Gross's for Sunlight soap: 'Why does a woman look old sooner than a man? Put a man at a washing tub, let him get heated with the hot suds until every pore is opened', caught attention in an era dominated by reiterated superlatives.

These examples highlight how difficult it is to assess the rhetorical, persuasive elements of advertising outside the historical context of production. The various historical debates and advertisements featured throughout this section testify to the existence of a detailed understanding among early practitioners and critics of the persuasive work successful advertisements had to do. However anachronistic the technique adopted might seem 'now', it is clear that 'then' many practitioners wanted their advertisements not simply to inform but to dazzle, entertain, amuse and, most importantly, persuade. The rhetorical strategies adopted to achieve this end have varied enormously over the years, but these different strategies should be considered in the context of the production system, for the simple reason that production has a formative influence on style. The involvement of occupational groups like writers, poets and journalists, the ongoing restrictions on visual display, and the growth of the agency system all contributed to the popularity of particular styles of verbal appeal at different stages. These factors were at least as important to the prevalence of different copy styles as more generalised beliefs and ideas about consumers and markets, and whether they had to be persuaded or simply informed.

the emotions: going for the jugular

They made her a grave too cold and damp
For a soul so honest and true
If they had been wise the dire necessity of opening the grave for one so lovely might have been averted, since 'Plantation Bitters', if timely used, are sure to rescue the young and lovely, the middle aged and the ailing from confirmed sickness. (Plantation Bitters advertisement, c.1860, quoted in Rowell, 1870: 147)

What a pity that a young man, the hope of his country and the darling of his parents, should be snatched from all the prospects and enjoyments of life by the consequences of one unguarded moment. (Perry's Purifying Specific Pills advertisement, c.1830–40 quoted in Nevett, 1982: 35)

The emotional dimension of advertising is, in many theoretical and practitioner accounts, uniquely associated with the late twentieth century. The perceived transition to emotional messages, or from a 'Unique Selling Point' to an 'Emotional Selling Point' based on audio-visual techniques rather than verbal propositions has been widely understood as a phenomenon specific to the period after the 1980s (Mort, 1996; Nixon, 1996). There is no question that technological changes in the form and nature of advertising media alone have produced a new range of possibilities for visual and aural communication.

Nonetheless, one of the questions being raised in this section is whether these changes in practice and technique can be reasonably understood as a 'new' structure of emotional appeal. Advertisements grounded in an emotional form of appeal can be traced to the seventeenth century. In this section some of the background to these early precedents is reviewed to help assess whether emotional appeals are best understood as the product of any given media or techniques. The aim is to try to uncover the contingency of emotional advertisements upon the specific assemblage of practices, media and technologies in use at given historical moments.

Johnson's question of whether advertisements played with the 'passions' was prompted not by the use of sounds and images to tap emotion, but by the words offered to do the same. Advertisements, he complained, promised and threatened too much. One particularly ruthless advertisement he cited was for a heavily advertised proprietary, the anodyne necklace.

> The true pathos of advertisements must have sunk deep into the heart of every man that remembers the zeal shown by the seller of the anodyne necklace, for the ease and safety of poor, toothing infants, and the affection with which he warned every mother, that she would never forgive herself if her infant should perish without a necklace. (Johnson, 1759: 226)

The anodyne necklace adverts, and those quoted above for Plantation Bitters and Perry's Purifying Specifics, use fear as a method of appeal. They rely upon the invocation of dire consequences arising from failure to use the product, and have had an enduring popularity in some categories of advertising. One of the most common of these in more contemporary advertising targets the fear of social embarrassment. This is particularly prevalent in certain product categories, especially those aimed at self-presentation and personal hygiene. Among the most influential campaigns of this type was one for Odorono deodorant prepared by the agency James Walter Thompson (JWT) from 1916. Deodorants at this time were a new, untested product, and extremely difficult to apply. In view of these challenges, the agency conducted research into the deodorant market to help target the campaign.

> This investigation developed the facts that Odorono was used by 22% of the women, competing products by 19%, and no deodorant by 59%. Of this 59% of non-users, 47% insisted that they did not need a deodorant. These facts were of the utmost importance. Obviously many of the women were incorrect in their statement that they did not need a deodorant. They did; they simply were not conscious of the fact. It was our task to make them realise it, and this furnished our advertising task with a new objective ... The need for a powerful appeal, yet one that was subtle to an unusual degree. (Account files, Box 13, JWTa)

The perceived need for a 'powerful appeal' provided the basis for James Webb Young's 1919 copy appeal 'within the curve of a women's arm'. The lengthy text, illustrated by a couple dancing, the woman's arm upraised, revealed the risk of inadvertently 'offending'. This mild-mannered reference to female perspiration caused outrage and resulted in 200 cancelled subscriptions to the *Ladies' Home Journal*. But it also increased sales by 112%. As a result, playing on similar fears of olfactory offensiveness became, and remains, standard practice in deodorant advertising.

This example suggests a relationship between the type of appeal, specific working practices and the nature of the product itself. The product, market context and particular methods of production can all act to pattern the type of appeal used. In the case of Odorono, JWT's use of market research and their sensitivity to the resistance the product was likely to encounter convinced them to use a potentially offensive, but strongly persuasive type of appeal. Products and markets in this respect do not determine the appeal; there is always a range of possibilities, but there is a relationship. This point is supported by the predominance of particular forms of appeal in particular product categories. Perfume adverts tend not to be based upon technical specification, whilst adverts for agricultural equipment tend not to rely on romantic appeals. This should not be taken to imply that these tendencies are simply dictated by the nature of the product. Rather, the nature of the product combines with the existence of particular practices, knowledge and precedents in the industry to mediate in favour of particular types of approach.

That this relationship is sometimes unpredictable emerges in another JWT campaign, for Chase and Sanborn's tea. This campaign employed an emotional appeal couched around the notion that tea has invigorating and stimulating qualities. According to *Fortune*, Chase and Sanborn's sales increased by several hundred per cent after the campaign; a particularly notable achievement as the company was one of the smaller players in the US's difficult, saturated tea market. American tea advertising at that point tended to be based on price, brand and flavour, making the JWT campaign a radical departure. According to agency records the campaign was informed by product research into the chemical composition of tea. This 'produced' a substance, *theol*, which was emphasised in the advertising. *Theol* was in fact a collective name for the fragrant oils present in tea. As such it has no chemical properties as a stimulant, but that was not the point.

J. Walter Thompson declared that Chase and Sanborn's tea was richer in *theol*, and that Chase and Sanborn's tea 'sways the senses' and provides an *emotional lift*. But nowhere did J. Walter Thompson actually say that the emotional lift was due to the *theol*. (*Fortune*, 1933: 38)

Senses are *Stirred*

Senses *Aroused*

An *Emotional lift*

Lifts your Senses up

Sways *the Senses*

Emotions Respond

to this tea—*richer* in theol

EXPERIENCE has taught Oriental races the beneficial effects of *tea*. They choose it because it stirs the senses . . . enriches emotional life . . . with no later, unfavorable reaction.

To get *all* the benefits of tea, it is important that you choose a tea rich in theol. This oil is the very essence— it carries the flavor and fragrance.

Chase & Sanborn's *Tender Leaf* Tea contains more of the precious theol than any but the most expensive blends. Picked during the dry season, the tender leaves which compose it are at the peak of flavor—and effectiveness.

Your grocer has this tea in quarter-pound and half-pound screw-top canisters.

Chase & Sanborn's *Tender Leaf* Tea

Courtesy Standard Brands, Inc.

WILL TEA BE MORE IMPORTANT TO THE NATION?

Figure 6.7

1930s Advertisement for Chase & Sanborn's tea (Source: Tea for Sale, Fortune, August 1935)

Product research in this instance helped provide JWT with a distinctive platform for the campaign, but the relationship between the research and the campaign is far from straightforward. The research was not designed to discover the 'truth' about tea, but to generate ideas. These ideas were then filtered through the individuals, their working practices and the agency culture – and the final campaign is thus configured by all these processes. It is also clear that JWT did not expect the emotional punch of the campaign to be carried by any individual element, but rather by a combination of typography, artwork and copy. Emotional appeals may thus be produced through different mechanisms, combining different elements, techniques and media.

The diverse, plural and contingent nature of emotional appeals also emerges in one of JWT's most famous historical campaigns, for Woodbury's soap (see Figure 6.8). The Woodbury's campaign, managed by JWT between 1910 and 1927, marks a decisive point in the development of JWT's approach to advertising. It was one of the first major campaigns produced during the transitional period from the management philosophy of James Walter Thompson to the very different one favoured by Stanley and Helen Resor. When JWT first took on the Woodbury's account sales were down, and the appropriation to be spent on advertising was cut from $253,000 to $25,000. Such a small appropriation intensified the need for memorable advertising. In addition, both the nature of the market and the product's history played a role in the strategy adopted. The product had previously been advertised to its predominantly female market using a proprietary-medicine appeal style which stressed, in fairly graphic terms, the soap's benefits as a 'treatment' for unsightly skin conditions. JWT was anxious to depart from this rapidly aging style, and aim instead for an address which was 'personal and human', but also 'scientific, restrained and dignified', and informed by insights emerging from psychology (Account Files, Box 1, JWTa).

This was to be embodied in an emotional appeal which graphically depicted the ultimate benefit resulting from the use of Woodbury's, an appeal selling masculine admiration and feminine envy as much as the product, and epitomised in the now world famous slogan 'a skin you love to touch'. (Account Files, Box 1, JWTa)

The copy, 'a skin you love to touch', was probably first written around 1912 by Helen Resor as part of a longer advertisement, before being picked up as a headline by another copywriter, James Webb Young, in 1914. While JWT's account files emphasise the planned and deliberate nature of the campaign, it is also clear that the final campaign was the outcome of a tentative and collective production process. The famous copy was not originally written as a slogan; its subsequent adoption as such occurred only after the

Mail the coupon below for a large size, full-color reproduction of this new pastel. It makes a very lovely picture.

A skin you love to touch

Painted by F. Graham Cootes

Why it is so rare

A skin you love to touch is rarely found because so few people really understand the skin and its needs.

They neglect it, then use some powerful remedy; or they take excessive care of it for a time, then forget it.

In fact, a famous professor of dermatology has repeatedly declared that few persons ever really cleanse their faces.

And that a skin which is not kept scrupulously clean, with its pores fresh and clear, is a constant invitation to various skin disorders.

This spasmodic care and neglect will never produce "a skin you love to touch."

Make this treatment a daily habit

Begin now to take *your* skin seriously.

You *can* make it what you would love to have it because, like the rest of your body, your skin is continually changing.

As the old skin dies and the new forms, you have an opportunity to make the new skin what you want it to be.

Just before retiring, rub in gently a warm water lather of Woodbury's Facial Soap—until the skin is softened, the pores opened and the face feels fresh and clean. Rinse in cooler water, then apply cold water—the colder the better—for a full minute. Whenever possible, rub your face for a few minutes with a piece of ice. Always dry the skin thoroughly.

Use this treatment persistently for ten days or two weeks and your skin will show a marked improvement. Use Woodbury's regularly thereafter, and before long your skin will take on that finer texture, that greater freshness and clearness of "a skin you love to touch."

Woodbury's Facial Soap is the work of a skin specialist. It is the result of thirty years' study of the skin and its needs. You will never know what a difference a soap can make in your skin until you try Woodbury's.

Woodbury's costs 25c a cake. No one hesitates at the price after their first cake. As a matter of fact it is not expensive, for it wears from two to three times as long as the ordinary soap. Tear off the illustration of the cake shown below and put it in your purse as a reminder to get Woodbury's today. Begin at once to get its benefits.

Woodbury's Facial Soap

JOHN H. WOODBURY'S FACIAL SOAP

John H. Woodbury

Sold by dealers everywhere throughout the United States and Canada.

* Mail coupon today for a copy of the beautiful picture above

A limited number of enlargements of the beautiful new picture by F. Graham Cootes, shown above, have been printed. They are lithographed in six colors, in soft, opalescent tones, which make them very lovely. The size is about four times as large as the picture shown here. No advertising matter appears on it. We will send you this large reproduction in full colors, and a cake of Woodbury's Facial Soap, large enough for a week's treatment, for 10c. Send for them now as the number of pictures is limited. Mail this coupon today. Address

The Andrew Jergens Co.
Dept. I-D, Cincinnati, O.
In Canada, address The Andrew Jergens Co., Ltd., Dept. I-D, Perth, Ontario

I enclose 10c for a full-color enlargement of F. Graham Cootes' new drawing, "A Skin You Love to Touch," and a cake of Woodbury's Facial Soap, large enough for one week's treatment.

Name

City   State
In Canada, address The Andrew Jergens Co., Ltd., Perth, Ontario

Figure 6.8

1914 Woodbury's Soap – 'emotional appeal' (Source: Andrew Jergen's Company, Account Files Box 1, JWTa)

emotional tone of the appeal was established as a definite success. The first advertisements JWT produced were actually much less romantic in tone, featuring a more cautious mixture of emotional and treatment-based appeals. It was only in view of the response to the emotional dimensions of the campaign that this aspect was further developed. Similarly, when sales began to fall back in the 1920s the company started to move away from this strategy, employing a range of treatment- and testimonial-based appeals in an attempt to regain the high performance of the previous decade. Through the success of campaigns like Woodbury's, JWT developed a reputation for expertise in emotional types of appeal.

> Again the Thompson Company, through Mr and Mrs Resor, was the first to recognise the possibility that psychology could contribute to the advertising business. That recognition grew out of the firm conviction that the emotions played the major part in the influencing of people to buy specific products. Whereas Lord & Thomas had been built largely on reason-why, the J. Walter Thompson company was built on a more complete recognition of the power of the emotions. Even today, I feel that heritage of emotional advertising still characterises the company. (Resor's File, Dawkins Papers; Officers and Staff series, Box 1, JWTa)

This reputation testifies to the strength of the belief within JWT, and other sectors of the industry at the time, that insights from the emerging discipline of psychology could be deployed 'scientifically' to produce more effective advertising. As the file notes remark, JWT's approach was sharply contrasted with the 'reason-why' method favoured by agencies like Lord & Thomas. 'Reason-why' and 'emotion' represent the two main approaches informing advertising practice in the period from 1880 to 1930. Curti (1967) and McMahon (1972) reviewed the premises informing the trade literature in this period and identified two opposing conceptions of the consumer, as inherently emotional and unreasonable on the one hand, and inherently logical and reasonable on the other. This dichotomy of emotion versus reason has had an enduring hold on practitioners, and remains a frequent source of debate in the trade press.

Yet, as important as such stylistic differences are, practitioners and theorists tend to overplay the opposition between reason- and emotion-based appeals. No matter how vociferously the differences between 'reason-why' agencies like Lord & Thomas and the psychological approach of JWT were articulated, in practice the techniques of production used in both agencies were probably very similar. Such assertions often say as much about agencies' own brand differentiation as they do about tangible differences in technique.[13] Furthermore, at some level even the most reasoned advertising appeal is, at the same time, an emotional appeal. As Curti notes, the appeal to consumers on the basis of their capacities for logic, discrimination and reason was often selected by those practitioners who perceived it to be flattering and a neat fit with the way consumers preferred to see themselves. In addition, in many emotion-based campaigns, like those for Odorono and Woodbury's soap, or even the eighteenth-century anodyne necklace ads, emotion is the reason for purchase.

Once again, the argument presented here is that emotion should be recognised as a dimension of appeal that is not resident within particular elements of advertising or facilities of media, but is contingent upon the system of production. Emotional appeals can thus be articulated quite clearly in written copy, as well as in image- or sound-based media, though the latter may well enlarge the possibilities. The visual and aural environment of late-twentieth-century advertising certainly produced new mechanisms for 'tapping emotion', but this, in itself, is not evidence of an unprecedented discovery of the promotional potential of 'emoting'. The emphasis on contemporary advertising as uniquely emotional may fit neatly into epochal diagnoses of our contemporary consumption-driven and 'aestheticised' society, but the evidence presented here suggests that early advertisers also had a well-developed comprehension of the selling potential of emotions. The methods they selected for doing so reveal far more about the local exigencies of context and circumstance than they do about the state of their promotional imagination.

concluding comments   Of all the attributes used to singularise contemporary advertisements, persuasiveness – judged as a combined outcome of the increased significance of images, rhetoric and emotions – is the most fundamental, and therefore the appropriate focus for a reconsideration of historical advertising. This reconsideration was not meant to demonstrate that pre-twentieth-century advertising, as a whole, was equally, more or less persuasive than contemporary versions, but rather that persuasiveness is always contingent upon the conditions of production. Thus direct comparisons of the persuasive capacity of twentieth-century television ads and eighteenth-century press advertisements based solely on text are of limited value. Both the texts and contexts of advertising have changed so much over time that some historical reconstruction is necessary before any assessment of their aims and intent can be attempted. In an effort to drive home the substance of these changes, this chapter reviewed the different ways in which different forms of advertising – puffs, advertisements and campaigns – have been defined historically by the context of their use. This line of argument was sustained throughout to help uncover the specific forces shaping the use of images, copy and emotional appeals at given moments.

Discussion of the historical role of the image and other forms of visual promotion uncovered the irregular path travelled by image-based advertisements. The development of images, in press advertising in particular, was patchy and uneven, with certain sectors of the press featuring display and illustrated adverts at certain times, while others did not. These mixed fortunes were driven by the interaction of technological limitations, a draconian politico-economic environment imposed in the form of stamp and advertisement duties, and a newspaper culture oppositional to display on a capricious mixture of grounds. Advertisers nevertheless sought by various means to design visually provocative advertising to be carried in the press, or failing that on posters and other media. Broadsides, handbills, tradecards and posters were not subject to the same restrictions as press advertising, and featured a range of type effects, including colour, small woodcuts and sometimes elaborate illustrations. Printed advertising, however, does not appear to have been used as a stand-alone medium; rather, it was deployed in conjunction with other media – banners, placard-bearers, exhibitions and carnival attractions – to produce a visual environment which was fundamentally calculated to act as a commercial stimulus. A very active visual imagination was thereby put to promotional uses in a way uniquely adapted to the particular historical circumstances.

This sort of contextual specialisation was also evident in the discussion of persuasive, rhetorical copy. Here, different styles of verbal appeal were considered in the context of the contemporary comment they attracted, and of the production system in which they featured. This crystallises the awkward truth that no matter how incomprehensible, bland or anachronistic historical copy might seem now, contemporary critics saw it differently. While critical reactions varied enormously they were united by an underlying preoccupation with advertising's capacity to have an effect. This is not the reaction that a simple, informational medium might be expected to provoke, and it signals the inadequacy of decontextualised readings of advertising copy. The popularity of the two main styles of copy featured – literary puffing and 'reason-why' – is explicable not by an overarching philosophy of consumption, but by their fit with the context of production. Literary puffing provided an efficient means of producing memorable copy, crucial in a context in which the use of images was so tightly circumscribed. Its popularity was also related to the involvement of freelancing poets and writers in the preparation of copy. Similarly, 'reason-why' gained ground as part of a broader institutional move away from 'carnivalesque' promotional styles towards more sober, rationalised, agency styles.

My argument was finally applied to the use of emotional strategies of appeal. Here, in contrast to the emphasis in some theoretical accounts, it was suggested that emotional appeals were neither specific to audio-visual media nor the exclusive preserve of the late twentieth century. Rather, emotional appeals exist in a variety of forms, and defined as such they have variable precedents. The surge in popularity in the early twentieth century of a new style of emotional appeal, in agencies like JWT, was partly enabled by the tools and knowledge emerging from psychology, but it was also shaped by the interaction of a range of forces, including the nature of products, markets and methods of production. The dichotomy between reason- and emotion-based advertising in any case caricatures the range of advertising propositions, all of which are at some level designed to produce an emotional response. No matter how they may look from a contemporary perspective, advertisements are never entirely 'innocent' in the sense invoked by critical theorists keen to draw a distinction between the manipulative accomplishments of present-day advertisers and the quaint announcements of their predecessors. Even information-rich advertisements seek to persuade – it is just that in certain contexts some strategies appear more likely to achieve that outcome than others.

notes

1 See Anonymous (1855), *Advertisements* Sampson (1874), Presbrey (1929), Hower (1939) and Rowsome (1959).

2 The attitude of many librarians and archivists to advertising can be illustrated by the common practice of removing the advertising sections of many magazines and journals prior to binding. See Rowsome (1959) and Pope (1983).

3 Caxton's advertisement of *The Pyes of Salisbury* around 1477 is often described as the first printed advertisement. See Anonymous (1855); *Advertisements* Sampson (1874); Presbrey (1929); Elliot (1962) and Nevett (1982) for discussions of the dates of the first advertisements.

4 Sampson (1874) and Anonymous (1855) *Advertisements* quote numerous examples of announcements in this vein.

5 See for example Spottiswoode's *The Triangle* (1909), Spottiswoode's Box, HAT archive; Sell's Services Presentation document c.1910 SL53, Sell's Box, HAT archive.

6 See also www.cc.gla.ac.uk/courses/scottish/ballads/.

7 See for example Bartholomew Faire: *A collection of advertisements,* [1687/1849 London], BL; Lysons, Daniel c.1825 *Collectanea,* BL; *Collection of Ballads, Broadsides etc,* BL; Daniel, George (compiler) c.1860 *A collection of illustrations,* 1746–1860, BL; Sivewright, (1820) BOD.

8 See Bellion (2002) on the widespread public fascination with optical tricks during this era.

9 See Chapter 5.

10 For more discussion of these tensions see Lears (1994) and Bogart (1995).

11 Addison's (1710) essay is another famous example, but other lesser-known parodies regularly featured in publications like the *Spectator,* the *Idler* and later *Punch.*

12 See also Chapter 2.

13 Nixon (1996) makes a similar point about agencies like Saatchi & Saatchi who marketed themselves as 'global' in the 1980s, and Bartle, Bogle & Hegarty's 'creative boutique' brand.

conclusion: devices and desires

It should be obvious that there is nothing like an economy out there unless and until men construct such an object. (Dumont, 1977: 24)

In this economy, inhabited by actors who are real professionals in product qualification and the profiling of goods, consumers are constantly prompted to question their preferences and tastes and finally, through the explicit debates that that implies their own social identity. ... Consumption becomes both more rational (not that the consumer is more rational but because (distributed) cognition devices become infinitely richer, more sophisticated and reflexive) and more emotional (consumers are constantly referred to the construction of their social identity since their choices and preferences become objects of deliberation: the distinction of products and social distinction are part of the same movement). (Callon et al., 2002: 212)

Callon et al. refer above to the upsurge of 'reflexive activity' in the emerging form of economic organisation they characterise as the 'economy of qualities'. The 'economy of qualities' turns on dynamic, reflexive processes of qualification and requalification of products and services facilitated by forms of organisation and socio-technical devices that act to enhance and intensify the links between consumption and production. Advertising is cast as one such socio-technical device equipped to offer consumers an ever-more refined basis on which to calculate and form preferences from the expanding array of 'qualities' on offer. As part of an apparatus that also comprises design, marketing and distribution, advertising refers subjects back to consumption as the crucial terrain upon which to negotiate their social identities. Once more advertising is thereby implicated in a profound epochal shift in the character of consumption, but this time to a more reflexive, and thus, a simultaneously 'more rational' and 'more emotional' basis. The debt here to theorists like Beck, Giddens, and Lash and Urry, who have sought to define the contemporary era as one of 'late', 'reflexive' modernity is clear (Beck et al., 1994; Lash & Urry, 1994), and, on the evidence presented throughout this book, much to be regretted.

Callon's formulation of economies and markets as defined and formatted by specific techniques, tools and devices was signalled in the Introduction as a productive way of thinking about advertising. Considered as a socio-technical device, advertising can be seen, by articulating the features, benefits and target consumers of specific products, to play a formative role in the definition – or the ongoing qualification and requalification – of markets. An investigation of how the operation of the mundane, material practices of advertising 'perform' markets, it was proposed through Chapters 1 to 3, offers a promising alternative to the textual hermeneutics which have thus far dominated critical work. Such an approach was advocated as a way of reinstating the significance of production-side activities to a field dominated by consumption-side analyses. It was, however – and this is where my disagreement with Callon et al.'s recent characterisation of the emerging economy comes into play – also advocated as a way to counter the anti-historical historicisisation of advertising in critical literature. This term is meant to invoke those narratives which describe advertising's evolution in reach and potency as the symbiotic companion of 'modernity', but which do not trouble to offer any detail of the past against which contemporary advertising is contrasted.

It is unfortunate that Callon's otherwise acute and sensitive portrayal of the role of calculative agencies, tools and devices in formatting the economic gives in to the epochal imperative that drives so much recent social theory. Aside from the tendency encapsulated so succinctly by Osborne (1998) to overdramatise and reduce the characteristics of social change, epochal theory runs on a kind of obsessive presentism that seems either unable or unwilling to do more than gesture to the past. Material, empirical circumstances are discounted, ignored or forgotten in the dualistic urge to differentiate what prevailed then from what is happening now. The past is thereby idealised or caricatured as the other to present circumstances. Nowhere is this more true than in the field of consumption and promotion, and the immediate casualty of this is our understanding of the scale, ingenuity and importance of prior promotional practices. A related consequence of course is the exaggeration of the novelty of the present, so that the character of contemporary consumption, and by extension promotion, is forever to be redefined in terms of a basis in desires, not needs; or symbolism, not instrumentality; or finally, in Callon et al.'s version, in the growth of rationality and emotionalism over, it can only be surmised, crude guesswork and functionality.

But if Callon and other theorists working to apply insights from the anthropology of science and techniques (AST) to the study of markets (Cochoy, 1998; Miller, 1998; Law, 2002; Slater, 2002a, 2002b) are correct in signalling the performative action of devices like advertising, it is reasonable to conclude that this is not a recently acquired characteristic. Buck-Morss (1995) traces the 'discovery' of the contemporary sense of economy back to the eighteenth century, when the processes of trade and exchange began to assume an increasing centrality in the everyday life of communities. Discovering the economy, of course, was not the result of an archaeological-style unearthing, but of the application of specific processes, tools and techniques. As Buck-Morss argues, in order for the economy to be envisioned it had to be inserted in a process of representational mapping which initially borrowed heavily from the tools of navigational mapping. Gradually an array of other techniques began to be developed to map, chart, measure and display the economy. This sort of representational work, as argued in Chapter 3, is absolutely intrinsic to 'thinking' the economy (see also Miller & Rose, 1990; du Gay, 1997; Miller, 2001). Representational work inevitably involves a kind of generative abstraction through which economic elements are codified and accorded material significance. This is not simply a matter of putting the economy into language, but is bound up with the development of those practices of calculation that constitute the economic.

Now, it is clear that the recent 'turn to the economy' in the anthropology of science and techniques has addressed itself in particular to the emergence of new calculative practices and the ways in which they 'alter the capacities of agents, organizations and the connections among them' (Miller, 2001: 379; Callon et al., 2002). This is an important line of enquiry, but not one that should obscure the productive consequences of older calculative practices. Perhaps the most significant insight for the sociology of economic life to come out of AST is a renewed commitment to the principle that economies and markets are not given, but the outcome of specific configurative processes. Clearly, this is a principle long accepted by those working within a broadly Foucauldian tradition of discursive constitution, among others (Dumont, 1977; Miller & Rose, 1990; Rose, 1990) but, as argued in Chapter 3, the particular contribution of AST has been to focus detailed attention on the productive or performative effects of mundane tools and practices. It makes little sense, however, to concentrate such an insight on new and emerging forms of economic organisation, when its distinction lies within the capacity to frame the interdependence between particular circumstances, agencies and forms of calculation at any given historical moment.

Callon et al.'s focus on the emergence of the 'economy of qualities' may be designed to articulate this sort of an interdependence, but the contention here is that in extrapolating a whole new form of reflexive consumption from an array of socio-technical devices and practices, Callon et al. have taken the argument into quite different theoretical terrain. This is terrain in which the minutiae of the local and specific give way to the global and the general; so, more prosaically, the distributive logic governing supermarket shelving practices becomes part and parcel of a shift to reflexive consumption. Perhaps Callon et al. are correct, and an unprecedented shift in the character of consumption is underway. But, as argued in Chapters 2 and 3, this is very familiar ground, and at the simplest level it raises questions about the past in which consumers did not reflect carefully on their consumption choices and did not relate them to their social status and identity. The evidence presented throughout Chapters 5 and 6 sought to show that advertising has had an enduring presence as a socio-technical device tuned to promote consumption through a wide variety of means, and certainly through both rational argument and emotional persuasion. Advertising is an extraordinarily mutable device that has assumed a diverse array of forms, incorporated divergent practices and utilised a vast assemblage of different institutions and media. Its shifting forms clearly relate to the exigencies of circumstance, whether technological, institutional or statutory, but it is much less clear that any protracted change in practice occurred in response to a substantive change in the character of consumption. Indeed the diversity of forms assumed by both promotional devices and the consumption practices they target makes it difficult to justify talking in terms of a single mode or character of promotion and consumption at all (cf. Fine & Leopold, 1993).

The underlying object of this book has been to demonstrate how a genealogical approach to advertising as a commercial, socio-technical device can both enhance understanding of its historical role and problematise teleological accounts which view advertising as an institution whose current potency derives from much larger transformative processes. As was argued through Chapters 1 to 3, contemporary advertising is characterised as a persuasive, pervasive and hybrid institution because the commodity logic driving 'capitalist' or 'consumer' societies requires it to be so. Underpinning this critical assertion is the belief that historical advertising functioned differently. Advertising at earlier historical moments is characterised as something of a rarity, deployed, where at all, to meet the 'simple', 'informational' objective of announcing the availability of goods. The investigation of the institutions, practices and products that have historically constituted advertising presented in Chapters 5 and 6 reveals a somewhat different picture. Advertising does not emerge from this as the product of a steady evolution, but as a plural and multifaceted *device* that is constantly adapting, in often contradictory ways, to changing circumstances. As Treasure notes, in advertising

conflicting trends and sub-trends emerge and disappear, ideas are expressed which find fulfilment many years later ... and organisations are transmuted into different forms so subtly that it is very difficult to pin down when change has actually taken place. (Treasure, 1977: 27)

Uneven and contradictory patterns of change are the result of advertising's sensitivity, in the first instance, not to the determinate economic or cultural logic underlying the singular character of consumption, but to immediate contextual circumstances. These circumstances or 'singular events' are the haphazard outcomes of entangled relations between the various players constituting the field of production. It demands a considerable effort of theoretical will to redraw them as small parts of an ideal, teleological continuity (Foucault, 1984b: 88). Formative events in advertising history, like stamp duty, were the result of particular politico-economic circumstances, and undoubtedly shaped the practice of advertising in identifiable ways, but not as part of a journey to a preordained destination.

There is, then, a disjuncture between critical characterisations of advertising and what can be surmised about historical practices. Throughout the book it has been posited that this disjuncture arises for both theoretical and empirical reasons. Theoretically, the representation of advertising as a medium whose evolution is a function of much larger transformational processes is extraordinarily powerful and compelling. Close examination of what such explanations involve in Chapters 1, 2 and 3 revealed a steady recurrence of certain themes, ways of thinking and modes of conceptualising key categories. The baseline critical understanding of advertising has been as a transformational medium acting upon meaning and reality, subjects and objects, and culture and economy, to reconfigure the nature of these entities and the relations between them. In Chapter 1, for instance, it was proposed that semiotic explanations of advertising derive their cogency from a materialist conception of meaning as properly based in an authentic reality. Chapter 2, meanwhile, posited that the transformational account of advertising required an essentialist conception of the continuity of human beings outside commodity systems of production. This line of argument was taken further in Chapter 3, with a review of the conceptualisation of culture and economy in critiques of advertising. In each instance, critical narratives about the role and impact of contemporary advertising employed very specific but not uncontested approaches to salient categories. In particular, categories like meaning, subjects and culture are deployed as if, outside the reconstitutive action of commodity systems of production, they had a fairly stable, bounded, ahistorical essence. But historical, anthropological and philosophical work acts as a reminder that such categories do not have a stable ontology, but are defined and instantiated through specific techniques and institutional formations external to themselves. 'Meaning', 'the subject' and 'culture' are meta-theoretical categories that should not be presumed to have a necessary continuity outside the strictly delimited context of their application. Rather, their contingency on historical and anthropological conditions external to themselves begs to be acknowledged.

Empirically, critical characterisations of the historical development of advertising have been hampered by their approach to evidence. As outlined in Chapter 4, despite offering a very particular narrative concerning the historical development of advertising, many of the most influential treatments include nothing substantive in the way of historical evidence, but base assertions on the changing nature of advertising simply on observations about the contemporary situation. It is entirely reasonable that theoretical accounts of advertising need not also be historical accounts, but where they are underscored by a teleological argument they should surely offer more than a discussion of the characteristics assumed to differentiate advertising in 'ideal type' economies. The argument advanced in Chapter 5 was that documenting increases in the pervasiveness or culturalisation of advertising is much less straightforward than critical accounts imply. Close historical study of advertising institutions, practices and products offers little solid evidence in support of the view that early advertising can be clearly distinguished from contemporary advertising along the lines so frequently described in these accounts. The evidence presented in Chapters 5 and 6 indicates that such changes have been much overplayed, leaving an impoverished account of the rich variety of the promotional field at different historical moments.

To be fair, a number of accounts do offer historical evidence (Ewen, 1976; Williams, 1980; Dyer, 1982; Leiss et al., 1986), but even these provide only a fairly sketchy and general outline of the development of specific institutions and practices. The historical development of the minutiae of industry practices is generally overshadowed by attention to advertising product, which is by far the most common sort of evidence presented in support of the evolutionary perspective. But, as Chapter 6 argues, interpretations of historical advertisements in the absence of any account of their context of production are scarcely an adequate guide to how they operated in their own time. An informed assessment has to consider the technological, organisational and institutional circumstances of production as these have a material import in shaping the final appearance of advertisements.

My concern throughout has been to offer a more informed history of advertising as a way of engaging with its characterisation in critical treatments. To this end, those criteria upon which the distinctiveness of contemporary advertising has so often been pinned – pervasiveness, hybridity and persuasiveness – have been reappraised in historical context. This exercise has highlighted the contingent, plural and differentiated nature of advertising. Advertising is inescapably the product of given historical circumstances, and it is entirely misleading to categorise the advertising of any era as a stage in the evolution of practitioners' knowledge. The history of advertising practice is marked by diversions and regressions as well as innovations, but any understanding of the significance of these has to make recourse to the context of production. This context is not just a matter of what was epistemologically possible, but also of what was technologically, legally, institutionally and organisationally possible. These contextual factors are of profound significance in shaping the practices, tools and techniques that have historically constituted advertising, and in turn the products, markets and consumers to which it addresses itself.

bibliography

published sources

Abbott, H. (1920) 'Doctor, Lawyer, Merchant, Chief – Which shall she be? Women's New Leadership in Business', *Ladies Home Journal*, July, 45 & 164.

Addison, J. (1710) *The Tatler* 224, Thursday, September 14.

Adorno, T. (1991) *The Culture Industry*. London & New York: Routledge.

Allen, J. and du Gay, P. (1994) 'Industry and the rest: the economic identity of service services', *Work, Employment and Society*, 8(2): 255–71.

Anderson, P. (1991) *The Printed Image and the Transformation of Popular Culture, 1790–1860*. Oxford: Oxford University Press.

Anonymous (1855) Advertisements. Art Vii. – 1, *Quarterly Review* cxciii, June.

Appadurai, A. (1986) *The Social Life of Things*. Cambridge: Cambridge University Press.

Baker, C. (1995) *Advertising Works 8*. Henley on Thames: NTC Publications Ltd.

Bakhtin, M. (1984) *Rabelais and his World*. Bloomington: Indiana University Press.

Barnard, M. (1995) 'Advertising: the rhetorical imperative', in C. Jenks (ed.) *Visual Culture*. London & New York: Routledge.

Barry, A. and Slater, D. (2002) 'Introduction: the technological economy', *Economy and Society*, 31(2): 194–217.

Barthes, R. (1967) *Elements of Semiology*. London: Jonathon Cape.

Barthes, R. (1973) 'Myth Today', in *Mythologies*. London: Paladin.

Barthes, R. (1977) 'The Rhetoric of the Image', in *Image – Music – Text*. London: Fontana.

Barthes, R. (1982) 'The Imagination of the Sign', in *Selected Writings*. London: Fontana.

Baudrillard, J. (1988a) 'Consumer Society', in M. Poster (ed.) *Selected Writings*. Cambridge: Polity Press.

Baudrillard, J. (1988b) 'The System of Objects', in M. Poster (ed.) *Selected Writings*. Cambridge: Polity.

Bauman, Z. (2000) *Liquid Modernity*. Cambridge: Polity.

Bauman, Z. (2001) 'Consuming Life', *Journal of Consumer Culture*, 1(1): 9–29.

Beck, U., Giddens, A. and Lash, S. (1994) *Reflexive Modernization, Politics, Tradition and Aesthetics in Modern Social Theory*. Cambridge: Polity.

Berger, J. (1972) *Ways of Seeing*. London: Penguin.

Bogart, M. (1995) *Artists, Advertising and the Borders of Art*. Chicago: University of Chicago Press.

Bourdieu, P. (1984) *Distinction: A Critique of the Judgement of Taste*. London: Routledge.

Bourdieu, P. (1993) *Sociology In Question*. London: Sage.

Buck-Morss, S. (1995) 'Envisioning Capital', *Critical Inquiry*, Winter: 434–67.

Burn, J. Dawson (1855) *The Language of the Walls, A Voice from the Shop Windows or the Mirror of Commercial Roguery*. London: Heywood.

Callon, M. (ed.) (1998a) 'Introduction: the embeddedness of economic markets in economics', *The Laws of the Market*. Oxford: Blackwell.

Callon, M. (1998b) 'An essay on framing and overflowing: economic externalities revisited by sociology', In Callon (ed.) *The Laws of the Market*.

Callon, M., Meadel, C. and Rabeharisoa, V. (2002) 'The economy of qualities', *Economy and Society*, 31(2): 194–217.

Campaign, (1998) *New Advertising Thinkers*, 24 July: 18–19.

Campbell, C. (1987) *The Romantic Ethic and the Spirit of Modern Consumerism*. Oxford: Blackwell.

Cochoy, F. (1998) 'Another discipline for the market economy: marketing as a performative knowledge and know-how for capitalism', in Callon (ed.) *The Laws of the Market*.

Cook, G. (1992) *The Discourse of Advertising*. London: Routledge.

Cousins, M. (1988) 'The Practice of Historical Investigation', in Attridge (ed.) *Poststructuralism and Questions of History*. Cambridge: Cambridge University Press.

Cronin, A. (2000) *Advertising and Consumer Citizenship: Gender, Images and Rights*. London: Routledge.

Cross, M. (ed.) (1996) *Advertising and Culture: Theoretical Perspectives*. Westport, CT: Praeger.

Curti, M. (1967) 'Changing concepts of human nature in the literature of American advertising', *Business History Review*, 41(4): 335–57.

Davidson, M. (1992) *The Consumerist Manifesto*. London: Routledge.

Davis, H. and Scase R. (2000) *Managing Creativity: The Dynamics of Work and Organisation*. Buckingham: Open University Press.

Dean, M. (1994) *Critical and Effective Histories: Foucault's Methods and Historical Sociology*. London: Routledge.

Deely, J. (1990) *Basics of Semiotics*. Bloomington, IN: Indiana University Press.

Derrick, P. (1907) 'The advertising agent as a factor in modern business', *Magazine of Commerce*, March.

du Gay, P. (1996) *Consumption and Identity at Work*. London: Sage.

du Gay, P. (ed.) (1997) *Production Of Culture/Cultures Of Production*. London: Sage.

du Gay, P. (2000) *In Praise of Bureaucracy*. London: Sage.

du Gay, P., Hall, S., Janes, L., Mackay, H., and Negus, K. (1997) *Doing Cultural Studies: The Story of the Sony Walkman*. London: Sage.

du Gay, P., Evans, J. and Redman, P. (eds) (2000) *Identity in Question*. London: Sage.

du Gay, P. and Pryke, M. (eds) (2002) *Cultural Economy*. London: Sage.

Dumont, L. (1977) *From Mandeville to Marx*. Chicago: University of Chicago Press.

Dunbar, D. (1979) 'The agency commission system in Britain: a first sketch of its history to 1941', *Journal of Advertising History* 2, January: 9–28.

Dyer, G. (1982) *Advertising as Communication*. London: Routledge.

Elliot, B.B. (1962) *A History of English Advertising*. London: Business Publications Ltd.

Ewen, S. (1976) *Captains of Consciousness: Advertising and the Social Roots of Consumer Culture*. New York: McGraw-Hill.

Falk, P. (1994) *The Consuming Body*. London: Sage.

Featherstone, M. (1991) *Consumer Culture and Postmodernism*. London: Sage.

Ferguson, H. (1992) 'Watching the world go round: atrium culture and the psychology of shopping', in R. Shields (ed.) *Lifestyle Shopping: The Subject of Consumption*. London: Routledge.

Field, E. (1959) *Advertising: The Forgotten Years*. London: Ernest Benn.

Fielding, H. (1741) Letter in the *Champion*, 19 December.

Fine, B. and Leopold, E. (1993) *The World of Consumption*. London: Routledge.

Fish, S. (1980) *Is There a Text in this Class?* Cambridge: Harvard University Press.

Fish, S. (1994) *There's No Such Thing as Free Speech: and it's a Good Thing Too!* New York, Oxford: Oxford University Press.

Fleming, T. (1976) 'How it was in Advertising: 1776–1976', *Advertising Age*, 19 April, 27–35.

Fortune (1933) 'Tea for Sale', August.

Foucault, M. (1972) *The Archaeology of Knowledge*. London: Tavistock.

Foucault, M. (1980) *Power/Knowledge*. Brighton: Harvester.

Foucault, M. (1981) 'Is it useless to revolt?' *Philosophy and Social Criticism*, 8: 5–9.

Foucault, M. (1982) 'Afterword; the subject and power', in Dreyfus and Rabinow, *Michel Foucault: Beyond Structuralism and Hermeneutics*. Brighton: Harvester.

Foucault, M. (1984a) 'What is Enlightenment', in Rabinow (ed.) *The Foucault Reader*. London: Penguin.

Foucault, M. (1984b) 'Nietzsche, genealogy, history', in Rabinow (ed.) *The Foucault Reader*. London: Penguin.

Fowler, N.O. (1889) *About Advertising and Printing*. Boston: L. Barta & Co.

Fowles, J. (1996) *Advertising and Popular Culture*. London: Sage.

Frederick, J.G. (1925) 'The story of advertising writing', in J.G. Frederick (ed.) *Masters of Advertising Copy*. New York: Frank-Maurice.

Galbraith, J.K. (1971/1958) *The Affluent Society*. Boston: Houghton Mifflin.

Gaukroger, S. (1986) 'Romanticism and decommodification: Marx's conception of socialism', *Economy and Society*, 15(3): 287–333.

Gentle, G. (1870) *Hints on Advertising Adapted to the Times*. London. British Library Catalogue.

George, D. (1926) 'The early history of Registry Offices', *Economic Journal: Economic History Supplement*, 1926–9: 570–90.

Giaccardi C. (1995) 'Television advertising and the representation of social reality: a comparative study', *Theory, Culture and Society*, 12: 109–31.

Glennie, P. (1995) 'Consumption within historical studies', in D. Miller (ed.) *Acknowledging Consumption*. London: Routledge.

Goffman, E. (1979) *Gender Advertisements*. London: Macmillan.

Goldman, R. (1992) *Reading Ads Socially*. London: Routledge.

Goldman, R. and Papson, S. (1994) 'Advertising in the age of hypersignification', *Theory, Culture and Society*, 11: 23–53.

Goldman, R. and Papson, S. (1996) *Sign Wars: The Cluttered Landscape of Advertising*. New York: Guilford.

Granovetter, M. (1985) 'Economic action and social structure: the problem of embeddedness', *American Journal of Sociology*, 91: 481–510.

Granovetter, M. (1992) 'Economic institutions as social constructions: a framework for analysis', *Acta Sociologica*, 35: 3–11.

Grossberg, L. (1998) 'Cultural studies crossroads blues', *European Journal of Cultural Studies*, 1(1): 65–82.

Habermas, J. (1989) *The Structural Transformation of the Public Sphere*. Cambridge: Polity.

Hall, S. (ed.) (1997) *Representation*. London: Sage.

Harvey, D. (1989) *The Condition of Postmodernity*. Oxford: Blackwell.

Haug, W. (1986) *Critique of Commodity Aesthetics*. London: Polity.

Hirst, P. and Wooley, P. (1982) *Social Relations and Human Attributes*. London: Tavistock.

Hindley, D. and Hindley, G. (1972) *Advertising in Victorian England 1837–1901*. London: Wayland.

Hodgins, E. (1947) 'J.Walter Thompson Company', *Fortune*, November.

Hopkins, C. (1990) [1929 & 1923] *My Life in Advertising and Scientific Advertising: Two Works by Claud Hopkins*. Chicago: NTC Business Books.

Horkheimer, M. & Adorno, T. (1973) *The Dialectic of Enlightenment*. London: Allen Lane.

Hower, R. (1939) *The History of an Advertising Agency*. New York: Arno.

Hunter, I. (1988) 'Setting limits to culture', *New Formations*, 4: 103–23.

Hunter, I. and Saunders, D. (1995) 'Walks of life: Mauss on the human gymnasium', *Body & Society* 1(2): 65–81.

Jameson, F. (1984) 'Postmodernism or the cultural logic of late capitalism', *New Left Review*, 146: 55–92.

Johnson, S. (1759) *The Idler* 40, Saturday, 20 January.

Jhally, S. (1987) *The Codes of Advertising: Fetishism and the Political Economy of Meaning in Consumer Society*. London: Routledge.

Kang, M.K. (1999) 'Postmodern consumer culture without postmodernity: copying the crisis of signification', *Cultural Studies*, 13(1): 19–33.

Kristeva, J. (1984) *Revolution in Poetic Language*. New York: Columbia University Press.

Laclau, E. and Mouffe, C. (1990) 'Post-Marxism without apologies', in E. Laclau, *New Reflections on the Revolution of our Time*. pp. 97–132. London: Verso.

Lash, S. and Urry, J. (1987) *The End of Organised Capitalism*. Cambridge: Polity.

Lash, S. and Urry, J. (1994) *Economies of Signs and Space*. London: Sage.

Latour, B. (1993) *We Have Never Been Modern*. Cambridge: Harvard.

Law, J. (2002) 'Economics as interference', in P. du Gay and M. Pryke (eds) *Cultural Economy*. London: Sage.

Lears, J. (1994) *Fables of Abundance: A Cultural History of Advertising in America*. New York: Basic Books.

Lefebvre, H. (1971) *Everyday Life in the Modern World*. London: Allen Lane.

Leiss, W., Kline, S. and Jhally, S. (1990/1986) *Social Communication in Advertising*. London: Routledge.

Leymore, V. Langholz (1975) *Hidden Myth: Structure and Symbolism in Advertising*. London: Heinemann.

Linton, D. (1979) 'Mr Mitchell's national work', *Journal of Advertising History*, 2, January: 29–31.

Lury, C. and Warde, A. (1997) 'Investments in the imaginary consumer: conjectures regarding power, knowledge and advertising', in M. Nava et al. (eds) *Buy This Book: Studies in Advertising and Consumption*. London: Routledge.

Macaulay, (1830) 'Mr Robert Montgomery's poems and the modern practice of puffing', *Edinburgh Review*, 194–210, April, ci.

Marchand, R. (1985) *Advertising the American Dream: Making Way for Modernity, 1920–40*. Berkeley: University of Califiornia Press.

Marcuse, H. (1964) *One Dimensional Man*. London: Routledge & Kegan Paul.

Marx, K. (1978/1844) 'For a ruthless criticism of everything existing', in R.C. Tucker (ed.) *The Marx Engels Reader*. New York, London: Norton.

Marx, K. (1978/1859) 'Preface to a contribution to the critique of political economy', in R.C. Tucker (ed.) *The Marx Engels Reader* New York, London: Norton.

Marx, K. (1978/1867) 'Capital. Vol. 1', in R.C. Tucker (ed.) *The Marx Engels Reader* New York, London: Norton.

Mattelart, A. (1991) *Advertising International: The Privatisation of Public Space.* London: Routledge.

Maxwell, E.L. (1904) *Modern Advertising.* London: Maxwell, Elliot & Moore.

Mayer, M. (1958) *Madison Avenue USA.* London: Bodley Head.

McKendrick, N. (1982) 'Commercialization and the economy', in McKendrick, N., Brewer, J. and Plumb, J.H. (eds) *The Birth of a Consumer Society.* London: Hutchinson.

McMahon, M. (1972) 'An American courtship: psychologists, advertising theory and the progressive era', *American Studies*, 13: 5–18.

McRobbie, A. (1998) *British Fashion Design: Rag Trade or Image Industry?* London: Routledge.

Miller, D. (ed.) (1995) *Acknowledging Consumption.* London: Routledge.

Miller, D. (1997) *Capitalism: An Ethnographic Approach.* London: Berg.

Miller, D. (2002) Turning Callon the right way up', *Economy and Society* 31(2): 218–33.

Miller, P. (1998) 'The margins of accounting', in Callon (ed.) *The Laws of the Market.*

Miller, P. (2001) 'Governing by numbers: why calculative practices matter', *Social Research*, 68(2): 379–96.

Miller, P. and Rose, N. (1990) 'Governing Economic Life', *Economy and Society* 19(1): 1–31.

Minson, J. (1985) *Genealogies of Morals: Nietzche, Foucault, Donzelot and the Eccentricity of Ethics.* Basingstoke: Macmillan.

Moeran, B. (1996) *A Japanese Advertising Agency.* Surrey: Curzon.

Montgomery, R. (1828) *The Puffiad: A Satire* London: Samuel Maunder.

Morris, M. (1988) 'Banality in cultural studies', *Block*, 14: 15–26.

Mort, F. (1996) *Cultures of Consumption.* London: Routledge.

Myers, K. (1986) *Understains: The Sense and Seduction of Advertising*, London: Comedia.

Myers, G. (1999) *Ad Worlds.* London: Arnold.

Nava, M., Blake, A., MacRury, I. and Richards, B. (1997) *Buy This Book: Studies in Advertising and Consumption.* London: Routledge.

Negus, K. (1992) *Producing Pop.* London: Edward Arnold.

Negus, K. (1997) 'The production of culture', in P. du Gay (ed.) *Production of Culture/Cultures of production.* London: Sage.

Nevett, T. (1977) 'London's early advertising agents', *Journal of Advertising History*, 1, December: 15–18.

Nevett, T. (1982) *Advertising in Britain.* London: Heinemann.

Nixon, S. (1996) *Hard Looks: Masculinities, Spectatorship and Contemporary Consumption.* London: UCL Press Ltd.

Nixon, S. (1997) 'Circulating culture', in P. du Gay (ed.) *Production of Culture/Cultures of Production.* London: Sage.

Nixon, S. (2003) *Advertising Cultures: Gender, Commerce, Creativity.* London: Sage.

Norris, J.D. (1990) *Advertising and the Transformation of American Society, 1865–1920.* Westport CT: Greenwood.

Osborne, T. (1994) 'Sociology, liberalism and the historicity of conduct', *Economy and Society*, 23(4): 484–501.

Osborne, T. (1998) *Aspects of Enlightenment.* London: UCL Press Ltd.

Pigott, S. (1975) *OBM 125 years.* London.

Pollay, R. (1977) 'The importance and the problems of writing the History of Advertising', *Journal of Advertising History*, 1: 3–6.

Pollay, R. (1979) 'Lydiametrics: applications of econometrics to the study of advertising', *Journal of Advertising History*, 2: 3–18.

Pollay, R. (1984) 'Twentieth century magazine advertising: determinants of informativeness', *Written Communication*, 1(1): 56–77.

Pollay, R. (1985) 'The subsiding sizzle: a descriptive history of print advertising', *Journal of Marketing*, 49: 24–37.

Pope, D. (1983) *The Making of Modern Advertising*. New York: Basic Books.

Pope, D. (1991) 'Advertising as a consumer issue: an historical view', *Journal of Social Issues*, 47(1): 41–56.

Presbrey, F. (1929) *The History and Development of Advertising*. New York: Greenwood.

'Puffs' (1855) *Puffs and Mysteries; or the Romance of Advertising*. London: Winchester [printed].

Punch's Almanac (1846) Vol. 10, Jan.–Jun.

Punch's Almanac (1846) Vol. 11, Jul.–Dec.

Ray, L. and Sayer, A. (1999) *Culture and Economy after the Cultural Turn*. London: Sage.

Reeves, R. (1961) *Reality in Advertising*. London: MacGibbon and Kee.

Robinson, E. (1963) 'Eighteenth century commerce and fashion: Matthew Boulton's marketing techniques', *Economic History Review*, 16(1): 39–60.

Rorty, A. (1994) 'The hidden politics of cultural identification', *Political Theory*, 22(1): 152–66.

Rose, N. (1990) *Governing the Soul*. London: Routledge.

Rose, N. (1996) 'Identity, genealogy, history', in S. Hall and P. Du Gay (eds) *Questions of Cultural Identity*.

Rothenberg, R. (1994) *Where the Suckers Moon: an Advertising Story*. New York: Alfred A Knopf.

Rowell, G. (1870) *Men who Advertise*. New York: Chesman.

Rowell, G. (1872) *Advertiser's Gazette*, 6, 9 October.

Rowsome, F. (1959) *They Laughed When I Sat Down: An Informal History of Advertising in Words and Pictures*. New York: McGraw-Hill.

Sahlins, M. (1976) *Culture and Practical Reason*. Chicago: University of Chicago Press.

Salmon, L. Maynard (1923) *The Newspapers and the Historian*. Oxford: Oxford University Press.

Sampson, H. (1874) *History of Advertising*. London: Chatto & Windus.

Saunders, D. (1992) *Authorship and Copyright*. London: Routledge.

de Saussure, F. (1960) *Course in General Linguistics*. London: Peter Owen.

Sayer, A. (1992) *Method in Social Science*. London: Routledge.

Sayer, A. (1994) 'Cultural studies and the "economy" stupid', *Environment and Planning D: Society and Space*, 12: 635–7.

Schlesinger, M. (1853) *Saunterings in and about London*. London: Nathaniel Cooke.

Schor, J. and Holt, D. (eds) (2000) *The Consumer Society Reader*. New York: The New Press.

Schudson, M. (1993/1984) *Advertising, the Uneasy Persuasion: Its Dubious Impact on American Society*. London: Routledge.

Scorah, K. (1987) 'The planning context,' in D. Cowley (ed.) *How to Plan Advertising*. London: APG & Cassel.

Simpson, A.W. Brian (1995) *Leading Cases in the Common Law*. Oxford: Oxford University Press.

Slater, D. (1997) *Consumer Culture and Modernity*. Cambridge: Polity.

Slater, D. (2002a) 'Capturing markets from the economists', in P. du Gay and M. Pryke (eds) *Cultural Economy*. London: Sage.

Slater, D. (2002b) 'From calculation to alienation: disentangling economic abstractions', *Economy and Society*, 31(2): 234–49.

Smith, C. Manby (1853) *Curiosities of London Life, or Phases, Physiological and Social of the Great Metropolis*. British Library Catalogue.

Soar, M. (2000) 'Encoding advertisements: ideology and meaning in advertising production', *Mass Communication and Society*, 3(5): 415–37.

Soar, M. (2002) 'The first things first manifesto and the politics of culture jamming: towards a cultural economy of graphic design and advertising', *Cultural Studies*, 16(4): 570–92.

Steichen, E. (1962) *My Life in Photography*. New York: Doubleday.

Sternberg, E. (1999) *The Economy of Icons: How Business Manufactures Meaning*. Westport, CT: Praeger.

Stuart, D. (1838) 'The newspaper writings of the Poet Coleridge', *Gentlemen's Magazine*, July.

Stuart, D. (1838) 'Anecdotes of public newspapers', *Gentlemen's Magazine*, August.

Stuart, R. (compiler) (1889) *Letters from the Lake Poets to Daniel Stuart*. London.

Sweet, M. (2001) *Inventing the Victorians*. London: Faber & Faber.

Times, The, History of The Times, Vol. 1 n.d.

Thornton, S. (1999) 'An academic Alice in Adland; ethnography and the commercial world', *Critical Quarterly* 4, 1 Spring.

Trimmer, M. (1826) *Siege of Pater Noster Row: A Moral Satire*. London.

Tudor, B. (1986) 'Retail trade advertising in the Leicester Journal and the Leicester Chronicle 1855–71', *Journal of Advertising History*, 9(2): 41–56.

Turner, C. (1992) *Modernity and Politics in the Work of Max Weber*. London: Routledge.

Turner, E.S. (1952) *The Shocking History of Advertising*. London: Michael Joseph.

Turton, A. (1982) 'The Archive of the House of Fraser Ltd – a rich source for the historian of advertising and a novel advertisement for the company today', *Journal of Advertising History*, 5, March, 1–7.

Twitchell, J.B. (1996) *Adcult USA*. Boulder, CT: Westview Press.

Vestergaard, T. and Schroder, K. (1985) *The Language of Advertising*. Oxford: Blackwell.

Walsh, C. (1999) 'The newness of the department store: a view from the eighteenth century', in G. Crossick, and S. Jaumain, (eds) *Cathedrals of Consumption: The European Department Store 1850–1939*. Aldershot and Vermont: Ashgate Publishing Ltd.

Walsh, C. (2000) 'The advertising and marketing of consumer goods in eighteenth century London', in C. Wischerman, and E. Shore, (eds) *Advertising and the European City: Historical Perspectives*. Aldershot and Vermont: Ashgate Publishing Ltd.

Wells, H.G. (1923) *Tono-Bungay*. London: Collins.

Wernick, A. (1991) *Promotional Culture: Advertising, Ideology and Symbolic Expression*. London: Sage.

Williams, R. (1976) *Keywords*. London: Fontana.

Williams, R. (1977) *Marxism and Literature*. Oxford: Oxford University Press.

Williams, R. (1980) 'Advertising: the magic system', in *Problems in Materialism and Culture*. London: Verso.

Williamson, J. (1978) *Decoding Advertisements*. London: Marion Boyars.

Winship, J. (1981) 'Handling sex', *Media, Culture and Society*, 3:25–41.

Wood, J. Playstead (1958) *The Story of Advertising*. New York: Ronald Press Co.

Young J. (1961) *The Toadstool Millionaires*. Princeton: Princeton University Press.

Zelizer, V. (1988) 'Beyond the polemics on the market: establishing a theoretical and empirical agenda', *Sociological Forum*, 3(4): 614–34.

unpublished sources

Websites

Bellion, W. (2002) 'Pleasing deceptions', *Common Place*, 3 (1) October. http://www.historycooperative.org/journals/cp/vol-03/no-01/lessons/bellion-2.shtml

Dictionary of Victorian London: www.victorianlondon.org accessed 12 February 2003

Helfland, W. 'Every man his own doctor', www.librarycompany.org/doctor/helfand.html#2B Exhibition catalogue essay accessed 12 February 2003

Hopkin, D. *Consuming a Broadside Ballad* www.cc.gla.ac.uk/courses/scottish/ballads/ accessed 12 February

Institute of Practitioners in Advertising, website www.ipa.co.uk

John Johnson Collection Exhibition (2001) *A Nation of Shopkeepers: Trade Ephemera from 1654 to 1860 in the John Johnson Collection*. http://www.bodley.ox.ac.uk/johnson/exhibition Accessed 14 February 2003

Semiotic Solutions website www.semioticsolutions.com

Primary sources

Abbreviations

HATa – History of Advertising Trust Archives, Norwich

JWTa – J. Walter Thompson Archive, Hartman Center, Duke University, North Carolina

HOYTa – Hoyt Archive, Hartman Center, Duke University, North Carolina

CBa – Charles Barker Archive, Guildhall Library, London

AYERa – NW Ayer Archive, National Museum of American History, Smithsonian Insititute

BL – British Library

BOD – Bodlein Library, Oxford

1906 Post Office Directory

Account files, Boxes 1, 2, 3, 6 & 13 JWTa.

Agencies Box, HATa.

Andrew Jergen's Company, Roll 45, Market Research microfilms, JWTa.

Charles Barker Letters Book 1825–1847 MS 20011, CBa.

Bartholomew Faire: *A collection of advertisements, cuttings from periodicals, prints ... drawings ... notes relating ... Fair*: [1687/1849 London], BL.

Bernstein Company History Files, *Biographical File Series, Box 4*. JWTa.

Browne, Reginald Bousquet (c.1975) *T.B. Browne Limited: the first 100 years*. Unpublished memoir. Agencies Box, HATa.

Butler, G. (1985) *Bush House, Berlin and Berkeley Square: George Butler Remembers JWT 1925–62*. Unpublished Manuscript edited by Jill Frith from conversations with George Butler. JWT Box, HATa.

Chipchase, P. (c.1977) Manuscript notes on Streets, Streets File, HATa.

Collection of Ballads, Broadsides etc, c116.i.4, BL.

Colmans file, HATa.

J and J Colman (1977) *The Advertising Art of J & J Colman*. Unpublished internal commemorative document.

Crowsley, E.G. c.1952 *James White*. Unpublished notes for the Charles Lamb Society, Whites Box HATa.

Daniel, G. (compiler) (c.1860) *A collection of illustrations, portraits, newspaper cuttings, extracts from books and sale catalogues, advertisements, manuscripts and playbills, relating principally to the Shakespeare Jubilee of 1769, and in particular to David Garrick's part therein. 1746–1860*, BL.

Darrow, P. (n.d.) *Recollections*. Oral History transcript, AYERa.

Dawkins Papers, Officers and Staff series, Box 1, 3 JWTa.

Derriman, J. (n.d.) *Something in the City: The First 100 Years of Charles Barker and Son*. Unpublished Manuscript Agencies Box. HATa.

Fleishmann's Yeast Roll 55, Market Research microfilms. JWTa.

Fleishmann's Yeast: 1920 *Report on Creative Properties and Food Value*. JWTa.

Hoyt, C. (1926) Agency Training Manual. HOYTa.

Institute of Practitioners in Advertising (1956) *Aims and Functions*. London: IPA.

Jordan, C. (n.d.) *Memoirs*. Oral History transcript. AYERa.

J. Walter Thompson (1919) *Standardisation Committee*. JWTa.

JWT Junior Newsletter (1936) February JWTa.

Kohl, H. (1956) Kohl celebrates 50 years with JWT in *Round the Square*, Dawkins Papers, Officers and Staff series Box 2. JWTa.

Lysons, D. (c.1825) *Collectanea; or a collection of advertisements and paragraphs drawn from the newspapers, relating to various subjects*. BL.

Norris, E. (1967) *From Memories*. Internal memoir. Sell's Box. HATa.

The Propelling Power (1908) SL43 Colour Promotional Leaflet, HATa.

Raymond, C.E. (1923) *Memoirs and Reminiscences*. Unpublished manuscript. Officers and Staff series, Box 1. JWTa.

Samson Clark Box, HATa.

Sala, G. (1891) 'The world's press and what I have known of it', in *Sell's Dictionary of the World Press*. Sell's Box. HATa.

Sell's Guardbook, 1891, Sell's Box, HATa.

Sell's Services Presentation document (c.1910) SL53, Sell's Box, HATa.

Sell's List of Suburban Newspapers (1888) Sell's Box, HATa.

Sharpe, L. (1964) *The Lintas Story*. London: Lintas Limited, HATa.

Sivewright, J. (1820) *A Series of 24 illustrated lottery advertisements*. BOD.

Spottiswoode's *The Triangle* (1909), Spottiswoode's Box, HATa.

Streets (n.d.) *The Story of Streets*. Unpublished Manuscript.

Treasure, J.A.P. (1976) *A History of British Advertising Agencies*. Edinburgh University Jubilee Lecture, HATa.

Twin Peaks (1996) *Exhibition Leaflet*. D&AD Festival of Design and Advertising, 27 November – 1 December.

Warreniana (c.1830) *Warreniana, a tale, after the manner of the Rejected Addresses*, BL.

RF Whites Box, HATa.

Index

Page numbers in *italics* indicate figures, *n/ns* refers to chapter note(s).